Everyday Glory

THE REVELATION OF GOD IN ALL OF REALITY

Gerald R. McDermott

Baker Academic
a division of Baker Publishing Group
Grand Rapids, Michigan

Published by Baker Academic
a division of Baker Publishing Group
PO Box 6287, Grand Rapids, MI 49516-6287
www.bakeracademic.com

Printed in the United States of America

Library of Congress Cataloging-in-Publication Data
Library of Congress Cataloging-in-Publication Data
Names: McDermott, Gerald R. (Gerald Robert), author.
Title: Everyday glory : the revelation of God in all of reality / Gerald R. McDermott.
Description: Grand Rapids, MI : Baker Academic, [2018] | Includes bibliographical references and index.
Identifiers: LCCN 2018020568 | ISBN 9780801098291 (pbk.)
Subjects: LCSH: Revelation—Christianity.
Classification: LCC BT127.3 .M43 2018 | DDC 231.7/4—dc23
LC record available at https://lccn.loc.gov/2018020568

Unless otherwise indicated, Scripture quotations are the author's translation.

Scripture quotations labeled ESV are from The Holy Bible, English Standard Version® (ESV®), copyright © 2001 by Crossway, a publishing ministry of Good News Publishers. Used by permission. All rights reserved. ESV Text Edition: 2011

18   19   20   21   22   23   24   7   6   5   4   3   2   1

This book is dedicated to our three wonderful daughters-in-law,
Darrah, Whitney, and Julie.

They have helped make our sons the splendid men they are,
and they have given us eleven precious grandchildren,
Augustine, Anastasia, Magdalen, Catherine, Piers,
Margaret Rose, Florence, BIP, Phinehas,
Simeon, and Thaddeus Bede.

Contents

Preface

Many years ago I happened upon a notebook that Jonathan Edwards (1703–58) had kept throughout his life. He titled the notebook "Images of Divine Things."[1] In this notebook, now about eighty-five pages, Edwards jotted notes on the resemblances to the Triune God and his ways that he saw in the world around him. By "world," I mean not only nature but also what we call human relations. I was immediately enthralled.

This notebook opened a whole new world to me. I began to see beauty and riches in the stars above and the world beneath and pointers to gospel truths in multiple dimensions of reality. Later when I started to explore the history of Christian thought, I discovered that this Edwardsean way of seeing the world was not uncommon in previous Christian theology. In fact, it was the norm.

But in the twentieth century this way of seeing was lost in many sectors of the Christian church for reasons that I will explain. The reasons are now understandable, but the effect was a terrible loss to the faith of millions.

This book is an attempt to retrieve a profoundly Christian way of seeing reality. My prayer is that it adds depth and beauty to the faith of believers in this new century. I hope it also speaks to seekers who have caught a glimpse of the wonder and beauty of life and wonder where those glimpses have come from.

1. *WJE* 11:51–135.

Acknowledgments

As always, my wife, Jean, was a daily inspiration as I wrote this book on sabbatical. We were living with our oldest son and his wife and their six kids at the time. My gratitude goes to them for putting up with Grandpa as he wrote and wrote, day after day, while enjoying their laughter, questions, and long conversations.

I am deeply indebted to my editor Dave Nelson, who is becoming one of this country's premier theological book editors. He has smoothed the way all along and made excellent suggestions throughout.

I am also grateful for the invitations of Dallas Theological Seminary to deliver their Griffith-Thomas lectures for 2017 and St. John Lutheran Church in Roanoke, Virginia, to be the speaker at their annual theological weekend. Both series helped me think through and then revise some of the chapters that follow.

Thanks are also due to the following readers who gave input: Michael McClymond, Mark Harris, Matt Franck, Robert Benne, Paul Hinlicky, Brian Bolt, Hans Boersma, Josh Reeves, Ralph Wood, Alan Pieratt, Sean McDermott, Ryan McDermott, and Mark Graham. I am sure I did not use their suggestions in the ways most of them thought I should, and whatever distortions remain should not be attributed to any of them.

Special thanks are due to Paula Gibson for what I think is a superb cover. Thanks are also due to my excellent student Justin Hendrix for his copy-editing work.

Abbreviations

AE *Luther's Works: American Edition.* Edited by Jaroslav Pelikan and Helmut T. Lehmann. 55 vols. St. Louis: Concordia; Philadelphia: Fortress, 1955.

AH Irenaeus, *Against Heresies.* In *The Ante-Nicene Fathers*, vol. 1, edited by Alexander Roberts and James Donaldson. 1885. Reprint, Grand Rapids: Eerdmans, 1988.

CD Karl Barth, *Church Dogmatics.* 14 vols. Reprint, Peabody, MA: Hendrickson, 2010.

CSCO Corpus Scriptorum Christianorum Orientalium. Edited by Jean Baptiste Chabot et al. Paris, 1903.

WA *D. Martin Luthers Werke.* Weimarer Ausgabe. 121 vols. Weimar: H. Böhlaus Nachfolger, 1883–2009.

WJE Jonathan Edwards, *The Works of Jonathan Edwards.* New Haven: Yale University Press. Vol. 2, *Religious Affections*, edited by John E. Smith (2009). Vol. 8, *Ethical Writings*, edited by Paul Ramsey (1989). Vol. 9, *A History of the Work of Redemption*, edited by John F. Wilson (1989). Vol. 10, *Sermons and Discourses, 1720–1723*, edited by Wilson H. Kimnach (1992). Vol. 11, *Typological Writings*, edited by Wallace E. Anderson and Mason I. Lowance Jr. (1993). Vol. 13, *The "Miscellanies," a–500*, edited by Thomas A. Schafer (1994). Vol. 14, *Sermons and Discourses, 1723–1729*, edited by Kenneth P. Minkema (1997). Vol. 16, *Letters and Personal Writings*, edited by George S. Claghorn (1998). Vol. 18, *The "Miscellanies," 501–832*, edited by Ava Chamberlain (2000). Vol. 20, *The "Miscellanies," 833–1152*, edited by Amy Plantinga Pauw. Vol. 23, *The "Miscellanies," 1153–1360*, edited by Douglas A. Sweeney.

1

Recovering a Lost Vision

Most people in the world wander through life without seeing its full meaning. Christians know its meaning but often miss the embedded meaning in the *world* all around them. They know that God created the world and that he will bring the world to an end. Some know that the end will not take his people to a heaven in the sky but to a renewed world right here. But most Christians have been trained not to see the meaning of the innumerable *parts* of this world, or the meaning of the world itself. They have been conditioned to see *beyond* the earth and its heavens to a realm fundamentally removed from what they can see. They miss the glory of the Lord that is all around them—in *this* world and *these* heavens—which the seraphim extolled to Isaiah (Isa. 6:3) and the great liturgies proclaim: "Heaven and earth are full of your glory!"

Let me try to illustrate how we can see and not see at the same time. Try staring at the four dots in the picture on the previous page for 30–60 seconds.[1] Next close your eyes, and then look at a bright wall. You will see an image of "the glory of God in the face of Jesus Christ" (2 Cor. 4:6 ESV). Of course this is only an image and not the refulgent glory. Yet it demonstrates my point: the glory of the Lord is right in front of us, but we usually don't see it.

1. Taken from http://www.eyetricks.com/jesus.htm.

Disenchantment

This gap between perception and reality was not always so large. For millennia the cosmos had seemed to most men and women to be a source of wonder, an infinitely complex mystery with unsearchable beauties and intriguing harmonies. They believed the universe was a sign with meaning, but that the meaning was often missed. As the twelfth-century theologian Hugh of St. Victor wrote,

> The whole sensible world is like a kind of book written by the finger of God—that is, created by divine power—and each particular creature is somewhat like a figure, not invented by human decision, but instituted by the divine will to manifest the invisible things of God's wisdom. But in the same way that some illiterate, if he saw an open book, would notice the figures, but would not comprehend the letters, so also the stupid and "animal man" who "does not perceive the things of God" may see the outward appearance of these visible creatures, but does not understand the reason within.[2]

By the "animal man," Hugh probably meant a person who sees nothing of God's glory, or else has a sense of a Creator but does not let it affect him or her. But in the beginning of this quote Hugh spoke for millions in the church who have seen God's glory through "the things that have been made," as Paul put it (Rom. 1:20). They not only sensed something beautiful in the glories of the world around and above and in them but also sensed something of what Hugh called "God's wisdom" in and through the creatures he made. They resonated with Jesus's saying that the lilies of the field and the birds of the air showed that God would provide for his people, since God provided for the lilies and the birds and yet loved his people even more (Matt. 6:26–30). And if God was speaking through lilies and sparrows, they surmised, then he was probably also speaking through wine and bread and vines and lights, as his connections to those things suggested.

But in the modern age fewer Christians have been able to see messages like this in the creation. They have been affected by two things: growing secularism, which refuses to acknowledge that we and the world are the creation of God, and certain theologies that discount even believers' abilities to discern meaning in the creation.

2. Hugh of St. Victor, *De tribus diebus* 4; quoted in Peter Harrison, *The Bible, Protestantism, and the Rise of Natural Science* (Cambridge: Cambridge University Press, 2001), 1.

We've all heard about the first cause of Christians being less able to understand the meaning of creation—secularism and its gradual disenchantment of the world. We have heard from historians and sociologists that as more and more people became convinced that the world's origin could be explained by science, the cosmos came to be regarded as a predictable machine made by God. Then, when faith in God dissolved, it was seen as a cold universe arising from randomness and therefore inimical to lasting personhood and love.[3]

Most of us learned in college history classes that this disenchantment of the world started with "the Copernican revolution," which made humanity the center and measure, replacing the infinite God with finite man, broken in his relationships and partial in his vision. It made sense to us that moderns started to turn their focus from what was beyond limit (God) to what they could know within their limits (human beings and their nearby world). If we took a bit of philosophy in college, we learned that the German philosopher Immanuel Kant (1724–1804) limited knowledge even further by arguing that we could never know things as they really are, either God or things closer to us, but only our own thoughts about God and things. We might have also read about the Danish philosopher Søren Kierkegaard (1813–55) and his so-called leap of faith (a term he probably never actually used). But there is little doubt that he persuaded generations of readers that they must leap *over* reason and this world to get to ultimate truth. (It is unfortunate if this is all they gained from Kierkegaard, for he rightly stressed the flip side of reason's inability to know the Triune God—namely, the *soul's* capacity for communion with the Triune God in its "subjective," or personal, knowledge.) University students in the last few decades often felt reinforced by Kierkegaard in what they already had intuited, both from their own experience and the atmosphere at most universities, that reason cannot prove God or say *anything* certain about God other than that his existence is doubtful.

There is also what could be called a denominational difference. The sixteenth-century Protestant Reformers argued that late medieval Catholic theology had too much confidence in reason. Luther and Calvin insisted that Roman theologians of their day failed to recognize sufficiently that reason, like every other part of the human person, was tainted by the fall and therefore could not be relied upon to see in the creation anything truthful about God. Since reason was a gift of nature and not grace, Protestants tended to conclude that the world of nature is fundamentally different from the sphere

3. On the universe as a machine, see such works as Richard S. Westfall, *The Construction of Modern Science: Mechanism and Mechanics* (1971; repr., Cambridge: Cambridge University Press, 1977), and Margaret C. Jacob, *The Cultural Meaning of the Scientific Revolution* (New York: Knopf, 1988).

of grace, so that the beauties of the world have no fundamental or primary relation to the beauty of God. Even if they do, sin has so damaged our eyesight that we cannot see that relation rightly. In fact, our sin-damaged eyes are not capable of seeing anything about the true God from reason and nature alone. But more important for Protestants, God has shown us everything we need to know in the Bible, and the main story there is about salvation and especially justification. According to the Protestant Reformers,[4] too many Catholics had misused the creation to argue for what Luther called a "theology of glory," which assumed that they could know what was important to know about God through reason and nature alone. Luther proposed that the only way to know the true God was through the cross of Jesus Christ. Protestants generally agreed with Luther's approach to God and the cross, as did many Catholic theologians in the next centuries. But while Catholics continued to sustain a robust theology of creation, Protestants tended to let their under-standing of creation become eclipsed by their overwhelming emphasis on redemption. Some even went so far as to claim that there is no such thing as revelation through the creation.

It didn't help matters that the formidable trinity of the long nineteenth century—Darwin, Marx, and Freud—seemed to confirm Western culture's growing disenchantment of the world. However much some Christians la-bored to reconcile macroevolution with God's creative work, Charles Darwin (1809–82) persuaded millions that God was not needed to begin or sustain the world. Karl Marx (1818–83) told moderns that God talk is merely a drug ("the opiate of the masses") enabling the weak to cope with their economic and so-cial hardships. Sigmund Freud (1856–1939) pointed not at society as Marx did but at inner desire, claiming that religion is wish fulfillment. Like Marx, Freud insisted it was only the weak who need religion. For all three of these modern "prophets," the world was no longer a beautiful mystery created by a glorious God but an arena for the survival of the fittest (Darwin) or for the exploitation of the proletariat (Marx) or for conflict between the superego and the id (Freud).

While Christians rejected the atheism of these three thinkers, many agreed with parts of their projects. Some Christians accepted the new creation story of natural selection but said God initiated and perpetuated that process. Most Christians sympathized with Marx's concern for the downtrodden and recognized the evil of economic exploitation, especially by one class against another. Many Christians also saw Freud as opening up the ways that sin

---

4. There were also Catholic Reformers who used the Council of Trent to refashion doctrine in response to Luther's critique. See John O'Malley, *Trent: What Happened at the Council* (Cambridge, MA: Harvard University Press, 2013).

works in child-parent relations and in the depths of the unconscious. Yet by training Christian attention on how nature might have originated species, on the manner in which history and human nature colluded to produce economic oppression, and on the ways that inner human nature was conflicted, these thinkers made it more difficult for Christians to see the glory of God in nature. Besides, Darwin faulted the church's literal interpretation of creation, Marx protested the church's acceptance of class differences, and Freud decried the church's teaching about sexual sin. Christians couldn't help wondering whether the church might be wrong about creation too. Perhaps the medieval church's assumption that nature speaks in a variety of ways was just another illusion that secular prophets were dispelling.

More recently, the New Atheists have claimed to lend the authority of science to the world's disenchantment. Richard Dawkins is probably the most famous of this new tribe. In his book *The Blind Watchmaker* (1986) he tried to refute the argument for God from the apparent design of the universe. In 2006 he published *The God Delusion*, which claimed that the more one uses reason to understand science, the more one sees that there is no God. When reason looks at the stars above, the earth beneath, and the soul within, one finds not God, he claimed, but final randomness and meaninglessness. The world does not care, and love is something we imagine but that is finally ephemeral. This conclusion should not surprise us, Dawkins said in a BBC documentary: "Why should it be anything other than bleak? I mean, there is no caring about the universe. Why should there be? Why should the universe care about what happens to us?"[5]

Most Christians do not pay great attention to Dawkins and his ilk. As Alister McGrath and David Bentley Hart showed, these new skeptics are astonishingly ignorant of basic philosophy and theology.[6] For example, they typically treat the Christian God as one more being in a world of beings; such a conception is radically alien to the God and metaphysics of the Bible. Scripture's God is Being itself and in fact beyond being, so that all beings and all the world are *in* him. As Paul put it to the Athenian philosophers on Mars Hill, "In him we live and move and have our being" (Acts 17:28 ESV). The New Atheists tend to conceive of God as the seventeenth- and eighteenth-century

5. This quote is from "Richard Dawkins Documentary," https://www.youtube.com/watch ?v=BLtOffrpsHQ (site unavailable because of copyright restrictions). See also https://www .edge.org/conversation/richard_dawkins-why-there-almost-certainly-is-no-god.

6. Alister McGrath, *Why God Won't Go Away: Engaging with the New Atheism* (London: SPCK, 2011); David Bentley Hart, *The Experience of God: Being, Consciousness, Bliss* (New Haven: Yale University Press, 2013).

deists did, as a finite being who created the world with its laws of nature and then sat back to observe it and occasionally intervene.[7]

Yet there is a way in which the New Atheists affect Christians. They concentrate on moral evil, which they think disproves a good God, for he does not stop the greatest human evils such as the German Holocaust, the Soviet Gulag, and the Cambodian Killing Fields. They delight in exposing the vicious killing of nonhuman nature, "red in tooth and claw,"[8] where life seems to require death on a regular basis. What appear to be innocent animals are routinely attacked and killed with savagery by bigger animals. Then they ask how a good and loving God could have invented such a vicious system of nature.

Christians know there are good replies to these objections. They know that sin started a chain of life and death, so that nature both outside and inside of us is fallen. It groans with us for its redemption one day (Rom. 8:22). So while nature contains immense beauty and grandeur, it is also wracked by what could be called tragedy.

Many Christians also find it ironic that many of these same skeptics (both readers who cheer the New Atheist rejection of traditional monotheistic religion and some of the New Atheists themselves) treat the natural world as divine. It is a growing belief in the West that the physical cosmos is animated by an impersonal spirit called "Gaia" or "the goddess"—although this spirit is not regarded as a person in the way that monotheists think of God. In other words, while the cosmos is regarded by these devotees as more than physical, with some sort of supernatural (i.e., "above or beyond" nature) power driving it forward, the power is an "it" or a "thing," not a "he" or a "she"—something like the Hindu Brahman or the Daoist Dao. Neither of the latter two is a person or god; rather, they are but the impersonal spirit or essence of all that is, what we might call a directed energy. The ironic element is that while the New Atheists and their readers mock Christians for believing that a good God created a good world, they treat that same world with a similar reverence for the spirit that lies in and behind it. Even Dawkins, who disdained the Gaia hypothesis for its suggestion that the cosmos works to optimize life, wrote glowingly of the cosmos's "appearance of design," which contains such "complexity and beauty" that William Paley "hardly even began to state the case."[9]

---

7. On God's intervening occasionally, see Gerald R. McDermott, *Jonathan Edwards Confronts the Gods: Christian Theology, Enlightenment Religion, and Non-Christian Faiths* (New York: Oxford University Press, 2000), 19–33.

8. Alfred, Lord Tennyson, *In Memoriam A. H. H.*, section 56, stanza 4.

9. Richard Dawkins, *The Blind Watchmaker* (London: Penguin, 1986), 21. Paley (1743–1805) was the English apologist who famously argued that the universe showed evidence of being designed, just as a watch's complexity reveals a watchmaker behind it.

So today's skeptics are not very convincing.
ordinate amount of attention in the media and
times have been so noisy that the atmosphere s(
echoes. Some Christians as a result have lost con(
to celebrate the creation as "full of the glory of
wonder what if anything nature tells us of the div(

Biblical Joy

Consider the irony: moderns are proud that they now know that the world is not enchanted. Yet these same moderns—indoctrinated by Darwin, Marx, and Freud—have run to psychiatrists and counselors because of more per capita depression than perhaps in any period of history. The biblical authors, in telling contrast, write of joy to be found amid suffering. At the heart of that joy is a vision of the world as full of the glory of God. As John Calvin put it, the world is a theater of God's glory.[10]

Calvin wasn't saying anything new. The Great Tradition—from Origen and Augustine through John of Damascus to Thomas and Bonaventure—saw the world as a thing of wonder studded with beautiful and mysterious signs pointing beyond themselves. They all agreed with what the fourth-century theologian Ephrem of Syria (306–73) wrote: "In every place, if you look, his [Christ's] symbol is there, and wherever you read, you will find his types. For in him all creatures were created, and he traced his symbols on his property."[11] Ephrem was articulating what most Christians believed for most of the church's first seventeen centuries—that the universe is an immense trinitarian symbol, with every corner of the cosmos bursting with divinely given meaning. All the Christian thinkers drew on what the biblical authors thought obvious to any reasonable person: "The heavens declare the glory of God, and the firmament proclaims the work of his hands" (Ps. 19:1). Only "the fool" who looks at the heavens above or the moral law within can say, "There is no God" (14:1 ESV). It seemed absolutely obvious to anyone not prejudiced that, as Paul put it, "What can be known about God is plain to [human beings] because God has shown it to them. Ever since the creation of the world God's eternal power and divine nature, invisible though they are, have been understood and seen through the things he has made [in the

10. John Calvin, *Institutes of the Christian Religion*, ed. John T. McNeill, trans. Ford Lewis Battles (Philadelphia: Westminster, 1960), 1.5.8; 1.14.20; 2.6.1.
11. Ephrem of Syria, *Hymn on Virginity* 20.12; quoted in Seely Joseph Beggiani, "The Typological Approach of Syriac Sacramental Theology," *Theological Studies* 64 (2003): 544–45.

e and the world below]. So they are without excuse" (Rom.
Paul went on to suggest that those who are intellectually honest
ook into their own hearts and realize that "what is written on their
earts" is what *God's* "law requires, to which the conscience bears witness"
(2:15).

Two modern Christian theologians teased out the implications of this
biblical vision. They accepted the biblical suggestions that all the world is full
of types and proceeded to lay out this vision with a clarity and fullness that
have not been duplicated. The first was Jonathan Edwards (1703–58), and
the second was John Henry Newman (1801–90). Let me outline the vision of
each, for with these two we can get a robust conception of what the historic
church has meant by its typological vision of reality.

Jonathan Edwards

Jonathan Edwards believed that every last bit of the cosmos is a sign that
speaks and shows. The message is as near-infinite as the universe itself because the universe was made by the infinite God. But the message has a code
that must be cracked—word by word, sentence by sentence—to tell the story
inscribed within. The story is of the infinite-personal Being who decided
to create a cosmos with a little speck called Earth populated by creatures
called human beings. These little creatures were somehow made to be like
God himself, at least like him insofar as they had a capacity to think and to
love and to enjoy. But they abused those spectacular privileges and rejected
him. Yet he won them back by becoming one of them, subjecting his infinite
self to their, by comparison, infinitely tiny capacities and permitting them
to disrespect him, abuse him, and then torture and kill him. But then he was
lifted from the dead and in the same body came back to life. It was through
that shocking series of events—the life and death and resurrection of the
God-man—that God won those magnificent but perverse creatures back to
himself.

According to Edwards, this counterintuitive story is told by every square
inch of the cosmos. To be more precise, a tiny part of the story is told by each
tiny part of the cosmos. But if a person does not have what Edwards called
the "sense of the heart," which is given by the Holy Spirit, then that person
will never crack the code. He or she will not get that little bit of the story,
and probably not the whole story at all. In other words, that person will not
be able to read the signs, for they will be in a foreign language. Edwards used
exactly those sorts of words for this story. He said it is a language one has

to learn, just like learning a language of this world. But you have to go to the other world, as it were, to learn the language of the message because the message comes from the other world about this world, even though every bit of this world is inscribed with a part of the story.

Here is Edwards on the extent of God's messaging: "I am not ashamed to own that I believe that the whole universe, heaven and earth, air and seas . . . be full of images of divine things . . . [so much so] that there is room for persons to be learning more and more of this language and seeing more of that which is declared in it to the end of the world without discovering [it] all" (*WJE* 11:152).[12] God has a reason for his method, said Edwards—namely, that he is "a communicating God" who is ever speaking, ever imprinting his creation with messages, and ever revealing more and more of his beauty. But that characteristic—of being an ever-communicating Being—is only penultimate, not ultimate. It is an end or purpose of his works, but not his final end. The last end of all he said and did, in creating and then redeeming, is to bring glory to himself. Eighteenth-century skeptics said that idea sounded selfish. Edwards replied that it was selfish only if bringing joy and beauty and love to his creatures is selfish (see *WJE* 8:450–53).

So the purpose of imprinting the entire creation is for the sake of God's glorifying himself, but that happens only when his creatures find their greatest joy in seeing his beauty. And that beauty is, in a word, love. And all the beauties of this world—from the beauty of the intricate design of a simple cell in a simple leaf from a simple tree, to the phantasmagoria of a distant galaxy seen from the top of a mountain on a cloudless night, to the splendor of Beethoven's *Moonlight Sonata*, to the beauty of the most beautiful woman in recent history, Mother Teresa (!)—all of these earthly beauties are but refractions of the beauty of the self-denying, servant love of the three persons of the Trinity.[13] In Edwards's language, all of these beauties are types or images for which the antitype (the referent, or thing to which the type points) is the eternal beauty of the mutual love among the Father, Son, and Holy Spirit.

Now Edwards had plenty of critics in his day, even on typology. Liberals of his day—and eighteenth-century liberals denied the Trinity and the blood atonement and an eternal hell, just as liberals do today—denied types. Others

12. See the abbreviations list for full information on the various volumes cited throughout of *The Works of Jonathan Edwards*.

13. To those who would object that the Father cannot be self-denying and a servant, I (not Edwards) would reply that, in giving his son over to a humiliating incarnation and horrible death, the Father was denying himself for the service of his sinful human creatures. And the Spirit denied his own glory by pointing to the Son.

criticized him for going too far, finding a type under every bush, as it were. Edwards's response was, in effect, No, there are really two under every bush—both the insects under the bush and the roots that feed the bush.

Edwards defended himself by going to the Bible. He argued the usual case that the Old Testament is full of types that point to New Testament antitypes, but then he went further. Not only is the exodus a type of salvation, and not only are Kings David and Solomon types of Messiah Jesus as King, but every stroke of the pen in the Old Testament is typical. How do we know that? Because Paul said in 1 Corinthians 10:11, after recounting certain events when the Israelites were wandering in the Sinai wilderness, that "*all* these things were written for our instruction."

> Thus almost everything that was said or done that we have recorded in Scripture from Adam to Christ, was typical of Gospel things: persons were typical persons, their actions were typical actions, the cities were typical cities, the nation of the Jews and other nations were typical nations, the land was a typical land, God's providences towards them were typical providences, their worship was typical worship, their houses were typical houses, their magistrates typical magistrates, their clothes typical clothes, and indeed the world was a typical world.[14]

Like much of the church for most of its last two thousand years, Edwards believed that "Mount Zion and Jerusalem are types of the church of saints" (*WJE* 11:153). But unlike much of the church, he was not a supersessionist who believed that the church entirely replaced Israel. Unlike many evangelicals who insist, in Enlightenment fashion, that every text has only one meaning, and unlike many Christians who think, like Occamite nominalists, that the simplest explanation is always the best, Edwards followed the Great Tradition's fourfold sense of Scripture and was able to see multiple layers of meaning in the same text.[15] He was also able to do ontology (i.e., talk about being and existence) in the way the Bible does it. In other words, he employed the christological principle of coinherence and the trinitarian principle of *perichōrēsis*, both of which mean that *God's* reality, and therefore creaturely realities, are able to have two or more things going on at the same time. Christ is both God *and* man. The Father is in the Son, *and* the Son is in the Father,

---

14. *WJE* 9:289; 13:435; see also *WJE* 13:325, 363–64, 431–33, 434–35; 18:335; 23:500–501.

15. By Occamite I mean those who think like philosopher-theologian William of Occam (ca. 1287–1347), whose "Occam's razor" is famous for suggesting that the explanation with the fewest assumptions is always best. The fourfold sense of Scripture was the oft-used medieval and early modern method of interpreting Scripture that saw four levels of meaning in most biblical texts—the literal (what the text asserts), the allegorical (or doctrinal, especially about Christ), the tropological (or moral), and the anagogical (or eschatological).

and the Two by the Spirit are in the believer, at the same time that the whole church is in Christ, and the whole world is in God in some mysterious sense—in him we live and move and have our being. Therefore a Scripture text about Jerusalem or Mount Zion can refer as a type to the future gentile church at the same time that it speaks in quite literal fashion about the future of Jewish Israel.

Edwards went further than most of the tradition on typology, insisting that the New Testament is full of types too. The dove on Jesus's head at his baptism was a type of the Holy Spirit; so were the tongues of fire on the heads of the 120 and the rushing of wind at Pentecost (*WJE* 11:151).

Furthermore, the New Testament itself teaches us to look outside the Bible for types. When Jesus proclaimed that he was the true light and true vine and true bread, he implied that all lights and vines and breads in this world are pointers to, or types of, their antitypes in Jesus. Paul did the same for seed and sowing in springtime when he used them in 1 Corinthians 15 to argue for the resurrection of bodies. Unless God intended seed and planting to be types of spiritual realities, Paul's argument would not have made sense: "If the sowing of seed and its springing were not designedly ordered to have an agreeableness to the resurrection, there could be no sort of argument in that which the Apostle alleges; either to argue the resurrection itself or the manner of it, either its certainty, or probability or possibility" (*WJE* 11:62–63).

If types are in nature, they can also be found in nonbiblical history. Edwards wrote in his enormous "Types of the Messiah" notebook (*WJE* 11:191–324) that "many things in the state of the ancient Greeks and Romans" were typical of gospel things. For example, his "Images" notebook contains a long entry comparing the celebration of a military triumph in the Roman Empire to Christ's ascension. Just as the Roman emperor's triumphal chariot was followed by senators and ransomed citizens, so Christ was accompanied on his return to glory by principalities and powers and ransomed citizens of heaven. The Roman procession was closed by the sacrifice of a great white ox; so too Christ at the ascension entered the holy of holies with his own blood. The Roman emperor treated the people in the capital with gifts, and Christ did the same for his church (*WJE* 11:191, 82–84).

Edwards went further still—to the history of religions. He proposed that God has planted types of true religion even in religious systems that are finally false. This idea is hard for most Christians today to fathom, but Edwards was nothing if not a daring thinker, yet always within the bounds of the Great Tradition of orthodoxy. His adventurous step was to say that the near-universal practice of *sacrifice* in world religions was planted by God as a type of the perfect sacrifice of God's Son. Even the ghastly practice of human sacrifice, inspired by the devil, was permitted by God to prepare peoples for the sacrifice made by the God-man. Edwards also taught that pagan *idolatry*, in which deities were believed to inhabit material forms, was a type of the true incarnation. Furthermore, he believed pagan sacrifices showed the heathen that sin "must be suffered for" and that they therefore needed God's mercy (*WJE* 13:405–6).

Yet Edwards warned that typology can go off the rails. It is not a problem to see types everywhere, because they *are* everywhere. But it *is* a problem to interpret them wrongly, as sometimes happens. Origenist speculation, as it has been called because of the tendency of Origen (ca. 184–253) to take the material things of Scripture as types of spiritual things, can flee from history (the proper domain of orthodox typology) to allegorical generalizations about human existence. Edwards said the guardrails on orthodox typology are twofold. First, it must stay within the orthodox story of redemption, which is rooted in historical events. They compose the great antitype. The story is a huge story with a near-infinite number of types, but it is a different story from the myriads of heretical stories and the varieties of human speculations that are not heretical but merely imaginary.

Second, typological interpretation takes practice, just as it takes practice to learn any language, to learn to read this story. Here are Edwards's words, worth quoting at length:

> Types are a certain sort of language, as it were, in which God is wont to speak to us. And there is, as it were, a certain idiom in that language which is to be learnt the same that the idiom of any language is, viz. by good acquaintance with the language, either by being naturally trained up in it, learning it by education (but that is not the way in which corrupt mankind learned divine language), or by much use and acquaintance together with a good taste or judgment, by comparing one thing with another and having our senses as it were exercised to discern it (which is the way that adult persons must come to speak any language, and in its true idiom, that is not their native tongue).
>
> Great care should be used, and we should endeavor to be well and thoroughly acquainted, or we shall never understand [or] have a right notion of the idiom of the language. If we go to interpret divine types without this, we shall be just like one that pretends to speak any language that ha[s]n't thoroughly learnt it. We shall use many barbarous expressions that fail entirely of the proper beauty of the language, that are very harsh in the ears of those that are well versed in the language. God ha[s]n't expressly explained *all* the types of Scriptures, but has done so much as is sufficient to *teach* us the language. (*WJE* 11:150–51)

John Henry Newman

Like Edwards, John Henry Newman (1801–90) believed the Old Testament is chock-full of types pointing to New Testament realities. Eve is a type of Mary, Rahab of Mary Magdalene, Moses of Christ, Pharaoh of the devil, just as Israel in the wilderness is a type of the church in the world. But for Newman, the Anglo-Catholic theologian who shocked all England by "swimming the Tiber" in 1845, the Old Testament's types pointed especially to high church and sacramental realities. The tree of life in the creation story, Melchizedek's bread and wine, and the milk and honey in the wilderness all were types of Christian Eucharist inaugurated by Jesus. As if to rebut what he thought to be evangelical antinomianism (the idea that in Christ we are free of law), Newman taught that Joshua's work was a type of the works that faith must produce if it is saving faith: Joshua showed that, once given an inheritance by God, we must seize it and fight the battles necessary to hold it. Newman said that the three Jewish orders of ministry—high priest, priest, and Levite—were types of the Christian orders of ministry: bishop, priest, and deacon.[16]

Similarly to Edwards, Newman saw a continuity of substance between type and antitype, but substance raised to a higher order. Church buildings continue to show that God maintains a special presence in a building consecrated to his worship, just as in Jerusalem's temple. The New Testament tells us in Colossians 2 that baptism is the new covenant antitype to the Old Testament type of circumcision; each sacrament brings the child into God's covenant with Abraham's family. The Jewish Passover is raised to its completion in Jesus's passion as the sacrificial lamb, and then in the church in the daily and weekly Eucharists. In each transition from type to antitype, there is a kind of correction but then restoration. For example, the Passover enables a special annual communion with the God of Israel, but the Eucharist enables it every day. Yet Passover's essential elements—atonement and communion—are restored.[17]

Newman wrote less about the world of nature "out there" than Edwards did. For example, he said that the blessings of rain and fruitful seasons and regular food and ordinary gladness in life are all types that show every human being that God is good, but he did not write in profuse Edwardsean detail about the hundreds of other ways in the natural world that we learn about

16. Jaak Seynaeve, *Cardinal Newman's Doctrine on Holy Scripture: According to His Published Works and Previously Unedited Manuscripts* (Leuven: Publications Universitaires de Louvain, 1953), 258–62; John Henry Newman, "Joshua a Type of Christ and His Followers," in *Sermons Bearing on the Subjects of the Day* (London: Longmans, Green, 1918), 159, 161, 165, 209–10.

17. Newman, "Joshua a Type," 204–5, 206, 207–11.

God. Yet he did surpass Edwards in his commentary on the types in *human* nature. In particular, Newman wrote often about conscience. He said that we humans hear God speak to us the most in our conscience. What we learn there, more than anything else, is that God is our Judge and that justice is an eternal principle. Sinners must be punished for their sins.[18]

There is another type in the world "out there" that teaches Christians and non-Christians alike, according to Newman. He called it the "government of the world" by God, which is close to what Edwards called "moral government." By these phrases they both meant things that happen in the world that teach observers that there is genuine moral retribution in the cosmos. For Newman, among the things taught by the "government of the world" was that evil is punished eventually, even if after a long time. Good is returned for good, not always but often, and sometimes after a long time. Newman saw this pattern happening through earthquakes and plagues, the rise and fall of states, the migrations of peoples, scientific and technological inventions and discoveries, and even the progress of philosophy and other realms of knowledge (313).

Again, like Edwards, Newman believed that the world religions contain types of truth, even though these religions are finally false. They teach lessons such as the following: "that punishment is sure, though slow, that murder will out, that treason never prospers, that pride will have a fall, that honesty is the best policy, and that curses fall on the heads of those who utter them" (313). But it is not only moral truth they teach; there are also truthful religious lessons. The most important is the "vicarious principle," which is the idea that "we appropriate to ourselves what others do for us." For example, parents work and endure pain so that their children may prosper, and children in turn suffer because of the sins of their parents. The punishment earned by the husband often falls on the wife, and benefits come to all from the dangerous or unhealthy toil of the few. Soldiers endure wounds or death for the sake of those who sit at home (315). This is a truth that other religions recognize in varying degrees but that Christian faith sees most clearly in Christ's vicarious satisfaction for our sins.

Two corollaries are the notions (1) that sacrifices for sin must offer something that is ours and unblemished, and (2) that there is meritorious intercession, whereby it is of the greatest merit for saintly people to intercede for sinners. There are strains of these two themes in many world religions, said Newman, and both are types fulfilled perfectly in Christ's unique mediation by the offering of his unblemished self for undeserving sinners (315–17).

18. John Henry Newman, *An Essay in Aid of a Grammar of Assent* (Garden City, NY: Image, 1955), 312, 304–5. In the next few paragraphs, page numbers in parentheses refer to *Grammar of Assent*.

Newman paid more attention to the fine arts than did Edwards. When we hear sublime and beautiful sounds emanating from so little—a mere "seven notes in the scale"—we cannot but conclude that the mysterious stirrings of heart that we feel have actually "escaped from some higher sphere." These earthly harmonies suggest to our inner religious ear that there must be an eternal harmony shared by saints and angels in another world. They even whisper to us that just as good music obeys mathematical and harmonic laws, so too there must be divine law for us to obey in the moral and religious realms. Music has a peculiar ability to pierce the veil that separates the visible from the invisible worlds.[19]

Newman talked about two levels or kinds of types. There are natural types for this world, visible in nature and history, that operate by what he called the "mystical principle." They are principally for unbelievers and show to them that there is another world beyond their sight. Then there are types of grace that operate by the "sacramental principle," which are for the church. They show *not* that there is a God who governs the world according to justice over the long haul (lessons from mystical principle) but that God redeems the world through the meritorious and vicarious intercession of his Son (lessons from the sacramental principle). Both kinds of types operate by analogy, which principle seen in its fullness shows that everything is connected to everything else. Even the two kinds of types—the mystical for the world of nature and the sacramental for the world of grace—are connected. Hence grace does not oppose nature but perfects it.[20]

Is It Legitimate?

For both Edwards and Newman, as for most of the Christian tradition until the twentieth century, this typological view of reality was a great blessing to believers and unbelievers alike. For believers it helped make sense of all of reality, showing that nature and grace are not opposed but complementary, one pointing to the other. It was also enjoyable, providing great satisfaction and fulfillment, both intellectually and aesthetically. Furthermore, it provided a kind of ethical enjoyment, adding conviction and strength to moral lessons that otherwise were harder to accept. For unbelievers, it offered an intellectual

19. *The Letters and Diaries of John Henry Newman*, ed. Charles Stephen Dessain (London: Nelson, 1969), 19:415.

20. John Henry Newman, "Milman's View of Christianity," in *Essays Critical and Historical* (London, 1871), 2:190, 192, 229; John Henry Newman, *Sermons 1824–1843*, vol. 2, ed. Vincent Ferres Blehl, SJ (Oxford: Clarendon, 1993), 382.

coherence to reality that reinforced Christian theological proposals that God is the author of not just redemption but also creation and that the two are concordant not disjunctive. For many, this perspective was helpful apologetically—assisting them in their own understanding of faith and explaining its coherence to others. This typological vision of reality served the church in these ways for more than nineteen hundred years.

In the twentieth century, however, many Christians, especially Protestants, lost sight of this vision. Part of the reason was the rise of Nazism and its "theology" of blood and soil. This was taken to be an example of "natural theology" (the name for Christian theologies that find meaning in this world) and therefore proof that claims for types in the world outside the Bible lead only to idolatry. The Swiss theologian Karl Barth (1886–1968) was particularly effective in persuading his fellow theologians that all natural theology is a betrayal of the biblical vision. For more on Barth's objections to natural theology and my analysis of those objections, see the appendix.

Barth is best known for his judgment that liberal theology rejected biblical revelation and replaced it with a system of thinking from outside the Bible. He called on Christians to recover "the strange, new world of the Bible" as a framework for viewing reality.[21] In the next chapter we will look at the Bible and its use of typology. Readers might find that the ways that Jesus and the apostles read the Old Testament typologically are strange and new. But even if they seem strange and new, I trust that readers will also find that the Bible's use of types is the key to discerning types outside the Bible.

---

21. Karl Barth, "The Strange, New World within the Bible," in *The Word of God and the Word of Man*, trans. Douglas Horton (Gloucester, MA: Peter Smith, 1978), 28–50.

2

The Bible

A World of Types, Key to Types in All the Worlds

Jesus said, "Moses wrote about me" (John 5:46). He told the two disciples on the road to Emmaus that there were "things about himself" in "*all* the Scriptures" (Luke 24:27). For this reason he said that the story of Jonah, for example, was not just the story of a Hebrew prophet preaching to pagan gentiles but a type of Jesus's coming death and resurrection: "Just as Jonah was in the belly of the great fish for three days and three nights, so the Son of Man will be in the heart of the earth for three days and three nights" (Matt. 12:40).

This was one of many examples where Jesus transposed the ancient context—and the biblical author's original intention—to interpret the Old Testament text as a massive typological system referring to himself. On another occasion he took a psalm about YHWH putting King David's enemies under his feet and reinterpreted it as testimony that God would put his own (Jesus's) enemies under his feet.[1] The author of another psalm (118) probably was giving thanks for how Israel had been chosen by God after being overlooked by the great powers of the world, but Jesus applied it to himself in Luke 20:17: "What then is this that is written, 'The stone which the builders rejected has

---

1. This was the meaning of Jesus's question in the temple about Ps. 110, "David calls him [the Messiah] Lord. So how is he [the Messiah] his [David's] son?" (Mark 12:37; Luke 20:41). The rabbis had been interpreting this psalm as a messianic psalm (Midrash Tehillim on Ps. 110), thus already thinking that there were two levels of meaning: the literal, in which someone else is writing about YHWH's exaltation of David, and the prophetic, in which YHWH was talking about the Messiah. Jesus followed the rabbis in focusing on the prophetic and not the literal sense.

become the cornerstone'? Everyone who falls on that stone will be broken to pieces; it will crush the one on whom it falls." In still another psalm David lamented that his "bosom friend" had "lifted the heel against [him]" (Ps. 41:9). Jesus said that this statement was really about Judas betraying *him* (John 13:18).

Modern Christians have often thought these were merely examples of Old Testament *prophecy*. The Old Testament author, they imagined, was predicting what would happen to or through the Messiah. But notice the way this interpretation misunderstands what is going on in these texts. Not only does it wrongly presume that the Old Testament author was self-consciously predicting something about the future Messiah, but it also fails to discern what Jesus was clearly suggesting. Jesus was implying that the Holy Spirit already knew everything about the Messiah's life, death, and resurrection when the Old Testament was being written and that the Spirit was guiding the authors to write things that would anticipate those details—even when the Old Testament authors themselves knew nothing about those future details.

In one sense these words *were* a kind of prophecy, for they do indeed predict details about the future. But as many have pointed out, it was "forth-telling" rather than "foretelling." For, as Peter said, even the prophets (and even less so the authors of the other parts of the Old Testament) did not know "which person or time" was meant when "the spirit of the Messiah" was guiding them to write what they wrote (1 Pet. 1:11). The Spirit knew, but the authors typically did not know how or even *if* what they wrote contained a level of meaning beyond their ken. So the author of Psalm 118 was rejoicing in how YHWH had lifted him up after years of ignominy, probably with no idea that his words were really about the future Messiah.

For this reason Jesus and the apostles read all the Old Testament as a massive typological system—one giant type. On the one hand, it has its own integrity as a story of the world and its meaning written by God's chosen people. But on the other hand, Jesus and the apostles suggested it was all about Messiah Jesus and his kingdom, and the ways in *that* kingdom that God takes sinners and makes them into a holy people.

Not only Jesus read the Hebrew Bible as a typological system. Think of Paul's remarkable testimony in 1 Corinthians 10. There he wrote that the whole story of Israel's redemption from Egypt and its wanderings for forty years in the wilderness was *typikōs*, or "for a type" (v. 11). All "these things took place as types [*typoi*] for us." The story of "our fathers" traveling "under the cloud" and passing "through the [Red] sea," eating the manna ("spiritual food") miraculously set out each morning, and drinking water ("spiritual drink") miraculously from the rock—all of those details in that long story were put there by God's Spirit in order to draw the Christians in Corinth closer to Christ and his kingdom. Paul said that these stories are to teach the Corinthians not to "desire evil as they did," not to be "idolaters as some of them were," and not to "partake in sexual immorality as some of them did" (vv. 6–8). If the Corinthians followed these bad examples, they might incur the same punishments—"twenty-three thousand fell in a single day," and others were "destroyed by the Destroyer" (vv. 8, 10). Nor were they to "put Messiah to the test, as some of them did and were destroyed by serpents" (v. 9).

Paul's point was that Torah was written, and the Old Testament events transpired, with all the details of Christ and his kingdom already directing their progress. As proof, Paul pointed to the Israelites in the wilderness, who "drank from the spiritual rock that was following them, and the rock was the Messiah [Christ]" (1 Cor. 10:4). Notice the two remarkable things Paul said here. First, the rock was "following" the Israelites in the Sinai. Nowhere in Torah is such a movement stated, but the rabbis during Paul's time were teaching it in their commentary on written Torah.[2] Second, the rock that gushed water was Christ! It was not just a *symbol* of the future Messiah that Moses imagined or a *sign* of his love that God sent. In some way that Paul does not explain, Christ himself was the rock miraculously spouting water.

Think of what this means for types in general. If this rock was a type—and Paul explicitly wrote that it was (using the very word *typos*)—and if he used this rock as his quintessential example of Old Testament typology, which he seemed to do, then he suggested that every other type in the Old Testament somehow participates in the ontological reality of the Messiah, Jesus. But I am getting ahead of myself. At the end of this chapter I will return to the question of what a type actually is, which is what theologians call the "metaphysics" of types. That is, is a type out in the world merely a sign that points to God? Or is it something more? In other words, does the setting and rising of the sun as a type of the Son in his death and resurrection, for example, mean anything more than that God uses the former as a pointer to the latter? Or is the sun somehow participating in the reality of the Son? This is the question I will address at the end of the chapter, and Paul's comments on the rock and other types will help us.

One more place where the New Testament suggests that all of the Hebrew Bible is a massive typological system with Christ and his redemptive kingdom at its heart is in Hebrews. The author of Hebrews repeatedly went to the book of Psalms for prophecies of the Messiah to come. In nearly every

---

2. Peter Enns, *Inspiration and Incarnation: Evangelicals and the Problem of the Old Testament*, 2nd ed. (Grand Rapids: Baker Academic, 2015), 139–41.

case this author wrenched the psalm out of its original context and assigned
a messianic meaning to the text that was undoubtedly not intended by the
original author. For example, Psalm 8 has humanity as a whole in mind when it
compares the heavens to puny men and women. The Hebrew uses a masculine
noun and singular masculine suffixes for humanity in general, as the English
language used to do until recently ("man" and "him" as inclusive references
for men and women both).

> When I look at your heavens, the work of your fingers,
>   the moon and the stars that you have established;
>   what is man that you are mindful of him,
>   the son of man that you care for him?
> Yet you have made him a little lower than God
>   And crowned him with glory and honor.
> You have given him dominion over the works of your hands
>   You have put all things under his feet,
> All sheep and oxen,
>   And also the beasts of the field,
> The birds of the air, and the fish of the sea,
>   Whatever passes through the paths of the seas. (Ps. 8:3–8)

While the psalm's author was thinking of "man" in general, the author of
Hebrews said it is not only about a coming messiah but Jesus in particular:[3]

> It has been testified somewhere,
>   "What is man that you are mindful of him,
>   the son of man that you care for him?
>   You have made him a little lower than the angels,
>   with glory and honor you have crowned him,
>   and all things you have put under his feet."
> . . . At this time we do not yet see everything subjected to him, but while he was
> made a little lower than the angels, we do see Jesus crowned with glory and
> honor because of the suffering of death. (Heb. 2:6–9)

It is not just in this place in Hebrews that the author read the Old Testament as a giant testimony to Jesus as Messiah.[4] There is also a telling reference
in chapter 8 to the entire system of Hebrew worship. In verse 5 the author

3. In the early church it was common to read Ps. 8 this way. See Paul's nearly identical exegesis
in 1 Cor. 15:27 and Eph. 1:22.
4. See, for example, the author's transposition of meaning in Heb. 1:5 (Ps. 2 and 2 Sam.
7:14); 1:6 (Deut. 32:43 LXX); 1:8 (Ps. 45); 1:13 (Ps. 110); 2:12 (Ps. 22); 5:5 (Pss. 2; 110); 8:5
(Exod. 25:40); and 10:5 (Ps. 40).

wrote of the Jewish liturgical leaders in the tabernacle (his Jewish readers probably understood this to apply to the second temple, from which they might have been excluded and were being called to leave),[5] "They worship the heavenly things according to a shadow and model [of those things], as Moses was instructed when he was about to construct the Tabernacle, 'See,' he [YHWH] said, 'that you make *everything* by the pattern [*typos*] that was shown you on the mountain.'" The author of this letter was quoting Exodus 25:40.

Notice what this author was suggesting—that "everything" in the tabernacle worship was *typical* of heavenly things. "Everything" in the tabernacle/temple was constructed according to "the pattern that was shown [Moses] on the mountain." Every little part was directed by God as a type of something going on in "heavenly things." This wording means that all the details that Christians usually dismiss as no longer applicable to them in the new covenant—the so-called ceremonial aspects of the law—are pieces in the massive pattern given by God, every part of which has some correspondence to what is now going on in heavenly worship.

In other words, it is not just the story of Israel's history, as Paul suggested, that bears typological meaning for us. It is also the whole system of Jewish sacrifice and worship that is spelled out in minute detail in the Torah and then discussed and refined throughout the rest of the Old Testament. Every last part of the law has meaning for Christians, and it all refers to the Messiah and his redemption. Even details such as compassion for animals: Paul told the Corinthians that the command in Torah not to "muzzle an ox while it treads out the grain" is really about paying a minister of the gospel. "Is it the oxen that God cares about? Isn't God talking about us? It was written for us because the plowman and thresher should plow in hope of sharing the grain" (1 Cor. 9:9–10).

Some have speculated that such a comment means that Paul had no use for the literal meaning of Torah commands—in this case, the command to let oxen eat while they are treading out the grain (Deut. 25:4). But this conclusion is mistaken. Paul made clear elsewhere that the law was to be obeyed, but with a new twist—in light of the Messiah and his resurrection. Because of these epochal events new spiritual meaning was added to the literal meaning.[6]

5. See Carl Mosser, "Rahab outside the Camp," in *The Epistle to the Hebrews and Christian Theology*, ed. Richard Bauckham et al. (Grand Rapids: Eerdmans, 2009), 383–404.
6. Paul insisted that the law was not to be overthrown now that faith had come (Rom. 3:31); that it is holy, righteous, and good (Rom. 7:12); and that Jesus had come so that the righteous requirement of the law might now be fulfilled in us (Rom. 8:4). The law had become "the law of Messiah" because Messiah Jesus had now shown us the law's inner meaning (1 Cor. 9:21;

So, for example, this command was not to be ignored at its literal level but was also to be interpreted in light of the Messiah and his kingdom. It was about *both* our duty to care for animals *and* the right of workers in Jesus's kingdom harvest to "reap material things" from that harvest (1 Cor. 9:11–12). The fulfillment (antitype) of the type does not destroy the type but completes it, just as Jesus said he came not to destroy the Law and the Prophets but to fulfill them (Matt. 5:17).

Why So Indirect?

Let me recap a bit. We have seen that Jesus, Paul, and the author of Hebrews used the Old Testament typologically—not in a straightforward manner reproducing the thinking of the original authors but as a system of patterns that points to the Bible's culmination in Jesus's redemption and kingdom. Later in this chapter I will outline some of the ways in which the Old Testament pictures these things. But before I do so, I must answer the questions that make typology a stumbling block for many moderns. They wonder why God would use such indirect means to teach his people about his Messiah and his redemption. Why use difficult-to-understand types? Why not tell them directly in clear statements? And why take thousands of years? Why didn't God reveal his highest truths directly at the very beginning?

A first answer to these questions is that typology seems to be God's preferred way to communicate. I say that because God has filled both all of reality and all of the Bible with types. In the next eight chapters we will see that God has filled all of reality—nature, science, law, history, animals, sports, world religions, and even sex—with types. And we have seen briefly—and will see more fully in the next pages—that the Bible is full of types. The Old Testament teaches that God often speaks in parables (Prov. 1:6; Ps. 49:4), which are verbal types, and YHWH often points to the future with *enacted* types rather than prophecies. For example, Jacob and Esau struggled in the womb, which was an enacted type of the future hostilities between the Israelites and the Edomites (Gen. 25:22–23). Jacob's hand grabbed Esau's heel during birth, which was another enacted type of the Israelites overcoming and supplanting their enemies (25:26). Moses was drawn out of the river as an infant, foreshadowing in action what would happen to the whole Israelite nation years later in the Red Sea (Exod. 2:1–10; 14:1–31). The burning bush that was not

---

Matt. 5:17–19). Lest his readers think the literal meaning of Tanakh can be ignored, he warned the early church not to "go beyond what is written" (1 Cor. 4:6), which seems to mean the text of the Old Testament.

consumed was a visible type of Israel's preservation in the fires of affliction in Egypt and elsewhere throughout its history (Exod. 3:1–22). Moses's rod that swallowed up the Egyptian magicians' rods typified the superiority of YHWH's power over that of all other gods (Exod. 7:12). God enabled David to kill a lion and a bear as types of his future destruction of Israel's enemies (1 Sam. 17:37). God used a bush to show Jonah human frailty when God suddenly grew the bush and just as suddenly withered it. The bush was a type of the people of Nineveh, for whom YHWH cared, just as Jonah cared about the bush (Jon. 4:6–11). In the Old Testament, then, God often uses not just words but enacted words—types—to foreshadow the future.

The New Testament tells us that Jesus "said *nothing* to the crowds without a parable" (Matt. 13:34). Paul suggested that all of biblical history can be seen as "two covenants" represented by two women, Sarah and Hagar. One was "from Mount Sinai, bearing children for slavery," and the other corresponds to "the Jerusalem above," which is free. Paul used this typology to distinguish between (1) a narrowly Pharisaic view of salvation that would come from law and (2) his own gospel of salvation by promise through the Messiah (Gal. 4:21–5:1). He intimated that the proper understanding of God's ways with Israel and the world comes through an "allegory," which in this case consists of two grand types: "Hagar is Mount Sinai," and "the other [woman, Sarah] is the Jerusalem above, and she is our mother" (Gal. 4:25–26). What Paul implied is that the grand story of redemption and its principal opposing story are best seen as two giant types. He depicted these types after three chapters arguing in propositional form that "a person is not justified by works of the law but by the faithfulness of Jesus Christ" (Gal. 2:16)[7]—not by our works but by Jesus's works. Paul turned in chapter 4 to typology as if to say, "If you aren't persuaded by my propositional argument, let me give you an image that might be easier to see."

You might disagree with Paul's apparent intent. Perhaps you think, as most of the West has thought in the last few centuries, that clear and distinct propositions are superior to images. You might wonder why God does not speak more directly all of the time instead of just some of the time. After all, he spoke clearly his moral will in the Ten Commandments, and he told the disciples directly that Jesus was his beloved Son in whom he was well pleased (Matt. 3:17; Mark 1:11). But the Old Testament is a special problem. If God's final revelation was of his Messiah, why was this whole first Testament—77 percent

---

7. My translation of *pisteōs Iēsou Christou* follows the argument of Richard Hays and others that, for Paul, it is the faithfulness of Jesus, not our faith, that saves us. See Hays, *The Faith of Jesus Christ: The Narrative Substructure of Galatians 3:1–4:11* (Grand Rapids: Eerdmans, 2002).

of the Protestant Bible!—merely a typological testimony to the Messiah rather than a clear statement of the Messiah? And what about the New Testament, which has its own share of mysteries? We read there of the "mystery" of marriage (Eph. 5:32), the "mystery" of Israel (Rom. 11:25), and "the mystery of iniquity" (2 Thess. 2:7 KJV)—not to mention the mystery of the church, in which gentile and Jew remain two but become one (Eph. 2:11–22; 3:8–9); the mystery of the Eucharist, in which somehow the body and blood of Christ are communicated through bread and wine (1 Cor. 10:16; Matt. 26:26–28); and the mystery of the Trinity, in which three are one (John 14:18–31; 17:11).

Thomas Aquinas, Jonathan Edwards, and Edward Pusey are of help here. Thomas (1225–74) spoke of sacraments as types that enact the gospel. Infant baptism, for example, brings the Holy Spirit to a baby who has done nothing to merit him. This act shows the gratuity of grace—that God's love comes to sinners who have done nothing to deserve that love. These enacted types are perfect for us, Thomas argued, because we are sensory creatures and because the sacraments use the senses to show us what they mean. Baptism uses water, and Eucharist employs bread and wine. They appeal to our senses of sight, sound, touch, taste, and smell. He added that they are well suited to us for another reason. We tend to like external (rather than merely mental) activities because we are created bodies with connections to other bodies and things external to us, and they are external means of receiving Christ's grace.[8] So Thomas might say that God prefers types because they involve the sensory and external world and we are sensory creatures in that world.

Edwards emphasized the fittingness of types to God's communicative disposition.[9] For Edwards, God is "a communicative being" whose most overwhelming disposition is to communicate his perfections. As Edwards argued in *The End for Which God Created the World*, this was the reason for the creation: apart from the creation and God's continuing exercise of his attributes toward the creation, many of God's attributes would lie dormant (*WJE* 13:410).[10]

But there was a problem. God is infinite, and his creation is finite. How could the sublime things of infinite divinity be communicated to finite minds? Edwards's answer was a paraphrase of Calvin's notion of accommodation: God accommodates his truth to our finite understandings just as human adults change their manner of presentation when teaching children. Ordinary

---

8. Thomas Aquinas, *Summa theologiae* III, q. 61, art. 1; q. 68, art. 9.

9. These paragraphs on Edwards are adapted from Michael McClymond and Gerald McDermott, *The Theology of Jonathan Edwards* (New York: Oxford University Press, 2012), 116–29.

10. See also *WJE* 8:429, 434–35, 438–39; see Janice Knight, "Learning the Language of God: Jonathan Edwards and the Typology of Nature," *William and Mary Quarterly*, 3rd ser., 48 (1991): 543–51.

discourse distorts heavenly things only because of the incommensurable gap between infinite, nonmaterial realities and human concepts expressed with words grounded in finite, material things (*WJE* 18:583).[11]

Therefore, God uses types, which, though also employing material images to express immaterial realities, nevertheless by the power of imagery suggest to the human mind what lies beyond the visible world. So types are employed by God because of their pedagogical value. Many types are pictures of sorts, and a picture is worth a thousand words—or at least a hundred. For example, Edwards wrote, "temple of the Holy Ghost" expresses in a few words what would otherwise take one hundred. "By such similitudes a vast volume is represented to our minds in three words, and things that we are not able to behold directly are represented before us in lively pictures" (*WJE* 13:181).

These pictures so cohere with human sensibilities—or, to put it in Edwards's terms, there is such an analogy or harmony between the pictures and our sensibilities—that the human mind is naturally led to see the substance that the types represent. "The affairs of the Jewish church are so much of a shadow, that a mind so prepared and exercised would naturally be led to the substance" if that mind is "of a poetical and gracious disposition" (*WJE* 13:363–64).

The types also have affective value. Because they are drawn from the sensory world and commonly employ material objects as images, fallen human beings, who are more familiar with the material than the immaterial world, can more easily understand them. They are more affected "by those things [they] see with [their] eyes and hear with [their] ears and have experience of" (*WJE* 14:140).

If types are more accessible because grounded in sensory experience, they are also more enjoyable. Types provide "pleasure" and "delight." We know they do, Edwards argued, from the great enjoyment people derived from "the imitative arts, in painting, poetry, fables, metaphorical language [and] dramatic performances. This disposition appears early in children." Perhaps because it is enjoyable, subjects taught by types are more easily remembered, and moral lessons taught are received with deeper impression and greater conviction (*WJE* 11:191).

God therefore adapts his teaching method to human nature. He instructs the human race in a way that is best suited to the creature. Types are an aid to memory, they reinforce their lesson with extra strength and conviction, and they bring pleasure and delight.

11. John Calvin, *Institutes of the Christian Religion*, ed. John T. McNeill, trans. Ford Lewis Battles (Philadelphia: Westminster, 1960), 2.11.13; 1.17.13; *WJE* 10:418; 20:188.

Finally, Edwards connected types to the arts. Both, he explained, appeal to the same aesthetic and erotic capacities. Each uses the principle of *mimēsis* (imitation of the true, beautiful, and good) and fulfills human desires for the dramatic and the beautiful. Types, then, are a part of the divine aesthetic, the way in which God unites pedagogy and aesthetics.

The nineteenth-century Anglican theologian Edward Pusey (1800–1882) warned Christians not to insist on precision and clarity when it came to knowledge of God. He reminded his students that it was the deists who refused to accept biblical truths that did not satisfy their understandings of clarity, and that Paul's highest revelations were of "things that cannot be told" (2 Cor. 12:4). Noonday beams from the sun contract our sphere of vision, he wrote. We see more clearly with diminished light when the sun is not so brilliant. Pusey argued that when we gain in precision we often lose our knowledge of depth, just as when we look closely at the surface of the ocean it is impossible to see into its depths. The more precise our knowledge of something, the narrower its range.[12]

Pusey insisted that to attempt to replace figures or types with abstract propositions was to evaporate much of the meaning of the Bible. There was no better way to understand the main gospel truths, he wrote, than through its figures—such as the sacrifice of Christ, the kingdom of God, and the temple of the Holy Spirit. Translation into other terms sacrificed depth. Besides, "The picture-language of the East was the very choice of God, in order to reveal Himself. Why should we be wiser than He and paraphrase His language?"[13]

Finally, Pusey developed Thomas's thinking on enacted truth in the sacraments. Pusey remarked on the extra power conveyed when we see and participate in the enactment of God's kingdom. We see in our mind's eye the mystery of the only begotten Son in the sacrifice of Isaac as it is enacted in the biblical story. We hear of it when we listen to the story of Passover as God saves his only son Israel from slavery in Egypt. And we enact the mystery ourselves when we participate in the eucharistic sacrifice at Holy Communion. "If the sight be more than hearing, how much more [does one find] oneself enacting the truth, and when appealed to, the typical service [worship with liturgical and sacramental types] had this advantage[—]that being, as it were, wound round the conscience and forming a part of the spiritual life, it furnished a mingled argument to the conscience and the understanding."[14] As it is often

12. Edward Pusey, "Lectures on Types and Prophecies in the Old Testament" (typescript made available to the author by Hans Boersma), 5–6.
13. Pusey quoted here "a thoughtful German" ("Lectures," 46).
14. Pusey, "Lectures," 61.

remarked, the gospel is *told* in the preached Word, but the gospel is *shown* and *made present* in the sacraments.

God prefers types, then, because they use sensory experience to appeal to us sensory creatures (Thomas), they use the material to express the immaterial in ways that are enjoyable and memorable (Edwards), and they communicate depth that cannot be expressed in abstract propositions (Pusey).

Why So Long?

But why did God take so long in his use of types? Why was it necessary to use types for more than a millennium in the history of Israel before the Messiah was finally brought to earth? One of the most interesting answers to this question was given by the church's first philosopher of history, the early church father Irenaeus (ca. 145–202).[15] Irenaeus's grand metaphor was God as pedagogue. A pedagogue is a teacher who patiently leads his students step by step through a careful educational process. God, the divine pedagogue, is teaching and training his flock through the course of history. But he can teach only so much at a time because he knows the limited capacities of his pupils. Irenaeus says that after the fall we were infants as a race, needing discipline, capable of milk, not meat. For this reason God revealed only a tiny part of his glory, saving the incarnation of his Son for many centuries later.[16] In his great treatise *Against Heresies*, Irenaeus wrote that man as a race was "a little one . . . a child" who had to "learn" how to love God. He had to grow and become strong.[17]

Not only was the human race young and undisciplined but it had also allowed its heart to become hardened. Because of both "human infirmity" and "incontinence," God permitted the enactment of certain laws, such as the Old Testament laws allowing divorce. Without these concessions to human weakness, too many would have turned away from God entirely. The Ten Commandments were one stage in the divine pedagogy. They kept humans from idolatry and trained them in what it means to "love [God] with the whole heart."[18]

For this reason Christ was not revealed at the beginning, and the incarnation did not come for many centuries. Human beings weren't ready for it. It

15. These paragraphs on Irenaeus are adapted from Gerald R. McDermott, *God's Rivals: Why Has God Allowed Different Religions?* (Downers Grove, IL: IVP Academic, 2007), 99–116.
    16. *AH* 4.38.1–2.
    17. *AH* 4.15.2; *St. Irenaeus: Proof of the Apostolic Preaching*, trans. Joseph P. Smith (New York: Newman Press, 1952), 12.
    18. *AH* 4.15.2.

would have been incomprehensible, too much to bear. They would not have been prepared. Using Irenaeus's reasoning, we would say that it is for the same reason we don't give a text on systematic theology to a new believer, or a test on calculus to the arithmetic student. Irenaeus's point was that God planned a gradual course of preparation for his people to receive and understand the incarnate Word. He prepared a long series of stages through history that eventually culminated in the supreme event. Without those stages of patient preparation, the final event would have been misunderstood. The student would neither have understood the advanced material nor have been able to graduate into the real world of communion with God.

God did the same in his preparation of Israel. He first taught his chosen people that sins must be expiated by the sacrifice of a life. The reason is that sin kills; it takes life. So another life must be given for the life that was taken away. Since blood is essential to life, shed blood was the proof that life had been sacrificed. As Israelites made sacrifices and learned by *doing* and *watching* that life with blood must be sacrificed to atone for life taken, they were prepared over centuries for the eventual blood sacrifice of the perfect Israelite for all the sins of Israel.

But Israel had to learn in stages, just as we learn in stages. First we study arithmetic, then algebra and trigonometry, and only after all that can we negotiate calculus. Israel had to be taught indirectly, just as we cannot look directly into the sun but only indirectly. We look at the sun's beams and not the source of the beams. Israelites learned about the Messiah *directly* only fairly late in their history, but they were being prepared for that revelation *indirectly* all along through types—particularly the type of sacrifice for sin.

They first had to sacrifice *animals* for human sin before they could accept the sacrifice of a *man*. They had to learn that an animal could substitute for a *man* before they could accept the substitution of the Messiah for *themselves*. They had to learn that the sacrificed animal must be unblemished and a (ritually) clean animal. They needed to see that at Passover it had to be a lamb, which was meek and gentle but suffered a violent death. They also had to learn through that annual festival that there needed to be a scapegoat to carry the sins of Israel into the wilderness, while the high priest of Israel was interceding for the people by sprinkling blood from the sacrifices on the mercy seat. All of these types of the Messiah and his redemption prepared the Jews to understand the words of the prophet Isaiah: "YHWH laid on *him* the iniquity of us all . . . because his soul was making an offering for sin" (Isa. 53:6, 10). They had to go through centuries of *repeated* sacrifices for sins until it could be revealed that one day there would come a *final* sacrifice for sin: "Seventy weeks are decreed about your people and your holy city, to *finish* the transgression [the Hebrew can mean "sin offerings"], to put an *end* to sin, and to atone for iniquity, to bring in *everlasting* righteousness, to *seal* both vision and prophet, and to anoint a most holy place" (Dan. 9:24 ESV).

The Great Antitype, or The Grand Theme of the Bible

Now that I have argued (1) that the Bible is full of types and that the Old Testament is one massive type, and (2) that God prefers to communicate through types because they communicate with greater depth than propositions alone, I want to propose the grand theme of the Bible. By grand theme I mean the antitype for all the types—that is, the reality toward which all the shadows of the biblical types point. That divine reality is the history of redemption by the trinitarian God. This is the project of making a sinful humanity into a holy church by the work of the Trinity, starting in eternity, typified by Israel's redemption from slavery, actualized by the Messiah's work in the incarnation, and applied to the saints in history through the church. I will sketch the biblical types of this grand theme by first outlining some Old Testament types of the redemption, and then sketching Old Testament types of the Messiah.

Types of the Redemption on the Road to Emmaus

What were the highlights of the most exciting theological lecture in history? I refer here to what Jesus said on the road to Emmaus as he explained to the two disciples "the things about himself" in "all" the Scriptures. Jonathan Edwards thought Jesus probably started with the creation, when "darkness was over the face of the deep" and God said, "Let there be light" (Gen. 1:2–3). Perhaps then Jesus told the two disciples that his coming was "the light that shines in the darkness," which "the darkness has not overcome" (John 1:5). And that he was the redeemer whose coming into the world was the "true light that enlightens every man" and gradually drives out the darkness from one's soul (1:9). Perhaps he also explained that his redemption was bringing a "new creation" for both believers and the world (2 Cor. 5:17; Rom. 8:18–25; Rev. 7:9; 22:2). And that the new creation of his kingdom is the antitype of the first creation, which is its type; that the redemption that is the kingdom is the Light that drives out all darkness.

There is little doubt that in that grand lecture to his two students, the world's greatest seminary professor talked about the Bible's first prophecy of redemption: "And YHWH God said to the serpent . . . 'I will put enmity between you and the woman, and between your seed and her seed. He will strike your head and you will strike his heel'" (Gen. 3:14–15). This was a

prophecy because it foretold what would happen, but it was also a type because it used vivid imagery without direct explanation of its meaning. The
serpent's striking Eve's seed on the heel was Satan's part in the killing of the
Messiah. The devil thought he had finally gotten rid of God's Messiah. But
this striking of the serpent's head by the seed (which means Christ; see Gal.
3:16) is a prophecy-by-type of Christ's victory over Satan at the cross. As Paul
suggested in his letter to the church at Colossae, just when Satan thought he
had defeated God and his Messiah, he discovered that the instrument he had
used to kill the Messiah was the same weapon God was using to bring victory:
God "cancelled the record of debt that stood against us . . . by nailing it to
the cross. God thereby disarmed [Satan's] rulers and authorities and shamed
them, by triumphing over them through it" (Col. 2:14–15).

If there is any doubt that Jesus told these two on the road to Emmaus about
the creation and the serpent, there is absolutely *no* doubt that he spoke of
Israel's exodus from slavery in Egypt as a type of his own redemption of God's
people. Surely he told these learners that, just as the Jews were liberated from
slavery to the tyrannical Egyptian regime, from early death at the hands of
their cruel overseers, and from bondage to the hated Pharaoh, *he* was saving
them from bondage to sin, fear of death, and control by the devil through
his life, death, and resurrection. For this reason John the Baptist proclaimed
that Jesus was "the lamb of God," the antitype toward which pointed all the
Passover lambs (unblemished one-year-old males) that were to be sacrificed on
the eve of the Passover feast each spring (Exod. 12:1–6). On the first Passover,
Israelites were told to smear the lamb's blood on the top of their doorposts
so that when the angel of death came to strike the firstborn, the angel would
"pass over" the homes with the blood. Paul thus wrote that "Christ is our
Passover lamb that has been sacrificed" (1 Cor. 5:7). His blood redeems us,
just as the lambs' blood at the first Passover redeemed Israel (Heb. 9:12).

Types of the Messiah

Let's continue imagining what Jesus told those two disciples. Apparently
he spoke more about the Redeemer than the redemption, for Luke said that
he "interpreted to them in all the Scriptures the things concerning *himself*"
(Luke 24:27 ESV). In other words, the bulk of his "lecture" was about how he,
the Messiah (remember, this is what "Christ" means), was in all the Scriptures.
Not types of redemption per se, but types of himself. Or—and we will get to
this possibility at the end of the chapter in our discussion of the metaphysics of types—perhaps he meant that the stories of redemption, such as the
exodus, are really about *him* at work and not just something that resembled

his future work. Edwards and others had called these "types of the Messiah" (see *WJE* 11:187–324). We will suggest a few of them here.

Let's begin with God's first address to Abraham, the father of Israel. God told him that through him and his progeny all the families of the earth will be blessed: "I will make of you a great nation . . . and in you all the families of the earth shall be blessed" (Gen. 12:2–3 ESV). Here the God of Israel proclaimed that blessing would come to the world through Israel, the progeny of Abraham. Jesus might have had this promise in mind when he told the woman at the well that "salvation is from the Jews" (John 4:22). In any event, God hinted to Abraham here that the Messiah would come from his loins, which meant that the Messiah would be descended from Abraham. He would be a Jew, one from the chosen people. Just as Abraham and his family would bring blessing to the world, so the Messiah and his family—the church, which is his body—would bring blessing to the world, for the head of the body is the Jewish Messiah, who is the foremost son of Abraham, and Abraham's family was to bless the world.

Perhaps the greatest son of Abraham before Jesus was Moses. He too was a type of the Messiah. It was by God but through Moses's leadership that Israel was delivered from death and destruction by Pharaoh and his armies. Moses led Israel through its own valley of the shadow of death. And as Paul wrote, Christ was there in the wilderness feeding Israel through Moses's faith. Moses was a type of Christ.

Joshua was captain of the armies of Israel during the conquest of Canaan. He brought God's people out of the wilderness into Canaan, the land flowing with milk and honey. He led them into battle and defeated their enemies. He was a type of the Messiah, who brought God's people out of their wilderness, fought their battles for them, and led them into a land of milk and honey.

Gideon was another type of the Messiah. Like Christ while he was in Galilee and facing the power of both Rome and Jerusalem, Gideon was small and weak and without weapons of war in his battles with Midian. He led a tiny number, a remnant of his own people. Christ too leads a remnant, his "little flock" (Luke 12:32), and he and his flock fight with spiritual and not earthly weapons.

Samson's name means "little sun," like Christ, who is the "sun of righteousness" (Mal. 4:2; Luke 1:78–79). Samson saved Israel from their enemies the Philistines. In this respect he was like all the little saviors of the Old Testament, who were little lights reflecting the true Light of the world.

Like the Messiah Jesus, David was a shepherd. Like Jesus, he was hated by his brothers. Like Jesus, David defeated the enemies of God's people. Like Jesus, David obtained his wife by risking his life in battle against Israel's greatest enemy and destroying it. David won Michal (1 Sam. 18), and Jesus won the church as his bride (2 Cor. 11:2–4; Rom. 7:4). Like Jesus, David was not only a king but also a prophet. Most strikingly, David was a mediator who stood between God and the people, averting judgments and punishments for sin by interceding for them and taking the punishment on himself (2 Sam. 24).

Solomon was another type of the Messiah. Just as the Messiah brought peace between sinners and God, so Solomon's was a reign marked by peace, feasting, and joy. At the beginning of his reign, the house of the Lord was filled with glory. Just as Jesus's disciples beheld his glory (John 1:14; Matt. 17:1–8), so Solomon's glory became manifest: the kings of the earth came to hear his wisdom and see the glory of his kingdom (1 Kings 4:29–34; 10:1–13).

But perhaps the greatest and most vivid of the Messiah's types was Joseph. Like the Son of God, Joseph was a beloved son (of Jacob). The sheaves of his brothers bowed down toward his, just as the kings of the world will one day bow to Messiah Jesus (Ps. 72:11). In Joseph's dream the sun, moon, and stars bowed down to him, just as the heavens are said to declare the righteousness of the Old Testament's "Lord," whom the early church took to be the Messiah (Gen. 37:9; Ps. 50:6; 97:6). Joseph was hated by his brothers, even though he later saved them from famine; so too our Messiah came to his own, but his own did not receive him (John 1:11). Just as Joseph saved from famine all the nations of the world around Egypt (Gen. 41), so Jesus's redemption is for all the nations (Matt. 28:19).

Before Joseph's later exaltation, he was first humiliated by betrayal and prison. He was a man of sorrows, an innocent man unjustly condemned. He was thrown into a place among prisoners, but he seems to have suffered with meekness. All these details were like those of the Messiah Jesus, who was also betrayed, was unjustly condemned, was thrown in with criminals, and suffered meekly throughout.

But then Joseph, like the Messiah, was exalted by the king and raised up to become ruler of all. He was put at the king's (Pharaoh's) right hand and given the king's ring and authority. Like Jesus, Joseph was a prophet who saw things no one else did and revealed secrets from God. Joseph was said to be distinguished above all other men because in him was the Spirit of God (Gen. 41:38). He was one to whom no one could be compared because of his wisdom and prudence (41:39). Biblically literate Christians know that all of these things were true of the Messiah Jesus. Isaiah wrote that the Messiah would be called "Wonderful, Counselor," and that "the Spirit of the Lord God would rest on [him]" (Isa. 11:2; 61:1).

As if these details were not enough, there were even more ways in which Joseph was a type of the Messiah. Pharaoh gave Joseph a wife, just as God gave a bride to Jesus, his Messiah (Gen. 41:45; Rev. 21:2). Joseph's brothers were grief-stricken and fearful because of their sins against him. When they came to him, they humbled themselves. Joseph first appeared to be angry toward them and was harsh. But then he made known his forgiveness and love for them (Gen. 44:1–45:15). So too our Lord first makes known to us his wrath toward our sin before he shows us his mercy. We lay hold of that mercy only when we have first seen the wrath.

Finally, Joseph gave his brothers a great feast of food and fellowship and invited them to come and live in his land, which happened after they had reconciled. So too believers share in the feast of Holy Communion, eating and drinking with Messiah Jesus as a covenantal renewal of the reconciliation he procured. This feast is an anticipation of the great wedding feast of the Lamb that is to come. Joseph's story is a type of the big issues of sin and redemption and of the renewal of God's people and the world.

What *Are* Types?

We have only scratched the surface of biblical typology. I will occasionally point to typology in the *New* Testament in the following chapters, but in this chapter I have focused almost entirely on the New Testament's use of Old Testament types. We have seen not only that Jesus and the apostles read the Old Testament typologically but that the Bible tells the story that all the types outside the Bible are *about*.

Now to the status of types: What exactly are they? I argue throughout that they are not merely things *we* notice but things or events that *God* has set in place. But even then, what *are* they? Take marriage, for example. Scripture tells us expressly that it is a type of the union of Christ with his church. If so, what is the relation between union in human marriage and union in the Christ-church marriage? Is the former merely a picture of the latter? Or is the relation something more?

It seems to me, on the basis of what Scripture tells us about types, that the type *participates* in the antitype—that is, it shares in the *being* of that to which it refers. Paul wrote in the 1 Corinthians passage we already examined that the rock that was following the Israelites in the wilderness, from which they drank water miraculously, "*was* Christ" (1 Cor. 10:4). This is nothing short of astonishing, and impossible for us to understand fully. But we *can* understand that this rock was not merely provided by Christ as a thing separate from Christ, in the way that Jesus was separate from a drink of water that he might have given to the woman at the well (John 4). No, the rock with its water flowing out of it *was* Christ. When those Israelites drew near to the rock, they were drawing near to their Messiah. When they drank from the rock, they were drinking Christ. The rock *participated* so fully in the reality of Christ that to experience the rock was to experience Christ. The rock was not merely a pointer but the presence itself—of Christ.

Hebrews 10:1 also suggests that types *participate* in the being of the realities to which they point. The author wrote, "The law has a shadow of the good things to come, but it is not the true form of the things." Much of this letter describes the furnishings, sacrifices, and worship of the desert tabernacle. We are told that these details were all "copies of the heavenly things" because they followed "the pattern" that God showed Moses on top of the mountain (8:5). Yet even though the tabernacle was only a shadow of the true form in heaven, "the glory of YHWH filled the tabernacle" (Exod. 40:34). The glory was so dazzling that "Moses was not able to enter the tent of meeting because the cloud settled on it—the glory of YHWH filled" it (40:35).

Note the implication: although the tabernacle was only a shadow of heavenly realities, it was nevertheless filled with the divine glory. But was this glory—the bright radiance of the divine presence—the same as the glory of God in the highest heavens? Paul wrote that there are different degrees or levels of glory: "There is one glory of the sun, and another glory of the moon, and another glory of the stars; for star differs from star in glory" (1 Cor. 15:41 ESV). Of course Paul was discussing the brightness of the heavenly bodies and not God's glory, but he suggested nonetheless that divine glory has levels or degrees. Hebrews makes clear that the things of the law such as the tabernacle were shadows of their heavenly counterpart, and so it is plausible that the glory of the tabernacle was also a shadow of the fullness of heavenly glory. If so, then it suggests that the shadow participates in the being of the fullness from which it draws. After all, an everyday shadow has no being without the light shining on the object that casts the shadow. And without the presence of the object there would be no shadow. So even at this phenomenological level, the shadow draws its *being* from the light and the object that create it.

The early church father Ambrose, who wrote much about types in the Bible and the world, taught that "the shadow is in the law, the image in the Gospel, the truth in heaven."[19] The Anglican theologian Richard Hooker also held to this metaphysics of types. He argued that since all things partake of God insofar as they are effects of God as their highest cause, types derive their

---

19. Ambrose, *On the Duties of the Clergy* 1.48, in *Nicene and Post-Nicene Fathers*, Series 2, ed. Philip Schaff (Peabody, MA: Hendrickson, 1994), 10:40.

being from their divine antitypes.[20] They don't merely point but participate in the realities to which they point.

Yet as Edward Pusey put it, types participate to different degrees. He called the antitype that is Christ and his kingdom "the Archetype."[21] This is the only Archetype in all of reality, and all the types draw their being and substance from this Archetype. But here's the catch: the types contain the substance to different degrees. Bread and wine in the Eucharist are so *full* of the substance that the types of bread and wine *become* the Archetype of Christ in his body and blood. Other types, such as the sun in the sky, do not participate to such a degree in the Archetype, but they draw their substance nonetheless from the Son. As we just suggested, the tabernacle participated in the glory of God but not to the degree to which a body of Christian worshipers, among whom Christ is more fully known, partakes of that glory. Yet even this glory is less than the glory of heavenly worship, where from the throne come thunder and lightning and before the throne is a sea of glass like crystal (Rev. 4:5–6).

Erich Auerbach (1892–1957) was a comparative literature scholar whose book *Mimesis* (1946) revolutionized modern understandings of typology in the Bible. He showed that for Western literature that drew from the biblical tradition, linear history was always connected "vertically" to divine realities. In fact, not only was everyday reality always connected to the divine world, but all the past and future were connected to every time and place. In this "figural interpretation of history . . . every occurrence, in all its everyday reality, is simultaneously a part in a world-historical context through which each part is related to every other, and thus is likewise to be regarded as being of all times or above all time."[22]

Auerbach described finding in a twelfth-century French Christmas play what recent Christian theologians describe as the presence of the future in the present. Auerbach wrote that in this Christmas play "it is clear that Adam has advance knowledge of . . . Christ's coming and redemption," so that "a thing of the future . . . [is] included in the present knowledge of any and all times."[23] This is what Matthew Levering meant when he said that "the historical includes a participation in realities known by faith."[24] It is

20. Richard Hooker, *Laws of Ecclesiastical Polity* 5.56.5, in *The Works of Richard Hooker*, ed. John Keble and Michael Russel (n.p.: CreateSpace, 2010).

21. Pusey, "Lectures," 14, 32.

22. Erich Auerbach, *Mimesis: The Representation of Reality in Western Literature*, trans. Willard R. Trask (Princeton: Princeton University Press, 1953), 156.

23. Auerbach, *Mimesis*, 157.

24. Matthew Levering, *Participatory Biblical Exegesis: A Theology of Biblical Interpretation* (Notre Dame, IN: University of Notre Dame Press, 2008), 6.

not only the realm of grace, he argued, that participates in divine realities but the order of nature too. So if bread is a type of Christ as our "bread from heaven" (John 6:32–33), it meant that eucharistic bread actually participates in the being of Christ insofar as he is our spiritual bread. This is true not only for matter and space, such as bread on an altar, but also for time. The future of the kingdom was already present when the biblical authors wrote, so that the details of their writings were being shaped by the details of the future. This was not predicting the future but absorbing the pressure of the future on their historical present. Thus the types that they depicted were already participating in the realities of the future kingdom, since those future realities were shaping the types. The antitypes were giving being and substance to the types. The types participate in the realities to which they point because the future is available to and pressing on the present.

Pusey wrote about the "sacramental union" between the type and its Archetype.[25] Because types communicate depth in ways that propositions cannot, the Archetype cannot be communicated fully *except* through types. For this reason the type and its antitype cannot be separated. The first is fulfilled by the other, and the second has no fullness without the first. Pusey said that "God has joined them together and man may not and can not [*sic*] put them asunder."[26] The antitype of Christ and his kingdom is joined to the type by the latter's participation in the first. The two are joined in being, even if at different levels or to different degrees.

In his book *Scripture as Real Presence*, Hans Boersma argued that when the fathers did "christological exegesis" of the Old Testament—and they did so voluminously—they "knew that prophecy chronologically precedes fulfillment, [but] they were convinced that in a more important sense it is fulfillment that *precedes* prophecy."[27] In other words, the future was already present. The Trinity was leading the prophets to construct types whose details corresponded explicitly to specific features of the incarnate Christ, who was already present before the incarnation. For this reason, according to Boersma, the fathers taught that believers can experience the sacramental presence of Jesus Christ when they read Scripture, for Scripture itself is a "typological system" that participates in the being of Jesus Christ.[28]

25. Pusey, "Lectures," 23.

26. Pusey, "Lectures," 23.

27. Hans Boersma, *Scripture as Real Presence: Sacramental Exegesis in the Early Church* (Grand Rapids: Baker Academic, 2017), 241 (emphasis added).

28. Boersma, *Scripture as Real Presence*, 278.

Signs, Symbols, and Types

In sum, types are not just *signs* that point. Nor are they simply *symbols* that human beings construct to connect the dots among different things.[29] Scripture suggests that God has filled both the Book of Revelation (i.e., Scripture) and the Book of Nature with persons, patterns, and things that not only show but also participate in the reality of what they show: Christ and his redemptive kingdom. Jesus said he did not come to abolish the Law and Prophets but to fulfill them. He proclaimed that he was their true subject, and his apostles suggested he (by his Spirit) was their author (1 Pet. 1:11). So just as the Word of God filled the Bible and all *its* types with his being, so he has shared his being—in many and different dimensions—with types in all of reality.

How Should We Then Discern?

Types are in all the world. Some of them can be seen and partially understood by those who are unsaved. As Paul put it in Romans 1:20, even the unconverted can see through "the things that have been made" that God exists and is all-powerful. They have God's moral law on their hearts (2:14–15), so they can make moral judgments. They can see these basic things—God's existence and power and most of the Ten Commandments—but little more. Because they do not have faith, they cannot see more than a few of the countless types sprinkled throughout the created world. Only those with faith can see more of them and learn how to interpret them.

But *how* do believers learn to interpret the types? How can they distinguish between types that God has implanted with the purpose of teaching—such as lilies and sparrows teaching God's providence, as Jesus suggested—and merely human analogies that the converted might observe but were not intended by God? Let me propose a few basic principles.

The first way we can know that something is truly a divinely given type outside the Bible is when the Bible says so explicitly. There are actually more of these biblical signals than we might think. We have already mentioned Jesus's pointing to the lilies and the sparrows and Paul's saying that seeds dying and germinating illustrate the resurrection (1 Cor. 15). Jesus said that the same process in seeds points to a second spiritual truth, that spiritual fruitfulness is preceded by a kind of death (John 12:24). He reminded his listeners that a

---

29. My use of the word "symbol" is meant to capture its popular sense today, not the theological sense of a sign that participates in the reality to which it points, as Paul Tillich famously put it. This theological sense is actually close to what I mean in this book by "type." See, for example, Tillich, *Systematic Theology* (Chicago: University of Chicago Press, 1951), 1:238–47.

tree is known by its fruit (Luke 6:44). As I have already said, Jesus's referring to himself as the true vine and true bread and true light suggests that all other vines and breads and lights in this world are intended by Jesus to make us think of him. Paul said that the typological meaning of human marriage is Christ's marriage to his church (Eph. 5); in other words, God instituted human marriage for the purpose of teaching something about his eternal kingdom. He also used the grafting of branches onto a tree to illustrate God's grafting gentiles into his family of Israel (Rom. 11). God told Noah that the rainbow would always be a natural type reminding the world of his promise never to send another worldwide flood (Gen. 9:8–17). He suggested to Isaiah that snow is a type of God's covering (by forgiveness) sins and the bloody wounds ("red") they have caused: "Though your sins be scarlet, they shall be white as snow" (Isa. 1:18). These are just a handful of the hundreds of places where Scripture uses nature and human institutions to illustrate features of God's kingdom.

Wait a minute, some may ask: How can I say that Scripture's use of nature or a human institution for illustration means that God intended for that thing to speak to us of something in his kingdom? Here is where the doctrine of creation comes in. Most would concede that when the Creator uses something he has created to illustrate something else in his creation or kingdom, he means that the former is made to point to the latter. This illustrative purpose might not be the *only* reason it was created, but it is *among* its purposes. Snow was presumably created by God for all sorts of reasons, but among them is its use as a beautiful type, a marvelous illustration of forgiveness. We know that purpose because God himself uses it in just that way in the revelation he gave to Israel.

But what about other types that are not stated explicitly in Scripture? Again we should recall the doctrine of creation, which teaches us that every part of this world, as broken as it is, was created by the Creator. Every part has been shaped by his hand, receiving something that reflects his patterns of creating. If so, then we should expect that the whole world, since it was made by the same infinite trinity of persons, would be full of traces of that Trinity.[30] We should be surprised if all the world were *not* "full of types."

The next step is to ask a nonintuitive and perhaps new question: Does God typically explain his types in Scripture? The answer is not always, perhaps not even most of the time. Consider all the types of the Messiah in the Old Testament. There are hundreds, probably more, but we will consider only the two most famous—Moses and the Suffering Servant of Isaiah 53. Moses

30. Peter J. Leithart, *Traces of the Trinity: Signs of God in Creation and Human Experience* (Grand Rapids: Brazos, 2015).

led the children of Israel out of slavery in Egypt, just as Jesus leads us out of slavery to sin, death, and the devil. The Servant in Isaiah was a man of suffering on whom the Lord laid the iniquity of us all, just as Jesus was a man of suffering on whom God laid our sins. The interesting thing to note is that God never explained in either Exodus or Isaiah that these two persons are types of the coming Messiah. Neither did God explain or interpret the many prophecies of the Messiah in all the Old Testament. In most cases where later readers, both Jewish and Christian, have discerned a messianic prophecy, this discernment has come from what Richard Hays calls "reading backwards," not from an explicit interpretation given by the text itself.[31]

Yet Jesus expected his disciples to have understood the Old Testament types pointing to him and precisely how these types worked. He rebuked the disciples on the road to Emmaus for failing to understand these things: "How foolish you are, and how slow of heart to believe all that the prophets have declared! Wasn't it necessary for the Messiah to suffer these things and then enter his glory?" (Luke 24:25–26). Earlier, before his death and resurrection, Jesus had criticized the apostles for failing to understand the types in his parables without his interpretation: "How could you fail to perceive that I was not talking about bread when I said to beware of the yeast of the Pharisees and the Sadducees?" (Matt. 16:11). He had kept hidden from the crowds the meaning of his parables and revealed that meaning only privately to his disciples (Mark 4:11–12). Yet we readers of the New Testament have only some of those private interpretations, not all.

Mark in fact called on the readers of his Gospel to understand things that he did not explain. When he quoted Jesus's warning about the "abomination of desolation," he added an aside, "Let the reader understand," without explaining further (13:14). When Jesus entered Jerusalem on a colt, Mark did not explain the prophetic meaning of this action (11:1–11). Jesus himself told his disciples, "For the Son of Man goes *as it is written of him*, but woe to that one by whom the Son of Man is betrayed!" (14:21), without explaining how the Old Testament predicted this betrayal. In the garden of Gethsemane as he was being arrested, Jesus told those listening, "Day after day I was with you in the temple teaching, and you did not seize me. *But let the Scriptures be fulfilled*" (14:49). We readers are never told which texts of Scripture this event was fulfilling.

In other words, Jesus expected his disciples to know where the prophecies and types were in Scripture and his teachings, *and* to be able to figure out

---

31. Richard Hays, *Reading Backwards: Figural Christology and the Fourfold Gospel Witness* (Waco: Baylor University Press, 2016).

the meanings without his having to explain them. God did not explain the types of the Messiah explicitly in the Bible, and Jesus did not always explain the meaning or application of the types in his own parables. He said that he came to fulfill all of the Law and the Prophets (Matt. 5:17–20) but suggested only occasionally and in very small part what those prefigurings and fulfillments looked like.

Jesus expected his disciples to infer where the types were and what they meant. He implied that his teaching, and the Old Testament as a whole, taught the types *indirectly*. As I have just suggested, the Gospel of Mark is well known for its indirection. Mark's "messianic secret" is famous for its concealment of Jesus's messianic status. Several times in the gospel Jesus actually forbids people from telling others that he was the Messiah. Richard Hays wrote that this indirection was characteristic of both Jesus and the God of the Bible overall. For example, when Mark described Jesus walking on water, he said that Jesus came toward the disciples on the water and "intended to pass them by" (Mark 6:48). Exegetes have wondered for centuries what that last phrase means. Hays argued convincingly that Mark had referred *indirectly* to the Septuagint's version of Job 9:4–11, where the text says that God "stretched out the heavens and *trampled the waves of the* sea . . . do[ing] great things beyond understanding, and marvelous things without number. Look, he *passes me by*, and I do not see him; *he passes me by*, but I do not perceive him." Hays added that the Greek verb that both Mark and the Septuagint used for "pass by" was the same verb used in Exodus 33 and 34 (Septuagint), where God is said to "pass by" Moses in order to reveal his glory indirectly.[32] The point is that God revealed his glory indirectly, just as Mark revealed Jesus's glory indirectly. So too types are indirect. They suggest without stating directly; they whisper rather than shout. They are shy, neither announcing their presence nor explaining their message. So just as the messianic types in the Old Testament are not expressly noted by the text, and the applications of the types in Jesus's teachings are not always spelled out, neither do the types or their meanings typically announce themselves in the Bible.

After all, the Bible is a premodern text, not a systematic theology. It prefers to speak with images and symbols, people and events, dialogue and action— not abstract principles with instructions on how to apply those principles in every conceivable case. It speaks of clean animals and unclean animals and of their various "kinds" rather than what we would call their species and genera. The stars are given to *us* to mark the signs and seasons (Gen. 1:14)

32. Richard B. Hays, *Echoes of Scripture in the Gospels* (Waco: Baylor University Press, 2016), 70–73.

and to show us the glory of God. We are not told the things scientists would want to know about them. The Bible is a beautiful story full of types and symbols and images, evocative of poetry and art, appealing as much to the right brain as to the left. Rather than being a drawback, this is part of its glory and beauty. Like all beautiful things, it often *shows* us rather than *tells* us its inner secrets. It is full of "spiritual things for those who are spiritual" (1 Cor. 2:13). To insist on clear instructions explicating all of its symbols is rather like asking Mozart to write a philosophical analysis of his music.

Does this mean that we are free to assign any meaning we choose to things in nature and history and call them God's types? Of course not. There are firm rules for discerning types when the Scriptures have not made them explicit.

First, things or events must fall within a clear range of biblical meaning. For example, we can say the anger of any large animal might be a type to show us something of God's wrath. For Scripture compares the Lord's anger to that of a she-bear mourning her cubs (Hosea 13:8; Isa. 59:11), and the anger of any other large animal would fall within that range of typical meaning. The fall of any proud empire in postbiblical history could plausibly be called an antitype prefigured by the fall of the proud emperors and their empires in the Bible, and all are types of the final judgment of proud empires at the end of history. Both of these things—the anger of large animals and the fall of empires—could be legitimate types and antitypes because they correspond to clear biblical counterparts.

Second, when something in nature or history does not have a clear biblical counterpart, it must nevertheless fall within the meaning of the whole story of redemption that the Bible tells. For example, Scripture alludes to sports but never directly addresses the subject or its key notion of winning and losing. But we can suggest, as I will in a later chapter, that because human beings seem to be instinctively competitive and so enjoy the struggle to win against opponents, and because winning and losing are part of the biblical drama of redemption, there might be something here of a type. The contest points to the eternal cosmic contest of the Bible, in which there will indeed be winners and losers—the redeemed and the unredeemed, the saved and the lost. This winning will be different, of course, from earthly victory, for the crown will go not to the swift or strong or wise or intelligent of this world (Eccles. 9:11) but to those the world considers foolish and weak.

Another way of putting this point is to say that true typology is *descending* rather than *ascending*. It starts on the mount, as it were, with orthodox faith that comes from a vision of the beauty of holiness of the trinitarian God of Israel, and then goes *down* from that vision—gained from the Spirit of Jesus, who showed his glory on the Mount of Transfiguration—to our world of experience in nature and history. It does not start with our own ideas about life in the world of the here and now and go *up* to construct a new idea of God. True biblical typology, the sort that the church enjoyed for seventeen hundred years, *illustrates* things in the orthodox vision of God that have been handed down to us by the Great Tradition. It does not construct or shape doctrine. It is not a priori, starting with preconceived ideas and then using them to construct theology. Instead it is a posteriori, which means it thinks *after* God's thoughts as they have been given to us by Scripture and the teaching of the orthodox church.

Third, we should measure all of our supposed types against the wisdom of the Great Tradition of theology and exegesis. Paul tells us that the church is founded on the apostles and the prophets (Eph. 2:20), and the pastors and the teachers (Eph. 4:11). The received wisdom of the orthodox church is a precious gift to us, our best protection against wild and fanciful typology. As James Jordan has noted, the excesses of "Origenist" allegory and typology resulted not from assigning meanings where Scripture was not explicit but from forcing Platonist categories onto Christian theology. The fathers were generally quite competent at distinguishing between biblically based typology on the one hand and allegory based on philosophy foreign to the biblical vision on the other, as Jean Daniélou showed.[33]

Therefore some types would be ruled out. If we were to think we saw types in nature or history that teach the virtue of same-sex marriage, we would be seeing not true types but fanciful imaginings. We can draw this conclusion because the Great Tradition's parsing of Scripture has already made it clear. So have all the great moral teachers of the universal church. The same goes for supposed types teaching universalism, the notion that all will eventually be saved. Jesus taught repeatedly that there are two destinies for the human race, with some finding God forever and others choosing against him forever. Christian theological tradition has denounced universalism as heresy, despite the recent claims of some.[34]

Every true type, imprinted by God on nature and history, will point to the great drama of redemption depicted in Scripture, taught by the orthodox theologians, lived by the saints, dramatized in the great liturgies, received

33. James B. Jordan, *Through New Eyes: Developing a Biblical View of the World* (Eugene, OR: Wipf & Stock, 1999), 17; Jean Daniélou, *From Shadows to Reality: Studies in the Biblical Typology of the Fathers*, trans. Wulstan Hibberd (London: Burns & Oates, 1960); see also John J. O'Keefe and R. R. Reno, *Sanctified Vision: An Introduction to Early Christian Interpretation of the Bible* (Baltimore: Johns Hopkins University Press, 2005); J. D. Dawson, *Christian Figural Reading and the Fashioning of Identity* (Berkeley: University of California Press, 2002).

34. Michael J. McClymond, *The Devil's Redemption: A New History and Interpretation of Christian Universalism* (Grand Rapids: Baker Academic, 2018).

in the sacraments, and portrayed in icons. It is the story of the Triune God saving sinners from sin, death, and the devil by the life, death, and resurrection of Jesus the Messiah, the Son of God. Thus a true type will point to the church, the body of Christ, which embodies that redemption in the world. Any type that does not illuminate and enliven that story as told by the church is not a true type.

The typological tradition of the church therefore invites us to a "conversion of the imagination."[35] Many of us have been blinded in part by our deep familiarity with the secular world and its foolish presumption that science explains the world. Recent trends in the church have shielded us from the historic church's dazzling vision of this world, which is thoroughly typological. As a result, we have missed out on abundant beauty, joy, and fulfillment. The following chapters are an invitation to be healed. They call on you to let the Spirit open your eyes to the riches all around you, the innumerable facets of the surrounding worlds that illustrate the glory of God.

35. Hays, *Reading Backwards*, 4.

3

Nature

Sermons in Stones

The great Anglican priest and poet George Herbert wrote about looking through a window,

> A man that looks on glass,
> On it may stay his eye,
> Or, if he pleaseth, through it pass,
> And then the heav'n espy.[1]

Two centuries later the Jesuit poet Gerard Manley Hopkins wrote of nature radiating the glory of God:

> The world is charged with the grandeur of God.
> It will flame out, like shining from shook foil.[2]

Both of these British poets were Christians who saw the world in the way much of the Great Tradition has seen it—not just spotted here and there with signs, some near and some far, but as a sign in and of itself, with meaning from top to bottom. In other words, it's not turtles all the way down (in the

1. George Herbert, "The Elixir"; quoted in Alister McGrath, *The Open Secret: A New Vision for Natural Theology* (Malden, MA: Blackwell, 2008), 68.
2. Gerard Manley Hopkins, "God's Grandeur" (1877), The Poetry Foundation, https://www.poetryfoundation.org/poems-and-poets/poems/detail/44395.

popular expression of infinite regress), but wheels within wheels of glory, each layer and dimension full of words and images pointing up and out to the Creator and Redeemer.

We should not be surprised, for as the early Christians in Syria argued, the world was created by the Logos, whose very name ("Word") suggests communication.[3] As we saw in chapter 1 from Ephrem of Syria, "In every place if you look, his [Christ's] symbol is there, and wherever you read, you will find his types. For in him all creatures were created, and he traced his symbols on his property." Ephrem added, "When he created the world, he looked to adorn it with icons of himself."[4]

The great Cappadocian theologians used the book of Wisdom (13:5 LXX) to argue for analogies between visible nature and invisible divinity: "The greatness and beauty of created things give us an idea of their Creator through analogy [*analogōs*]."[5] They conceded that there was hiddenness and dissimilarity in every analogy that suggested similarity, but they believed the eyes of faith could nonetheless see divinely planted symbols in nature.[6] Basil of Caesarea (329–79), for example, wrote that "by the sight of visible and empirical realities," the human mind was "led, as by a hand, to the contemplation of invisible realities." So even "a single plant, a blade of grass, is sufficient to occupy all your intelligence in the contemplation of the *technē* [skill] that produced it."[7] For Gregory of Nyssa (335–94), the sunlight's beauty teaches us something of God's beauty, the solidity of the sky points to the unchangeableness of the Creator, and the vastness of the heavens suggests the infinity of power that holds up the universe.[8]

The conviction that nature is full of God-inscribed types runs throughout the Christian tradition. Maximus the Confessor (580–662) wrote that God the Word speaks in the infinite diversity of all things.[9] According to Bonaventure

3. Joseph Beggiani, "The Typological Approach of Syriac Sacramental Theology," *Theological Studies* 64 (2003): 543–57.

4. *Des heiligen Ephraem des Syrers Hymnen de Virginitate*, ed. and trans. Edmund Beck, CSCO 223 (Leuven: Secrétariat du Corpus, 1962), 70–71. English translation: Sidney Griffith, "A Spiritual Father for the Whole Church: St. Ephrem the Syrian," *Sobornost* 20 (1998): 30–31.

5. *Septuaginta* (Old Greek Jewish Scriptures), ed. Alfred Rahlfs (Stuttgart: Württembergische Bibelanstalt / Deutsche Bibelgesellschaft [German Bible Society], 1935).

6. Jaroslav Pelikan, *Christianity and Classical Culture: The Metamorphosis of Natural Theology in the Christian Encounter with Hellenism* (New Haven: Yale University Press, 1993), 61–72, 101–6.

7. Basil, *In Hexaemeron* 1.6; 5.3; quoted in Pelikan, *Christianity and Classical Culture*, 65, 101.

8. Gregory of Nyssa, *Contra Eunomium* 2.475–78; quoted in Pelikan, *Christianity and Classical Culture*, 62.

9. Maximus the Confessor, *Ambiguum* 7.

(1221–74), all of creation speaks of God by its origin, magnitude, multitude, beauty, plenitude, operation, and order. Nicholas of Cusa (1401–64) taught that all three persons of the Trinity speak through the creation, which he said is an infinity of signs or mirrors.[10] Luther, as we have seen, wrote that creation is "the most beautiful book of the Bible; in it God has described and portrayed Himself."[11] The Irish philosopher George (Bishop) Berkeley (1685–1753) held that all material things are signs or words in the divine language, and the German Lutheran philosopher Johann Georg Hamann (1730–88) wrote of paradise, in which "every created thing was a living word."[12]

These Christian thinkers expressed what they thought was the teaching of the Bible. They took seriously Job's suggestion:

> Ask the beasts, and they will teach you;
>   the birds of the heavens, and they will tell you;
> or the bushes of the earth, and they will teach you;
>   and the fish of the sea will declare to you.
> Who among all these does not know
>   that the hand of the LORD has done this? (Job 12:7–9 ESV)

According to most of the great thinkers in the Great Tradition, Job was suggesting what they themselves had sensed after hearing the word of salvation and then looking at nature: the beasts and birds and bushes and fish were talking. They were saying, "The Lord made me, and he is glorious!" Most Christians for most of the last two thousand years have thought Jesus was suggesting the same thing when he regularly pointed his hearers to the world of nature for confirmation of what he was teaching. "Take a look at the lilies of the field, how they grow. They neither labor nor spin. Let me tell you, not even Solomon in all his glory was arrayed as one of these. If God clothes the grass of the field that is here today and tomorrow is thrown into the oven, don't you think He will care for you, O you of little faith?" (Matt. 6:28–30).

Permit me to paraphrase Jesus in a pedestrian way: "The world of nature is constantly talking, reinforcing what I, Jesus, am teaching you." Little wonder that Jesus's parables regularly use things in nature to illustrate kingdom

10. Bonaventure, *Itinerarium mentis ad Deum* 1.14; Nicholas of Cusa, *De filiatione Dei*, in *Compendium* 8.

11. Quoted in Heinrich Bornkamm, *Luther's World of Thought* (St. Louis: Concordia, 1958), 27.

12. George Berkeley, *Alciphron* 4.7–15; Johann Georg Hamann, *Ritter von Rosenkreuz*, in *Sämtliche Werke* (1949–57), 3:32; all of these quotations are cited in David Bentley Hart, *The Beauty of the Infinite: The Aesthetics of Christian Truth* (Grand Rapids: Eerdmans, 2003), 291–92.

principles. They point to what happens to houses built on sand and houses built on rocks when storms with floods come; they point to trees that produce good fruit and trees that produce bad fruit; they note what happens to seeds thrown onto a path, rocky soil, thorny soil, and good soil; they refer to tiny seeds that produce huge bushes; they evoke the way a bit of leaven spreads itself through a lump of dough and the way weeds and wheat grow together in a field. He granted that many people see nothing about God in any of these things of nature, but that for those with eyes to see, there are "sermons in stones," as Shakespeare put it, lessons about the kingdom of God.[13]

For Paul, this connection between nature and the kingdom ought to be obvious to a Christian. He seemed exasperated that the Corinthian Christians didn't see from *nature* that there must be a resurrection of the body: "You foolish person! What you sow does not come to life [again] unless it dies. And what you sow is not the body that is to be, but a bare kernel, perhaps of wheat or some other grain" (1 Cor. 15:36–37 ESV). Nature has been teaching us all along, Paul was saying, that out of death comes new life that is different from its first form.

James B. Jordan suggested that there are understandable reasons why all of nature is one giant type containing an infinite number of types. "God is infinite and man is finite. We simply cannot grasp God's infinite tri-personality all at once. For this reason, God chose to reveal the infinity of His personality in the diversity of this world. Various things in the world reveal various things about God."[14]

John Frame, a Reformed theologian, was not hesitant to say—as some Reformed theologians of the twentieth century *have* been reluctant—that this world of nature is full of analogies to God.

> Everything in creation bears some analogy to God. All the world has been made with God's stamp on it, revealing Him. Creation is His temple, heaven His throne, earth His footstool. Thus Scripture finds analogies to God in every area of creation: inanimate objects (God the "rock of Israel," Christ the "door of the sheep," the Spirit as wind, breath, fire), plant life (God's strength like the cedars of Lebanon, Christ the "bread of life"), animals (Christ the "Lion of Judah," the "lamb of God"), human beings (God as king, landowner, lover; Christ as prophet, priest, king, servant, son, friend). . . . All this can be boiled down to a simple fact: The universe and everything in it symbolizes God.[15]

13. William Shakespeare, *As You Like It*, act 2, scene 1, line 564.
14. James B. Jordan, *Through New Eyes: Developing a Biblical View of the World* (Eugene, OR: Wipf & Stock, 1999), 22.
15. John Frame, *The Doctrine of the Knowledge of God* (Phillipsburg, NJ: P&R, 1987), 230.

Rabbi Barry Kornblau told the story of the famed Israeli rabbi Avraham Kook (1865–1935), who took a walk one day with a friend in the fields around Jaffa. When the friend plucked a twig or flower, Rabbi Kook gently reproved him: "Believe me—in all my days, I have taken care never to pluck a blade of grass or flower needlessly, when it had the ability to grow or blossom. You know the teaching of the Sages that there is not a single blade of grass below, here on earth, which does not have a heavenly force above telling it, Grow! Every sprout and leaf of grass says something, conveys some meaning. Every stone whispers some inner message in its silence. Every creature utters its song (of praise of the Creator)."[16]

Rabbi Kook drew from the Jewish sages of the Talmud, whose thinking was shaped deeply by the Mishnah, the written version of the same body of oral law that Jesus and Paul fed upon. But as we saw in chapter 2, some theologians rejected the idea that we can talk about God using things in nature. Some insisted that the minds of even the regenerate (spiritually reborn) are so fallen that we inevitably distort our view of God and turn him into an idol, something that is a caricature of the true God. Others said that to use something in finite creation to speak about the infinite God is myopic and perhaps laughable, for it presumes that the Being who is Being itself can be represented in any way by a tiny part of being, something like (using an analogy they would probably also reject) an inert hammer representing the human being who made it. The differences are so great that any similarity between the two misinforms more than it informs.[17]

But as Peter Leithart pointed out, the biblical writers did not have this anxiety. They compared God to rocks and fire and fathers and shepherds. They used ordinary language to talk about the God from whom language comes. In fact, by their use of images from nature, they testified that God himself had used nature—and that part of nature called human being—to talk about himself. He inspired the biblical authors to call him a rock (Gen. 49:24; Matt. 21:44) and fire (Deut. 4:24; Heb. 12:29), and compared his Son to a lamb (John 1:29) and a lion (Rev. 5:5). God called himself Father, which made hearers and readers compare him to the fathers they knew. Jesus called himself the bread of life, which called to mind ordinary Palestinian bread. In short, God and his Son were not as fearful as most theologians are to use ordinary human language about familiar things in

16. R. Barry Kornblau, "Elegy of a Tree," *Torah Musings*, October 30, 2012, http://www .torahmusings.com/2012/10/eulogy-for-a-tree.

17. See Peter Leithart's discussion of protests against these kinds of analogizing coming from Kathryn Tanner, Lewis Ayers, and Bruce McCormack in Leithart, *Traces of the Trinity: Signs of God in Creation and Human Experience* (Grand Rapids: Brazos, 2015), 147–53.

the world of nature and humanity to talk about themselves. They had no trouble saying that heaven and earth are full of glory (Ps. 19:1; Isa. 6:3), thereby suggesting that everything the divine persons created says something about the divine glory.

So the biblical writers testified that all the world is full of types, and the whole world is one massive type. But the presence and meaning of the types are not visible to those who cannot see. Like the Pharisees who searched the Scriptures but missed its inner meaning (John 5:39), the world is full of people who fail to see the meaning of the world. They miss the riches that lie under every rock, the message behind every bush. The eyes of their hearts need to be healed, said Augustine.[18] But if they seek that healing and their eyes are opened, then the sound of the world around them, as Michael Polanyi suggested, changes from noise to music.[19]

Edwards on Types in Nature

As one of my grad-school teachers used to put it, let's now move from sharpening knives to cutting meat. Let's look at what two modern typologists have actually done with nature, reading the signs in it to discern the types. We will look first at Jonathan Edwards, to whom we have already been introduced, and then at Peter Leithart (b. 1959), a contemporary Reformed theologian.

Edwards insisted that he was not merely inventing correspondences as "Origenists" would. Those typologists went beyond the bounds of biblical teaching and inference, finding meaning in nature that had little or nothing to do with scriptural stories or symbols. Those are the ones, said Edwards, who "are for turning all into nothing but allegory and not having it be true history" (*WJE* 11:151). As I suggested in chapter 1, Edwards believed that his typology stuck to biblical history and its inferences. After sketching his vision of types in nature, I will pause to ask whether his typology of nature followed the biblical grammar.

We will look at Edwards's natural types in three realms—the heavens and the atmosphere, living things among the flora and fauna, and the human person.

First, nature out *there*. The sun is Edwards's primary type in the heavens. Scripture makes clear the sun is a type of Christ because Scripture speaks of Jesus as the "sun of righteousness" and the "light of the world." Besides, the

18. Augustine of Hippo, *Sermo* 88.5; cited in McGrath, *Open Secret*, 197.
19. Michael Polanyi, "Science and Reality," *British Journal for the Philosophy of Science* 18 (1967): 191.

sun withdrew its light at the crucifixion of Jesus, and his resurrection took place at the same time as the rising of the sun (*WJE* 11:120).[20]

So what does the sun show us about Messiah?[21] The answer for Edwards was severalfold. The sun never diminishes in light or heat throughout the ages, which shows the "all-sufficiency and everlastingness of God's bounty and goodness." Nature's dependence on the sun ("vegetables growing and flourishing, looking green and pleasant") shows us our need for the Holy Spirit's "effusions" to be spiritually healthy (54).

But the sun is not perfect, Edwards observed. If you view it "with glasses" (a rudimentary eighteenth-century telescope), you see that it has spots. When examined closely even the most excellent created beings have imperfections. The sun's absence, in times of clouds and rain and darkness, highlights those imperfections. Plants need those times of rain and relative darkness in order to take advantage of the times when the sun is bright and clear. This cycle shows, according to Edwards, that the "rains of affliction" are necessary to prepare the soul for "the clear shining of the Sun of Righteousness." If a person receives only comfort and light and is "not prepared by humiliation," then comfort and light make "the heart worse." Pride then grows in the soul as a disease and eventually destroys it (125, 85).

The rising and setting of the sun are full of types. Overall, they are a type of the death and resurrection of Messiah. As the sun rises and brings the world out of darkness into light and warmth, so Messiah at his rising brings the church with him to happiness, life, and glory. The sun's setting is red and promises a fair day on the morrow, because Messiah's death was "with blood and dreadful sufferings" and brought us "a fair day" (64, 66, 81–82).

According to Edwards, the moon is a type of the church. Just as the moon forever changes, rising and falling, waxing and waning, moving from full splendor to total extinction, so too the church's lot on earth is to rise and fall in outward prosperity, succeeding and suffering intermittently through time. The moon's glory represents the prophets and apostles of the early church, and "possibly" that of "the Blessed Virgin Mary," because their glory is a reflection of the glory of Christ, just as the moon reflects the light of the sun (65–66).

Edwards also reflected on the seasons as types. *Spring* is meant to make us think of an outpouring of the Spirit of God. Seeds sprout, even those sown in

20. Page numbers in parentheses at the end of the next several paragraphs refer to *WJE* vol. 11, which contains Edwards's notebook "Images of Divine Things."

21. I replace "Christ" with "Messiah" from time to time in this book for two reasons: because some of these materials are inspired by Edwards's notebook "Types of the Messiah," and because we need to be reminded of the Jewishness of Jesus, which is often obscured by our use of the English transliteration (Christ) of the Greek translation (*Christos*) of the Hebrew (*mashiach*).

rocky ground. They look fair for a while, but then because of dry and shallow conditions, their pretty flowers wither and come to nothing. So too for souls in times of the Spirit (times of spiritual revival), who talk excitedly about God for a while but whose affections then dry up. This is the difference between birds and frogs in the spring, both of whom lift up their voices then. The birds are the saints, whose songs delight God during times of revival, while frogs are hypocrites, whose croaks bring him no pleasure (105–6).

The blazing heat of *summer* that dries up pools of water and withers herbs and plants that shot up in the spring should remind us of trials and sufferings that kill the shallow affections of hypocrites. Just as "sound fruit" persists through this heat, so too does the faith of the truly regenerate (88).

The fading of leaves, grass, and flowers and all their glory in *winter* is a sharp contrast to the unfading brightness of the heavens—which is the same in summer and winter, age after age. God means for us to be reminded of the great difference between, on the one hand, "earthly glory, riches, and pleasures," which fade like the flower of the field, and, on the other, "the glory and happiness of heaven which fadeth not away." This typology of the seasons, he argued, is "agreeable to many representations in the Scriptures" (96).

Second, Edwards turned to the world of flora and fauna. Flowers are innumerable, he wrote, and so few of them become ripe fruit. The same is true of the near-infinite number of seeds that are sown, so few of which sprout. It seems so great a waste, unless we recognize that God created these as types of the disproportion between those who endure in the faith and those who do not. So few are saved of the many, many who hear the Word. We are reminded by flowers and seeds that many are called but few are chosen (70).

The progress of fruit is a type of growth in Messiah. When fruit is young, it is very tender and "easily hurt" by frost or heat or vermin. So too for young converts, who are easily led astray. They must grow in perfection all through the course of their lives, just as fruit requires a term of growth before it is ripe. Fruit taken too early, when green, is bitter and sour; it becomes sweet and pure only after suffering heat and other pressures. Usually it becomes red or its juice starts to look like blood, just as the blood of Christ "fitted" the fruit of the tree of life for us. Young believers must suffer afflictions and persecutions—in a word, the cross of Christ—if they are to become sweet with meekness and Christian love. If heat destroys some fruit, so too affliction accomplishes nothing for hypocrites. But when true believers are ripe, they are ready to quit this life for heaven, just as ripe fruit is ready to quit its tree at the touch of the hand (115–16, 123, 93).

The flowers that eventually become trees start with slender shoots. Notice, Edwards observed, that when trees are young they are easily bent, representing the more pliable nature of children and the necessity of reaching children with the gospel while they are still malleable. Just as with a tree, so too with people: with age comes stiffness, until it is impossible to direct it in another direction without destroying the tree (59).

Trees more fully grown represent human beings and the church. Each starts with a tiny seed, barely visible. Each becomes either barren or fruitful. Each is known by its fruit. The church is signified by special trees—grape (vines), olive, palm, and apple trees (57, 80–81, 89, 98).

Finally, there is the world of animals. Edwards saw meaning in a number of classes of animals, and so the following are only a few of the ones he mentioned. Birds are images of heaven's inhabitants. For that reason they are more beautiful than other animals. When they sing, they sound like they are praising God. And their early morning songs are like preachers who wake up sinners from their spiritual sleep (84–85).

While it is not a pleasant music, the cockadoodling of the cock at dawn is a type of preachers of the gospel, who wake up sinners out of their sleep. This is also represented by the special singing of birds in the spring, which, we have already seen, is a type of an outpouring of the Spirit of God (92–93).

Fish, said Edwards, typify the inhabitants of hell. We know this, he wrote, because water is the place for the dead in Scripture. The Rephaim, whales, and sea monsters in the Bible represent devils and the wrath of God. Scripture portrays the miseries of death and God's wrath as the sea, the deeps, floods, and billows (84–85).

Third, consider the types Edwards found inside of *us*. Deep inside of us he found filth, which also is a type. Here Edwards meant the filth that is inside our bowels, the dung, which represents our inner corruption and filthiness, typified by the self-glorifying pride that thinks God is lucky to have us. Edwards believed that the twisting and turning of our intestines stood for the wiliness and shiftiness of our hearts in their natural self-deception. The fact that all of this is hidden from the outer eye means that our inner corruptions are secret, known in their fullness only to God (and perhaps those with whom we live!) (92, 94).

The filth is not a recent development in us but goes all the way back to our beginnings. This is seen by our condition at birth. There too we emerged in filth, signifying our inner pollution. We were naked, representing our spiritual nakedness before God. We were crying, showing that sorrow fills much of our lives. We were born "backward" (most babies in Edwards's day were delivered face down), with our backs facing God and heaven, and our faces to the earth and hell, to demonstrate "the natural state of our hearts" (54, 57, 96).

The natural state of our physical life, dependent on every breath of air we inhale, is also a type. The Bible teaches this lesson in Ezekiel's story of the dry bones coming to life by the Lord's breathing on them, and in Jesus's breathing on the apostles to impart to them the Holy Spirit in John 20. Just as our physical life depends on breath every moment, so too our spiritual life depends on the breath of the Spirit of God infilling us. Job said, "Our lives are but a breath" (7:7), like a blast of wind that blows past and does not return. So too when the warm heat of our breathing goes out of us, cold death "suddenly" comes in to replace it. It is a comfort to believers that when they see the sudden cold come to a corpse, they can reassure themselves that they have the supernatural breath that will keep us warm forever (55, 70–71, 100, 129).

Lastly, among "us" we can see types in children and assemblies. Children gradually grow into adulthood, showing us by their gradual growth not only the gradual spiritual growth of every saint (no room for Christian perfection here!) but also the gradual perfecting of the church into knowledge, holiness, and blessedness (61).

The great assemblies of the human community have much to teach us of the kingdom of God. Because they are the assemblies of *natural* men and women, they teach us of nature's types. The solemnity of a prince's coronation (and a president's inauguration?) is a "shadow" of the procession we will see at the end of the world as the saints receive their crowns of glory. This is also a shadow of what happened at Christ's ascension, when he was crowned "in his person" (119).

The solemnity of great criminal trials and executions of criminals is a type of the great solemnity that will pervade the final judgment. So too the joy we experience at weddings is a type of the joy the saints will taste at the great wedding supper of the Lamb (119).

Are Edwards's Types Biblical?

How did Edwards do? Are his types as solidly grounded in Scripture as he claimed? Perhaps not as securely as he imagined, but most are plausible.

His scriptural warrants for the sun as a type of God and his Messiah are clearly set out above. They seem apt. So his inferences from there to defects in the sun and the creation's need for times of darkness are plausible. Scripture more than a few times likens people to trees (Deut. 20:19; Judg. 9:8–15; Pss. 1:3; 92:8) and uses dung as a symbol of judgment (1 Kings 14:10; Ps. 83:10; Isa. 25:10). It is clear that breath is a sign of divine life (Ezek. 37) and that children are types of spiritual immaturity (1 Cor. 14:20). There are hundreds of references by the biblical authors to seeds representing God's words (e.g., Matt. 13:27), flowers symbolizing the fragility of beauty (e.g., James 1:10–11), and fruit as a type of spiritual growth (e.g., Matt. 7:17–19).

Other Edwardsean images are not as clearly set forth in the Bible. Birds are represented as symbols of faithfulness (Jer. 8:7) but not departed saints per se. The Old Testament depicts the ocean as the locus of judgment (Eccles. 9:12; Ezek. 26:5, 14; 29:3–7; Amos 4:2; Hab. 1:15–17), the cosmic sea as the threat of chaos (Job 38:8–11; Jer. 5:22), and the beast from the sea in Revelation 13 as a general in the devil's army. But the only things that would suggest that fish represent the denizens of hell are these dark images of the ocean. I have found no place where the Bible suggests that the moon is a type of the church.

Yet none seems to me to approach the allegorists' departure from biblical history that Edwards decried. In his essay "Types" he criticized "those that are for turning all into nothing but allegory and not having it to be true history"—probably meaning Anglo-Catholic preachers Lancelot Andrewes, Jeremy Taylor, and John Donne (*WJE* 11:20, 151). All of Edwards's more questionable inferences were rooted in the biblical history. So even if we cannot find the church referred to as the moon, Edwards pointed its waxing and waning to the mixed fortunes of the church in biblical history and prophecy. The Bible nowhere suggests that fish are the damned, but Edwards went to the events of biblical eschatology for warrant. Biblical history is still the screen on which his types were displayed, and they find their meaning within that story, not inside a system of meaning centered somewhere else.

Beauty as the Ultimate Type

One last point should be made about Edwards's vision of types in nature. It is the most beautiful part of that vision, for it has to do with beauty itself, which for him was the inner secret to all of nature. Deep within the structure of nature, he suggested, is beauty as a type of the divine beauty. This is not a major theme in the Christian tradition, and even those who wrote extensively on the subject fell short of Edwards in the centrality he gave to it.

In 1992 Patrick Sherry published *Spirit and Beauty: An Introduction to Theological Aesthetics*, in which he argued that the three greatest names in the history of theological aesthetics are Augustine, Balthasar, and Jonathan Edwards.[22] Of the three, he insisted, the one who made beauty most structurally central to his vision of God was Edwards. For Edwards, beauty was

22. Patrick Sherry, *Spirit and Beauty: An Introduction to Theological Aesthetics* (Oxford: Oxford University Press, 1992).

more descriptive of who God is than anything else. Listen to this claim by
the American theologian: "God is God, and distinguished from all other beings, and exalted above [th]em, *chiefly* by his divine beauty, which is infinitely
diverse from all other beauty. . . . This is the beauty of the Godhead, and the
divinity of the Divinity (if I may so speak), the good of the infinite Fountain
of Good; without which God himself (if that were possible to be) would be
an infinite evil" (*WJE* 2:298).

For Edwards, not only was beauty the innermost meaning of who God is,
but it was also the key to all the types in nature, both "out there" and "in here."
Being and beauty are interconnected and perhaps interchangeable, and both
are refractions of God's inner beauty. "God is the foundation and fountain
of all being and all beauty, from whom all is perfectly derived, and on whom
all is most absolutely and perfectly dependent; of whom and through whom
and to whom is all being and all perfection; and whose being and beauty is
as it were the sum and comprehension of all existence and excellence: much
more than the sun is the fountain and summary comprehension of all the
light and brightness of the day" (*WJE* 8:551). What we see of beauty around
us is a type of the divine beauty: "All the beauty to be found throughout the
whole creation, is but the reflection of the diffused beams of the Being who
hath an infinite fullness of brightness and glory" (*WJE* 8:550). But what did
Edwards mean by beauty, and how is it seen in nature?

Beauty for Edwards was most essentially proportion or consent. It might be
a simple proportion or agreement between two apples, or a complex proportion or harmony of a beautiful human face. There are simple and complex
beauties. The latter is a harmony among things that are different and even
jarring. It might contain partial irregularities or even ugly disagreement. But
if those partial or ugly features are parts of a larger harmony, then the ugliness or disproportion is *aufgeheben*, lifted up into a higher harmony that is
a complex beauty.

So while there is the symmetrical harmony of a French garden at the Versailles, there is also the asymmetrical harmony of a Japanese garden or of
a jazz chord that sounds dissonant when played alone but fits well within a
progression of chords.

In nature we can see harmony among dissonance in a mountain range.
When I am hiking on a mountain trail in Virginia, I look at other mountains
around and see no particular pattern or harmony, just irregular shapes and
seemingly random piles of rocks and trees. But when I look down from an
airplane at these same mountains, I see a beautiful pattern called the Blue
Ridge Mountains, with their long patterns of ridges that snake this way and
that but run generally in the same direction and often are nearly parallel to

each other. The pattern is pleasing to the eye and seems to have been designed by an intelligent Designer. But it is not only here. In every dimension of nature, from subatomic particles to distant galaxies, we see things that are discordant, different, and in disharmony when observed close-up but that form beautiful harmonies when seen from afar.

Edwards said the same pattern is in that part of nature called human and its moral relations. Morally it seems wrong to be selfish, seeking our own interest. But Adam Smith observed 250 years ago that when a man tries to make money by making and selling something out of self-interest, he learns that he must make it well to please his customer so that the customer comes back to buy another. If he prices it too high, the customer will go to another maker. The smart artisan, then, will make a good product and keep the price within an affordable range. What seems ugly—self-interest—after a while takes on a certain attractiveness because society constrains that self-interest so that it serves the interests of others. That overall pattern has a certain beauty to it.

Now, I know you will say that life is not so simple. That artisan could collude with other artisans of the same product and fix the price, keeping the product out of reach of all but the upper classes. Or a multinational corporation could buy up all the raw materials and producers and fix the prices similarly. But as Winston Churchill once said about democracy, the free market is the worst economic pattern for society—except for all of its alternatives. And I would venture to say that a twenty-first-century Edwards would say the same, that in this fallen world with its imperfect market systems, and despite all of these problems that come ultimately from sin, there is a certain beauty when I can go to a store in Alabama to buy fresh coffee that was harvested on the other side of the world. I am satisfied, and the small farmer in Africa is able to support his family. This is a kind of harmony that joins interests not initially allied to produce a limited but genuine harmony. This is a type in the very *natural* realm called human society and its economics.

Now let's move it up a little. Let's say that one of the middlemen in this global coffee chain decides to live at a lower standard of living because he is impressed that the Second Person of the Trinity decided to do the same. So he takes half the profit he could otherwise have made. The result is that he is able to buy coffee beans from 40 percent more African farmers than otherwise. Thus more poor farmers are able to have the self-respect of working to be able to support their families. This is a moral and spiritual beauty, Edwards would say, that is a type of the ultimate beauty, which is the proportion and consent in the mutual love and service among the three divine persons. In this way the patterns in nonintelligent nature and human society that join discordant members to form a higher concordance point toward, and are types of, the ultimate harmonies of self-denying service and love among the Father, Son, and Holy Spirit.

The ultimate picture of that inner-trinitarian service and love is the culmi-nation of the redemption. I say culmination because for Edwards the history of redemption started in the garden of Eden—not at the cross—and required the entire history of Israel. The repristination of that history in the whole *life* of Jesus is what saves us (Rom. 5:10). There we see ultimate harmony, which is self-sacrificial love in the midst of the greatest evil of all history, the murder of the Son of God. In this unspeakable evil and ultimate ugliness, genuine beauty is created by the mutual love of three persons—the Father suffering the passion and death of his Son, the Holy Spirit feeling the pain of the Father, as it were, and enabling the Son to endure the horrors, and Jesus himself taking on the physical tortures we deserve.

This is the culmination of the whole history of redemption that is pre-figured or typed in all of nature. As Edwards and Newman and others have pointed out, all of nature is full of life coming out of death, and so a figuring or typing of resurrection proceeding from death is found in nature. This is but one of the millions of other correspondences—types—in nature to the world of supernature.

This is Edwards's version of the analogy of being, as John C. Cunningham has put it. The spiritual beauties of God are communicated "ectypically" (by that part of God's infinite knowledge that we finite beings are able to receive) into created nature as forms of beauty.[23] The person who sees these beauties in nature, as well as their pointers to the divine beauty, sees what Edwards called "the beauty of holiness," which is the epistemological key to reality: "He that sees the beauty of holiness sees the greatest and most important thing in the world, which is the fullness of all things, without which the world is empty, no better than nothing" (*WJE* 2:274).

Translation: the person who sees the patterns of beauty in nature, even amid what seem to be disharmony and ugliness, sees the ultimate antitype, which is the meaning of all reality. Edwards suggests that perception then en-ables, or is the very sign of, union with the Creator of all reality (*WJE* 2:274). Hence ontology is connected to epistemology. To see the types of nature and to see their fullness, which means their beauty as symbols of the trinitarian beauty, is to be one with the Creator of nature, who is beauty incarnate.

The contemporary theologian David Bentley Hart sounded similar themes in his book *The Beauty of the Infinite: The Aesthetics of Christian Truth.*

---

23. John C. Cunningham, "Jonathan Edwards and the Trinitarian Shape of Beauty" (PhD diss., University of Virginia, 2015), 74.

Hart spoke of creation's surface as "a shining fabric of glory whose inmost truth is its correspondence to the beauty of divine love, as it is eternally expressed by the Trinity: a sacramental order of light." One can know what creation is only by seeing that it is beauty. The gap between analogies in nature and the divine beauty in which they participate is found not in nature being "utterly alien" but in God's being "infinitely more beautiful" than the beauty of creation.[24]

Leithart on *Perichōrēsis* in Nature

If Edwards saw the *beauty* of the Trinity in all of nature, Peter Leithart saw a trinitarian *pattern* in all of reality. Leithart wrote about *perichōrēsis*, or mutual indwelling, as a "trace of the Trinity" that is imprinted on creation and human life at every level.[25] This is a "reciprocal penetration" modeled by the three persons of the Trinity. Just as the Father is in the Son and the Son is in the Father, and their mutual indwelling is by the Holy Spirit, so too the church dwells in the Father and the Son by the Spirit: ". . . even as you, Father, are in me and I in you, that they also might be in us" (John 17:21). Disciples dwell in God because they are participants in the mutual indwelling of Father and Son. "The church is not merely an *image* of the eternal dance of triune life, but is introduced to the dance as a bridal partner" (140). The result is mutual indwelling of God and church: God dwells in the church, and the church lives in God. Every believer has Christ for a home (Col. 3:3), and Christ lives in each believer (Gal. 2:20).

Leithart found this trinitarian pattern in every dimension of nature. Most basically, we mutually indwell the world. We don't live in the world unless the world lives in us. Sound waves must penetrate our ears in order for us to hear the noise of the world. Light waves must penetrate us, or we cannot see the world. Molecules that create odors must enter our nostrils in order for us to smell the world. Only by the world penetrating us can we successfully live in the world (9–13).

Similarly, we live in *time*, and time lives in us. It is obvious that we are *in* time, unable to escape into the past or the future. Yet time inhabits us. We cannot think of the present without its immediately becoming part of the past. All of our thinking about the present is based on what we know from the past, even if only a few minutes before. The glass of water beside me

24. Hart, *Beauty of the Infinite*, 252, 253, 300.
25. Leithart, *Traces of the Trinity*, 137. In the next several paragraphs, page numbers in parentheses refer to *Traces of the Trinity*.

reminds me that I poured it twenty minutes ago. The words in front of me keep reminding me of my goal to finish this chapter by Friday, and this book by the end of the summer. I can rarely think of the now without immediately thinking of what's next. And not just the next day but the next season and year and, sometimes, the end of my life. Time dwells within me, even as I dwell in time (56–59).

Leithart pointed to mutual penetration in the way *language* works. Every word, he noted, is a union of the sensible and the intellectual. Take the word "swan." It relies on marks on the page shaped as letters we can see or, if spoken, a sound we can hear. Those sensory marks or sounds convey a picture of a bird, another sensory image. When we see one of those birds swimming elegantly on a pond and say, "That's a swan," we know that the sound "swan" is not precisely the bird but a word-sign for the bird we see. The real bird dwells within that sound pronounced "swan," even as the word dwells in the bird as we look at it (77). The bird we see is stored in our memory with the help of the word, and the word depends on the real bird to continue to have meaning. "Language is more like a Mobius strip in which inside and outside form a continuum. Sense and sound, sense and marking, fold back on each other. Ideas penetrate sound and marks" (73).

Literary texts also display this pattern of indwelling. Leithart referred to the story of Abraham being told to sacrifice Isaac. This story was retold by the Jewish philosopher Philo (d. AD 50), the Reformed theologian Theodore Beza (d. 1605), the philosopher-theologian Søren Kierkegaard (d. 1855), and the English novelist Thomas Hardy (d. 1928). Leithart observed that all of their texts were indwelt by the Genesis text, and each of their retellings enriched the original text, so that *our* understandings of the biblical story are filled with not only the biblical story but their retellings. We live in them as they live in us (80–81).

Music shows the same mutual indwelling. Leithart noted that when we hear music, it fills whatever space we are in, whether it be a cubbyhole or large room. Sound fills space without taking up space. We listen to a chord and cannot tell where one note ends and the other begins. Even when striking a single note, we hear half-heard overtones sounding within and around it. A chord consists of overtones on top of overtones.

Leithart cited composer and theologian Jeremy Begbie, who wrote about the interpenetration of music. Begbie described the way that sounds interpenetrate one another when more than one sound is present. They occupy the same space but remain audibly distinct. The tones of a chord can be heard *through* each other. In a three-tone major chord, for example, there are three distinct, mutually enhancing sounds, together occupying the same aural space.

Even when notes are not played at the same time, they require each other. The C in the C scale, for example, "leans ahead" to the D (88–89).[26]

Edwards conceived of the heavenly community as a singing society. It is a "society in the highest degree happy" that expresses "their love, their joy, and the inward concord and harmony and spiritual beauty of their souls by sweetly singing to each other" (*WJE* 13:331). Their choral music is a thing of beauty, thus exemplifying the beauty of the Trinity, but also a *society* in ways that are physical as much as spiritual. Bodies are distinct, but their combined voices become a single body as it were, and a single musical instrument. As Leithart put it, the voices mutually penetrate one another: each voice is a room in which the others dwell, and each dwells in the room that the others provide. Sopranos provide a house for the basses, and basses lay a foundation for all the others in which to live and move and have their being (93–94).

Leithart saw this same mutual indwelling in *knowing* (I know about a thing or person to the extent that the thing or person lives within me), *love* (an availability in which I make room in myself for others), and *imagination* (where concepts contain traces of their opposites, such as divine sovereignty and human freedom) (122–27). On imagination, Leithart wrote, "God's knowledge and human freedom depend on each other. Human freedom is embedded in God's infallible knowledge of the future, and God's infallible knowledge of the future somehow indwells human freedom" (126). Here I think Leithart meant that God knows what we will freely choose in the future, and it is his knowing that makes possible our free choosing. This seems to be what Paul meant when he wrote that our good works are the ones "*God* prepared beforehand" (Eph. 2:10). We "work out our salvation with fear and trembling" because *God* is "at work in [us], both to will and to work for his good pleasure" (Phil. 2:13). We live in God's knowing what we will, and God's willing and doing live in us.

Nature, then, is full of signs, testimonies, and voices. As Gregory of Nyssa put it, all of creation is a hymn to the power of the Almighty.[27] Every part of the creation speaks. There is meaning in every little bit. We will never be able to hear all the songs being sung or all the poems being spoken. But we can be confident, from the testimony of Scripture and the church, that all of nature is full of types. There is meaning everywhere—to be discovered by eyes that can see and ears that can hear, opened by the Holy Spirit.

26. Leithart cited Jeremy Begbie, *Theology, Music and Time* (Cambridge: Cambridge University Press, 2000), 24.

27. Gregory of Nyssa, *In inscriptiones Psalmorum* 1.3.30–33; paraphrased by Hart, *Beauty of the Infinite*, 275.

4

Science

The Wonder of the Universe

For most of his life Oxford philosopher Antony Flew (1923–2010) was known as a formidable opponent of belief in God. As Karl Giberson put it, "Whenever arguments supporting belief in God appeared, Flew was there, logical rapier in hand, to demolish them with counterarguments."[1] Yet in his last decade the intellectual world rocked with the news that Flew had become a theist of the deistic sort (a believer in a God who created and then left the universe on its own).

What had changed his mind? In his words, "recent scientific discoveries" in cosmology (investigations of the origins of the universe) and biogenesis (the origins of life). Flew never made the move from belief in an Aristotelian God of power and intelligence to the trinitarian God of Christian faith. But he insisted, against fellow philosophers who began to ridicule him, that he was continuing his lifelong practice of following the evidence where it leads, and that modern science showed new evidence—which he acknowledged is not the same thing as proof—for the propositions that (1) the universe did not come about by chance, and (2) without an organizing intelligence it was improbable for life to have emerged from nonlife.[2]

In this chapter we will see that we moderns have more reason than the ancients to say that the heavens and the earth are full of the glory of God. We

1. Karl W. Giberson, *The Wonder of the Universe: Hints of God in Our Fine-Tuned World* (Downers Grove, IL: InterVarsity, 2012), 9.
2. Giberson, *Wonder of the Universe*, 9–12.

will look first at the last century's discoveries in cosmology, and then at the strange way that beauty itself has led scientists to new discoveries. Part of the beauty comes from the surprising existence of mathematics as an idiom by which the cosmos seems to speak. Then we will turn from the macrocosm of the universe as a whole to the microcosm of the living cell and its embedded codes in DNA. At the end of the chapter we will ask what these things mean for typology and faith in the trinitarian God.

In our first chapter we mentioned the scientific discoveries that convinced most of the world that neither the earth nor humanity was the center of the universe. Even if recent historians are right to say that this conclusion did not necessarily lead to humans feeling less significant, it did lead some thinkers to question previous assumptions about God and the universe.[3] As astronomers came to see that the Milky Way galaxy contains billions of stars and the cosmos holds billions of galaxies, our little human world on planet earth seemed to be, with each new discovery, smaller and smaller. As science seemed to be able to explain more and more of what takes place on our planet, there seemed to be less and less need for a God to explain things.

Then along came new scientific developments. As science writer Kitty Ferguson explained, "The more we discover about both the cosmic and the microscopic levels of the universe, the more we seem to find ourselves again mysteriously reinstated as the kingpin."[4] About a century ago cosmologists started finding that the laws and constants set up at the origins of this universe were so precise that if they had been even slightly different, we would not be here. This discovery caused the agnostic physicist Sir Fred Hoyle to quip, "It looks like a put-up job."[5]

The story begins about a century ago when there were the first signs of a beginning to the universe. The early evidence came from astronomer Edwin Hubble's observations in 1929 that galaxies were drifting apart, which suggested an expanding universe. Many leading scientists found it hard to believe. Albert Einstein wrote that the idea of expansion "irritates me."[6] Allan Sandage, a physicist whose work was used to confirm the expansion theory,

---

3. Ronald Numbers, *Galileo Goes to Jail, and Other Myths about Science and Religion* (Cambridge, MA: Harvard University Press, 2010), 50–58. Thanks to Josh Reeves for alerting me to this volume.

4. Kitty Ferguson, *The Fire in the Equations: Science, Religion, and the Search for God* (Grand Rapids: Eerdmans, 1994), 163.

5. Fred Hoyle, "The Universe: Past and Present Reflections," *Annual Review of Astronomy and Astrophysics* 20 (1982): 16; cited in Alister E. McGrath, *A Fine-Tuned Universe: The Quest for God in Science and Theology*, The 2009 Gifford Lectures (Louisville: Westminster John Knox, 2009), 134.

6. Einstein in a letter to Willem de Sitter, cited in Ferguson, *Fire in the Equations*, 75.

nevertheless remarked that expansion was "such a strange conclusion . . . that it cannot really be true."[7] To counteract the possibility of a beginning, with its religious implications, Hoyle developed a countertheory, Steady State, that pictured a universe that expands because it continually creates matter but has neither beginning nor end. But when the discovery of cosmic microwave background radiation in the 1960s confirmed the existence of an initial cosmic explosion dubbed the Big Bang, many cosmologists had to rethink their earlier dismissals of a cosmic beginning. As American astronomer Robert Jastrow wrote,

> This is an exceedingly strange development, unexpected by all but the theologians. . . . The development is unexpected because science has had such extraordinary success in tracing the chain of cause and effect backward in time. Now we would like to pursue that inquiry farther back in time, but the barrier to further progress seems insurmountable. . . . For the scientist who has lived by his faith in the power of reason, the story ends like a bad dream. He has scaled the mountains of ignorance; he is about to conquer the highest peak; as he pulls himself over the final rock, he is greeted by a band of theologians who have been sitting there for centuries.[8]

The upshot is that we moderns have more evidence than the ancients had for believing that the universe had a beginning. Yet modern science gives us many more advantages than this. Recent cosmology shows us stunning evidence for order in the universe, far more order than the ancients could see when they appealed to order for evidence of God's existence.

For example, in Newtonian physics space and time were distinct. But in Einsteinian physics space and time make up one symmetrical four-dimensional space-time manifold. Space is not uniform in the way that gravity works on objects but can vary with time, suggesting an ordered unity of realities—space and time—that were once thought to be inherently disconnected.[9] Another example of cosmic order was the nineteenth-century discovery by James Maxwell that the electric and magnetic fields, which had been thought of as distinct, are actually unified. Then there is the remarkable unification of mass and energy, which in Newtonian physics were conceived separately but now are seen as mutually convertible in Einstein's famous formula $E = mc^2$. Furthermore, every one of the four basic forces (gravity, electromagnetism,

7. Allan Sandage, "Science: The Infinite Universe," *Time*, December 30, 1974, 48.
8. Robert Jastrow, *God and the Astronomers* (London: Norton, 1992), 107.
9. Stephen M. Barr, *Modern Physics and Ancient Faith* (Notre Dame, IN: University of Notre Dame Press, 2003), 102.

the strong force, and the weak force) is now seen to be "based in a profound way on principles of symmetry."[10] And there is more: particle physicists who explore the tiny interworkings of atoms are increasingly convinced that another kind of symmetry, called supersymmetry, exists in nature. It is said to pertain not only to the four dimensions of space-time but to other dimensions as well. There are many theoretical reasons for physicists to believe in supersymmetry, but no hard proof yet.[11] Nature, then, has an elegance and unity that run through it all, from top to bottom, that was never seen by ancients except intuitively. We now have scientists telling us of an inner principled harmony that ties together all of what is seen and unseen in the natural world.

Fine-Tuning

The most spectacular evidence of this invisible harmony is a new discussion among cosmologists and other scientists who talk about the "fine-tuning" of the universe. By this they mean the remarkable array of physical conditions in the cosmos that seem precisely calibrated for the emergence of conscious life. If they were to have been different in the tiniest ways, this universe would not exist. That is, if any of these conditions—which now exist—had varied in the most minute of ways, this universe would never have developed, and human life as we know it would never have been possible.[12] Let's look at eleven of these conditions of the universe that seem to have been "fine-tuned."

1. *Water* is absolutely essential for life. Yet it is so rare in the cosmos as to be statistically nonexistent. In other words, just as, when doing an inventory of your house, you would not include pennies that accidentally fell between the cushions of the living room couch, so too water is so rare that it wouldn't make the list in a cosmic inventory. Almost all spaces between stars are too cold for water, and stars are too hot. Only on planets orbiting at just the right distance from their suns is water possible. Its formation depends on the fine-tuning of all the constants in the rest of this list.[13]

2. *Carbon resonance* is required to make carbon, which is the all-essential molecule for life. This resonance is a level of energy required to complete an extremely complicated process of atomic fusion that produces carbon. If

10. Barr, *Modern Physics and Ancient Faith*, 102.
11. Barr, *Modern Physics and Ancient Faith*, 103.
12. Of course an omnipotent God can do anything, including creating human life without the requirements for these conditions. But then we would not be as we are, humans with these requirements. The question remains of why humans with *these* requirements are in a world precisely fitted for such beings.
13. Giberson, *Wonder of the Universe*, 84.

the resonance were a fraction of a percent lower or higher, the process would not work, and carbon would not be created. Life would then be impossible.[14]

3. The carbon resonance in turn depends on the *strong nuclear force*, which holds protons and neutrons together in the nucleus. This too is extremely delicate, meaning it would not work to create the possibility for life if it were not at precisely the right value, neither slightly more nor slightly less. If it were just 10 percent weaker, the basic elements would never have formed. If it were only 4 percent stronger, stars would last for so short a time that life would never have had a chance to evolve.[15]

4. Even the *weak nuclear force* seems to have been tuned to just the right level. After the first second following the Big Bang, cosmologists estimate that the ratio of protons to neutrons was six to one. This ratio was necessary for life. If it had been much weaker than it is, that ratio would never have been achieved, and life would not have been possible. A stronger force by a factor of ten would also have prevented life.[16]

5. *Gravity* was essential for the development of the present universe and the life it supports. If it had been just a tiny bit stronger than it is, all the matter exploding out of the Big Bang would have been sucked back into a black hole, snuffing out any possibility of life. If it had been just a wee bit weaker, that initial matter created by the primal explosion would have dispersed so quickly that it never would have collected into stars, one of which eventually created an environment for life.[17]

6. The *ratio of the electromagnetic force to the force of gravity* measures the relationship of the force that holds atoms together (by keeping electrons in orbit around the nucleus) to the force between atoms. If that ratio had been only slightly smaller, the universe would not have lasted long enough for creatures larger than insects.[18]

7. The *weights of the parts of the atom* make an enormous difference. If the neutron were lighter than it is by a fraction of 1 percent, isolated protons would be able to decay into neutrons, which means they would not be available for the creation of critically important atoms. Life would be impossible.[19]

8. The *overall density of energy and matter* in the universe, conventionally denoted as Ω, is just right. If the present density were slightly larger than it is,

14. Giberson, *Wonder of the Universe*, 116–18.
15. Barr, *Modern Physics and Ancient Faith*, 120–21.
16. Peter Bussey, *Signposts to God: How Modern Physics and Astronomy Point the Way to Belief* (Downers Grove, IL: IVP Academic, 2016), 105–6.
17. Giberson, *Wonder of the Universe*, 120–21.
18. McGrath, *Fine-Tuned Universe*, 119.
19. Giberson, *Wonder of the Universe*, 121–22.

the gravitational attraction of the matter and energy would pull the universe back in upon itself. If Ω were slightly smaller, the universe would expand too quickly and the gravitational pull of the matter would not be strong enough for the formation of galaxies.[20]

9. Concerning *initial entropy*, cosmologist Roger Penrose said that just after the Big Bang there was such a high degree of order that matter was spread out throughout its initial volume with an astounding evenness. There are many ways in which this could have been different, but only in this one way was there a possibility for eventual life to develop. This was a fine-tuning that raises all sorts of questions.[21]

10. A *very special planet* is needed for life. As we saw in number 1, the planet has to be just the right distance from a star to have a temperature that would permit liquid water. It seems to need a large moon to be able to stabilize its rotation and to need a larger protective planet further away to steer comets and asteroids in another direction. It also needs certain plate tectonics to provide both oceans and dry land. No one knows whether other planets in the universe have this combination of features that supports life. But ours has all the right characteristics.[22]

11. We take *air* for granted. But the density of the air we breathe is 10^{27} times the average density of matter in the universe. "Places in the Universe with a density at least as large as the air in a room are cosmically rare."[23] We are in this extremely rare location in an unthinkably vast cosmos.

The remarkable range of these eleven phenomena has convinced even nonreligious scientists that the universe shows signs of having been designed. We saw above that it helped convince Antony Flew that there must be a God, albeit deistic. Physicist Freeman Dyson was a colleague of Albert Einstein and Robert Oppenheimer at the Princeton Institute for Advanced Study and one of the earliest leaders of quantum mechanics research. His reaction to the ways that the laws of nature moved the universe toward the sustenance of life was to suggest intelligence at the beginning: "The more I examine the universe and study the details of its architecture, the more evidence I find that the universe in some sense must have known we were coming."[24] Even the famous atheist biologist Richard Dawkins acknowledged that it *seems* "as if our universe were set up to favour our eventual

20. Bussey, *Signposts to God*, 98–99.
21. Bussey, *Signposts to God*, 102–3.
22. Bussey, *Signposts to God*, 109.
23. Geraint F. Lewis and Luke A. Barnes, *A Fortunate Universe: Life in a Finely Tuned Cosmos* (Cambridge: Cambridge University Press, 2016), 18.
24. Freeman Dyson, *Disturbing the Universe* (New York: Basic Books, 2001), 250.

evolution."[25] Dawkins said he rejects "a divine knob-twiddler" because such a being would have been "at least as improbable as the settings of his knobs."[26]

But despite Dawkins's skepticism, "there is widespread agreement among astronomers, cosmologists and other theoretical physicists that our universe is in a very real sense 'fine-tuned' for our human existence."[27] Paul Davies, another physicist who is not a traditional believer, estimated that there are twenty knobs that had to be set just so in order for the laws of physics to start working. Some of them may depend on others among this set of twenty, and some might not require the same precision as others. But the fact that they all are in place in such a delicately interconnected way, that setting just one or a few of them differently would have doomed things from the start, caused him to say that studying them is like looking into "the mind of God."[28]

Owen Gingerich, Harvard astronomer and science historian, suggested that "if we are allowed to think of God in anthropomorphic terms, we would have to say, 'Good planning.'"[29] Nobel Prize–winning physicist Frank Wilczek "lost faith in traditional religion" yet said that this astonishing set of fine-tuning reveals a Creator of stunning artistry.[30]

Of course there are other physicists who saw this evidence for fine-tuning and shrugged their shoulders. They said it simply meant that we were extraordinarily lucky to have wound up in *a* universe that was able to produce us. Their most common alternative explanation has been the "multiverse." This is the idea that "ours is just one of many universes that appeared spontaneously out of nothing, each with different laws of nature."[31] Some astrophysicists proposed that there is an infinity of other universes out there, each with a different set of physical laws. In such an infinity we should not be surprised that there is one like ours.

Is this believable? Critics replied that while theoretically possible, it is not plausible. Unlike most physics, it does not describe any physical reality that

25. Richard Dawkins, "Why There Almost Certainly Is No God," Edge.org, October 25, 2006, https://www.edge.org/conversation/why-there-almost-certainly-is-no-god; quoted in Giberson, *Wonder of the Universe*, 176.

26. Dawkins, "Why There Almost Certainly Is No God," quoted in Giberson, *Wonder of the Universe*, 176.

27. Bussey, *Signposts to God*, 111.

28. Paul Davies, *The Mind of God: The Scientific Basis for a Rational World* (New York: Simon & Schuster, 1993).

29. Owen Gingerich, *God's Universe* (Cambridge, MA: Belknap Press, 2006), 53.

30. Frank Wilczek, *A Beautiful Question: Finding Nature's Deep Design* (New York: Penguin, 2015), 2.

31. Giberson, *Wonder of the Universe*, 180.

can be measured and examined. For science writer Martin Gardner, "There is not the slightest shred of reliable evidence that there is any universe other than the one we are in. No multiverse theory has so far provided a prediction that can be tested. As far as we can tell, universes are not as plentiful as even *two* blackberries."[32] Paul Davies dismissed the theory as hovering "on the borderline between science and fantasy."[33]

But is "fine-tuning" (also called the "anthropic theory," from the Greek word for "human being") just another "God of the gaps" illusion? That is, is it another example of religious believers claiming that gaps in present scientific knowledge prove the need for God? At one time scientists thought there was nothing beyond the planets, and then later that there were no other galaxies. As we have seen, scientists until fairly recently thought that the universe had no beginning. Are the fine-tuning phenomena we have described simply temporary limits to our knowledge? Will scientists one day see that there are reasons for all these phenomena?

In one sense, yes. Scientists *already* know that without any one of these numbers calibrated precisely as they are, most and perhaps all the others would be different, and this universe would not exist. In fact, physicists and cosmologists tend to agree that the more scientists learn, the deeper the fine-tuning goes. According to Australian astrophysicist Luke Barnes, "We have found fine-tuning as deep as we can go. . . . [It] follows us down. It shows no signs of disappearing on deeper levels. We can explain the proton mass in terms of, amongst other things, the quark masses; those in terms of the properties of the Higgs field; those, perhaps, in terms of supersymmetry. Anthropic constraints appear at all levels."[34] American physicist Stephen Barr wrote similarly: "The universe does not appear more and more flawed the more closely one looks at it, as one might expect if its regularity were a matter of luck. Rather, its *fundamental* patterns appear more and more wonderfully perfect the more closely they are examined."[35]

What these parameters show is not a series of gaps that the credulous replace with the God-hypothesis but a *boundary* in the knowledge of scientists—"beyond which lies something quite extraordinary."[36] Some scientists are simply unwilling to go beyond that boundary. Fred Hoyle's distaste for a Big Bang led him to develop the Steady State theory because he could not

---

32. Martin Gardner, "Multiverses and Blackberries," *Skeptical Inquirer* 25, no. 5 (September/October 2001), http://www.csicop.org/si/show/multiverses_and_blackberries.

33. Davies, *Mind of God*, 185.

34. Lewis and Barnes, *Fortunate Universe*, 345.

35. Barr, *Modern Physics and Ancient Faith*, 108 (emphasis original).

36. Giberson, *Wonder of the Universe*, 189.

live with the suggestion of a cosmic beginning, which sounded too much like the biblical story he had rejected.[37] Harvard biologist Richard Lewontin is similar. He and other scientists of like mind are committed materialists, who want above all else not to allow a divine foot in the door. "It is not that the methods and institutions of science somehow compel us to accept a material explanation of the phenomenal world, but, on the contrary, [it is] that we are forced by our a priori adherence to material causes to create an apparatus of investigation and a set of concepts that produce material explanations, no matter how counter-intuitive, no matter how mystifying to the uninitiated. Moreover, that materialism is absolute, for we cannot allow a Divine Foot in the door."[38]

For scientists like Lewontin who are committed materialists, the pattern we have just seen is barely visible to them. It slips through their categories in the way that fish smaller than three inches slip through a net with three-inch openings, prompting the proverbial fisherman to conclude that the sea doesn't contain fish smaller than three inches in diameter.[39] But many scientists are not so dogmatic. Some, like the ones we have just cited, see the evidence of fine-tuning to be what C. S. Lewis called a "clue to the meaning of the universe."[40] Like Einstein, they are amazed that we are able to understand a universe whose "eternal mystery . . . is its comprehensibility."[41] For if the universe were indeed a product of undirected and random forces that are finally irrational, it is extremely odd that the deeper scientists go into its macrocosmic structures (we shall see its microcosmic structure in a few pages), the more they see patterns they can understand and map in rational ways.

Beauty

But are we imputing our own rational designs to a nature that is dumb and mute and without inner rationality? One *might* be able to make this argument if there were not so many precise constraints, all of which together

37. Giberson, *Wonder of the Universe*, 76–77. Later in his life Hoyle came to doubt his doubts of theism, concluding that "because of this incredible chain of subtlety," the universe was purposive after all. See Bussey, *Signposts to God*, 70.

38. Richard Lewontin, "Billions and Billions of Demons," *New York Review of Books*, January 9, 1997, http://www.nybooks.com/articles/1997/01/09/billions-and-billions-of-demons.

39. Giberson, *Wonder of the Universe*, 187–88.

40. "Right and Wrong as a Clue to the Meaning of the Universe" is the title of book 1 in Lewis's *Mere Christianity* (London: Bles, 1952).

41. Albert Einstein, *Out of My Later Years* (New York: Philosophical Library / Open Road, 2015), 64.

were required to produce the only planet we know in which humans could develop. Yet there is something else that supports the notion that this universe is not the product of mindless random forces. Frankly, it is not something that I knew until I did the research for this book: the pervasive beauty in the hidden structures of the universe. Of course I have seen beauty in nature, the sort of beauty that caused the biblical authors to see the glory of God in the heavens and the earth. But what I did not know was the extent to which modern physicists and cosmologists talk about the elegance and loveliness deep in the recesses of the physical cosmos that we nonscientists never see.

Actually, some of the world's great minds saw this cryptic beauty long before the last century. Plato saw that the world in its deep structures embodies beauty: his demiurge was an artisan whose world became a work of art.[42] Newton had a preternatural gift of discovering the "dynamical beauty" of the laws governing the universe, at least at one level.[43]

But it wasn't until the last century that physicists learned that the same equations that govern atoms and light also govern musical instruments and sounds. It was only recently that scientists have come to see that light is a form of matter, and "that matter in general, when understood deeply, is remarkably light-like."[44] In other words, scientists have come upon a deep symmetry that connects what most of us have never imagined could be connected—matter, light, and music. Physicists call such connections a sign of deep beauty.

But what do they mean by "beauty"? Physicist Frank Wilczek said there are two hallmarks of what he calls "nature's artistic style." The first is symmetry, by which he meant nature's "love of harmony, balance, and proportion." The second is "economy—satisfaction in producing an abundance of effects from very limited means." This second hallmark, nature's uncanny ability to produce near-unlimited results from limited means, has been noticed by others. Robert Wright called it "nonzero-sumness."[45] By this he meant that the whole is more than the sum of its parts, and the whole can keep getting bigger while its parts seem to remain the same. In other words, there is a deep productiveness or fecundity whereby parts of the cosmos keep on giving while not losing anything of their own substance. Paradoxical but beautiful. Wright used game theory to describe how biological evolution has worked in economic and political history, but he also believed it worked in the whole of

42. Plato referred to the demiurge frequently in his *Timaeus*. For the demiurge as an artist, see Wilczek, *Beautiful Question*, 5, 47.
43. Wilczek, *Beautiful Question*, 112.
44. Wilczek, *Beautiful Question*, 8, 13.
45. Robert Wright, *Nonzero: The Logic of Human Destiny* (New York: Vintage, 2001).

nature.[46] This was his way of describing the deeply laid symmetry that many physicists have found in the universe.

Wilczek called this beauty a "miraculous harmony of Mind and Matter."[47] Ferguson said it is "the coming together of many disparate elements in a way that seems inevitable, effortless, intensely pleasing, beyond our expectations." It has to do with "a falling-into-place that appears little short of miraculous."[48] Its appearance is simple and elegant, demonstrating consistency and creativity.

Beauty has become so pervasively recognized by physicists that it has become a criterion of a true theory. If it is not beautiful, in other words, it is probably not true. Einstein himself said he believed his theory of general relativity was so beautiful that it *could* not fail.[49] Renowned physicist Stephen Weinberg, an atheist, implied that this criterion was widely recognized in the field: "I believe that the general acceptance of general relativity was due in large part . . . to its beauty."[50] Other leading physicists agreed. The mathematical physicist Paul Dirac wrote, "It is more important to have beauty in one's equations than to have them fit experiment."[51] Wilczek said it was beauty and symmetry that guided James Maxwell to see that the primary ingredients of nature are not point-like particles but space-filling fields. He was guided by "inspired guesswork" directed by a vision of beauty. This vision is now a staple of modern science, said Wilczek. The idea that symmetry dictates structure "has come to dominate our understanding of physical reality."[52]

This conclusion is stunningly odd. Even agnostics and atheists among these scientists (and not all physicists by any means are unbelieving) agreed that there are deep structures of harmony and symmetry holding together the physical cosmos. It is odd because it is illogical—on atheist assumptions—for a universe that has originated from unintelligent random processes to have deep structures that are beautiful. Logic suggests that randomness would be

46. Some wonder how nature governed by laws (such as those in evolutionary theory) can be compatible with a personal God, who would seem not to need laws but instead to run the world by regular direct intervention. Although Jonathan Edwards was not familiar with evolution, he wrote frequently about Newton's discoveries of the laws of nature. He believed that those laws described God's usual ways of sustaining the world and that miracles were occasions when God sustained things in extraordinary ways. See Michael McClymond and Gerald McDermott, *The Theology of Jonathan Edwards* (New York: Oxford University Press, 2012), 107–10.

47. Wilczek, *Beautiful Question*, 12.

48. Ferguson, *Fire in the Equations*, 60–61.

49. Einstein, quoted in Giberson, *Wonder of the Universe*, 67.

50. Steven Weinberg, *Dreams of a Final Theory: The Scientist's Search for the Ultimate Laws of Nature* (New York: Vintage, 1994), 98.

51. Paul Dirac, "The Evolution of the Physicist's Picture of Nature," *Scientific American*, May 1963, 47.

52. Wilczek, *Beautiful Question*, 7, 48.

without symmetry or harmony. For this reason Wilczek, who is not a traditional believer, observed that "the beauty of Nature's deep design . . . is as
strange as its strangeness is beautiful."[53]

What might be even odder is that this strange beauty is, in a word, perfect.
Hermann Weyl, one of the great mathematical physicists of the twentieth
century, wrote that although there is plenty of evil in the world, scientists
have found that at the deepest levels of nature there is perfection: "In [his-
tory] we evidently have not yet succeeded in raising the veil with which our
human nature covers the essence of things. But in our knowledge of *physical*
nature we have penetrated so far that we can obtain a vision of the flawless
harmony which is in conformity with sublime reason."[54] As Barr put it, nature's "fundamental patterns appear more and more wonderfully perfect the
more closely they are examined."[55] How strange!

This is one of many reasons why physicist John Polkinghorne concluded
that "modern science seems, almost irresistibly, to point beyond itself."[56]

The Strange Nature of Mathematics

Mathematics is a part of that beauty. Centuries ago the great astronomer
Johannes Kepler (d. 1630) found that math enabled him to predict the relative distances between the various planets and the sun. This finding made
him feel "possessed by an unutterable rapture," bedazzled by "God [thereby]
signing his likeness into the world," symbolizing "all nature and the graceful
sky" by "the art of geometry."[57] Modern scientists, such as the pioneer quantum physicist Paul Dirac, were similarly struck. "[The] fundamental physical
laws are described in terms of a mathematical theory of great *beauty* and
power. . . . One could perhaps describe the situation by saying that God is a
mathematician of a very high order and He used very advanced mathematics
in constructing the universe."[58]

If mathematics has impressed many of its greatest theorists with its beauty,
many scientists have been equally struck by the peculiarity of its ability to

53. Wilczek, *Beautiful Question*, 166.
54. Hermann Weyl, *The Open World: Three Lectures on the Metaphysical Implications of
Science* (New Haven: Yale University Press, 1932), 28–29.
55. Barr, *Modern Physics and Ancient Faith*, 108.
56. John Polkinghorne, *One World: The Interaction of Science and Theology* (Princeton:
Princeton University Press, 1987), 75.
57. Johannes Kepler, *Mysterium Cosmographicum*, quoted in Wilczek, *Beautiful Question*,
50–51.
58. Dirac, "Evolution of the Physicist's Picture of Nature," 45 (emphasis added).

map nature. The Nobel laureate physicist Eugene Wigner wrote a celebrated essay about how the ability of math to tell us about nature is "unreasonable."[59] Einstein said that our ability to make sense of the universe with mathematics is a "miracle,"[60] for a universe arising from randomness would not be expected to be so rational as to correspond with such precision to the precise system that mathematics is. In his book *The Mind of God* Paul Davies registered his surprise at this correspondence. "Much of the mathematics that is so spectacularly effective in physical theory was worked out as an abstract exercise by pure mathematicians long before it was applied to the real world . . . and yet we discover, often years afterward, that nature is playing by the very same mathematical rules that these pure mathematicians have already formulated."[61]

Is there a link between the beauty of mathematics and its description of nature? There is—in music. Millennia ago the Greek philosopher Pythagoras noticed that musical tones are in harmony if their tensions are ratios of the squares of small whole numbers. These rules, translated into frequency, state that notes sound good together if their frequencies are in ratios of small whole numbers. He was the first major thinker to see the connection between nature and music through the medium of mathematics. This "music of the spheres," which Pythagoras thought was created by the harmonies among the sun and moon and planets, is the same "heavenly harmony" that Kepler described. The physicist Wilczek said they were on to something profoundly true. Atoms, he wrote, are tiny musical instruments. "In their interplay with light, they realize a mathematical Music of the Spheres that surpasses the visions of Pythagoras, Plato, and Kepler. In molecules and ordered materials, those atomic instruments play together as harmonious ensembles and ordered materials."[62]

So mathematics links the world of nature and our minds by a kind of music. But do we comprehend it because we have created mathematics? Is it just another artificial human construct that we have imposed on the world? We have already seen that the fit between mathematics and the world is so close and precise that artificial imposition is unlikely. In fact, there is something about mathematics itself that suggests it has a life of its own completely apart from its use to describe nature. In other words, it seems to have its *own* existence and nature, quite removed from the physical world. As particle physicist Peter Bussey argued, mathematics is not physics, even though physics depends on

59. Eugene Wigner, "The Unreasonable Effectiveness of Mathematics in the Natural Sciences," *Communications in Pure and Applied Mathematics* 13, no. 1 (February 1960): 1–14.

60. A. Einstein, "Physics and Reality," *Journal of the Franklin Institute* 221 (1936): 313–48; cited in Bussey, *Signposts to God*, 55.

61. Davies, *Mind of God*, 151.

62. Wilczek, *Beautiful Question*, 225.

math. "Mathematics seems to have a life of its own."[63] Musician and science writer Kitty Ferguson told of the day when it dawned on her that mathematics has an objective reality apart from its use in science. "I remember clearly when it first dawned on me that human beings might have discovered mathematics, not invented it; that it might lie waiting in nature; that mathematical truth might be a part of independent reality. It wasn't in mathematics class, but in music theory, when I studied the harmonic series. It seemed to me that this pattern could not be a human way of sorting things out. It would have existed even if human beings had never existed."[64]

Astrophysicist Roger Penrose also noted that mathematics has a transcendent, objective character. "There often does appear to be some profound reality about these mathematical concepts, going quite beyond the mental deliberations of any particular mathematician. It is as though human thought is, instead, being guided towards some external truth—a truth which has a reality of its own, and which is revealed only partially to any one of us."[65]

Once again, then, we are faced with oddities. This world seems to have been fine-tuned not just with one or two parameters but with many. If a few or perhaps even one of them were different, we would not be here. These evidences of fine-tuning are strange enough, but the fact that there is beauty at the deepest physical levels of the universe, and that it has been noticed by agnostic and believing scientists alike, is also odd. Why would a randomly formed universe be beautiful? Furthermore, why would the beautifully rational system of mathematics so perfectly describe the way this world works? If this world is finally *irrational*, which is what one would expect from a cosmic accident (as it is said to be by atheists such as Richard Dawkins), then one would never expect a *rational* system like mathematics to fit it so closely and usefully.

Signature in the Cell

Stretched a bit more, the oddities continue. We looked in the last section at the macrocosm of cosmology. Here we consider the microcosm of the living cell. We will see that the oddities of beauty and rationality are there as well. Only this time, deep within the cell, there is a new element even more rational and surprising: *information*.

63. Bussey, *Signposts to God*, 50.
64. Ferguson, *Fire in the Equations*, 130.
65. Roger Penrose, *The Emperor's New Mind* (Oxford: Oxford University Press, 1989), 95; cited in Ferguson, *Fire in the Equations*, 131.

We have learned from physicists that matter and energy are convertible, and we might have concluded that those are the only real elements in the universe, or maybe just energy, with matter being one of its forms. But we would have been wrong. Stephen C. Meyer, a philosopher of science, wrote an award-winning book called *Signature in the Cell* that showed the ways in which information is the critical third component necessary for life to exist, after matter and energy.[66]

Meyer showed that this information needs to be phenomenally complex and specific in order for it to produce what is necessary for life. DNA, RNA, and proteins store and carry the information that cells in organisms need for replication and growth. The most important information is stored in DNA molecules arranged on long strands, wrapped around spool-like structures called nucleosomes. Meyer told his readers to imagine a large wooden spool with grooves on the surface. Two strands form a helical cord that wraps around the spool so that the cord lies exactly in the hollowed-out grooves of the spool. "Imagine the grooves hollowed in such a way that they exactly fit the shape of the coiled cord—thicker parts nestling into deeper grooves, thinner parts into shallower ones" (97–98). The irregularities of the cord match the grooves in the spool precisely. But the matching is even more precise, because the positively charged places on the surface of the spool (histone proteins) match perfectly the negatively charged places of the double-stranded DNA cord that wraps around it. This explains the shape of the proteins that make up DNA.

But it is not just the shape of the proteins that makes for specificity. It is also the *arrangement* of the proteins that specifies what information is being transmitted, and this arrangement is based on the sequence of the amino acids that make up the proteins. The specific sequence of the amino acids determines the three-dimensional structure of the whole chain (98).

In other words, life is transmitted by the transmittal of information contained in the DNA molecule. It is not just matter and energy that are exchanged in the transmittal of life, but highly complex and specific information. And the transmittal of information involves exceedingly complex and specific processes. Meyer distinguished complexity on the one hand and specificity on the other from complex specificity. Crystals exhibit beautiful order but not complexity. Mixtures of random polymers (large molecules) are complex but lack specificity. Human artifacts and technology, in contrast, such as paintings, signs, written text, spoken language, machine codes, computer hardware and

66. Stephen C. Meyer, *Signature in the Cell: DNA and the Evidence for Intelligent Design* (New York: HarperOne, 2009). In the next several paragraphs, page numbers in parentheses refer to *Signature in the Cell*.

software—all these are *both* complex *and* specific. So too is the information in DNA, found only in living organisms.

This is barely the tip of the iceberg of the complexity involved in the information that is stored and transmitted through DNA and RNA in the mystery of living organisms. Volumes of textbooks explain the intricacy of these processes that produce new life from existing life and then grow an organism once it has been produced. Since we are exploring signs of the divine, there are two fascinating things to note for our purposes. The first is a mystery that has now become familiar—the intriguing capacity of mathematics to read the highly specific information in DNA. If one realizes the explanation often given for the origins of life—that it arose from undirected natural selection and random mutations—it is something on the order of shocking that "the treatment of DNA and English text is 'mathematically identical.' Both systems of symbols or characters can be analyzed the same way" (108). Why shocking? Because, once again, randomness rarely if ever creates order that is complex and mathematically systematic.

The second strange feature of the cell's information system is its similarity to human-designed computers. Even Dawkins acknowledged that "the machine code of the gene is uncannily computer-like," and so did Bill Gates: "DNA is like a computer program" (368). Information theorist Hubert Yockey confirmed this conclusion when he wrote that "the genetic code is constructed to confront and solve the problems of communication and recording by the same principles found . . . in modern communication and computer codes" (368–69). A software engineer working with molecular biologists showed Meyer *Design Patterns*, a standard text for software engineers. He told Meyer that all the strategies for processing, storing, copying, organizing, accessing, and correcting digitally encoded strings of information were at work in the cell, but that the cell's methods were far more elegant. "It's like we are looking [in the cell] at 8.0 or 9.0 versions of design strategies that we have just begun to implement." The engineer told Meyer that studying the way the cell processes information gave him "an eerie feeling that someone else figured this out before we got here" (369).

One of the biggest mysteries in biology specifically and science generally is how life arose in the first place. Dawkins admitted in 2008 that "no one knows" the answer to this question.[67] "Leading scientists—Francis Crick, Fred Hoyle, Paul Davies, Freeman Dyson, Eugene Wigner, Klaus Dose, Robert

---

67. Final interview with Richard Dawkins in Ben Stein's documentary, "Expelled: No Intelligence Allowed," https://www.youtube.com/watch?v=V5EPymcWp-g; cited in Meyer, *Signature in the Cell*, 333.

Shapiro, Dean Kenyon, Leslie Orgel, Gerald Joyce, Hubert Yockey, even Stanley Miller—[have] all expressed skepticism either about the merits of leading theories, the relevance of prebiotic experiments, or both" (333). One of the popular theories was based on prebiotic simulation experiments in which scientists such as Stanley Miller tried to simulate the production of amino acids and other building blocks for life on the early earth. But in every case undesirable by-products have reacted with desirable building blocks to form inert compounds, such as a tar, called melanoidin—without the intervention of the scientist. Whatever success these experiments had always relied on manipulating chemical conditions both before and after performing "simulation" experiments. No life arose without the activity of a conscious, deliberate mind from the outside (334–35). Evolutionary algorithms supposedly showed the creative power of mutation and selection to generate functional information for early cells. But to the extent that any algorithm modeled a realistically biological process, it depended on an information-rich instruction set provided by computer programmers. In other words, in no case did an experiment or computer model successfully show the possibility of life coming from random mutations and natural selection alone (335–37).

Alister McGrath, who received a PhD in molecular biology from Oxford University, argued that RNA and DNA are such complex structures that the probability of their arising spontaneously is "widely conceded to be vanishingly small." McGrath recalled Hoyle's warning: "The chance that higher life forms might have emerged in this way is comparable with the chance that a tornado sweeping through a junk-yard might assemble a Boeing 747 from the materials therein." McGrath said Hoyle overstated his case a bit, neglecting "the apparent capacity for self-organization within the biochemical world." Yet he also showed that there is a massive gap between the origin of carbon, nitrogen, and oxygen in stellar cores and the origins of life itself. Therefore he concluded that the origins of life "are unquestionably anthropic." They require the fundamental constants of nature to have been fine-tuned in ways that we have already discussed. In and of itself the Big Bang was not capable of producing the basic building blocks—carbon, nitrogen, and oxygen. The formation of stars needed the gravitational constant, and the weak nuclear force could not have been different by one one-hundredth, or life would never have been possible.[68]

Barr argued that natural selection is insufficient to explain life because it requires life for it to be able to operate. In other words, it requires self-reproducing organisms that are able to pass on their traits genetically. How can it produce the first life if it needs life to operate? Another problem is that even the first

68. McGrath, *Fine-Tuned Universe*, 131, 134, 142.

"primitive" life form was enormously complicated. It appears to have had an elaborate structure involving dozens of different proteins, a genetic code containing at least 250 genes, and many tens of thousands of bits of information. "For chemicals to combine in random ways in a 'primordial soup' to produce a strand of DNA or RNA containing such a huge amount of genetic information would be as hard as for a monkey to accidentally type an epic poem." Barr raised the possibility of an infinite number of planets making theoretically *possible* a monkey typing *Hamlet*, but then suggested that such a comment might simply be a way for skeptical scientists to avoid allowing the divine foot in the door.[69]

Barr conceded that there is evidence that natural selection has taken place. What he doubts is that natural selection is sufficient to drive the whole process of evolution. Consider the Cambrian Explosion, he argued, a mere five-million-year period during which evolutionary changes took place one hundred times faster than any evolutionary scientists dreamed possible. It was not only the *time* that appears implausible but the *complexity* produced. The information required to put together a bacterium would fill the *Encyclopedia Britannica*. The human brain contains one hundred million neurons, each of which is connected to as many as a thousand other neurons. It dwarfs in sophistication any computer we know. Yet this brain—think of that of Mozart, Shakespeare, Einstein—is said to have evolved from an ape's in five million years. Based on what evolutionary scientists have told us, this is impossible. The complexity that had to be produced in this short period of time is nearly unimaginable. To conceive of this vast complexity, Barr drew a comparison. Humans are capable of building a jumbo jet, he said, but nothing "as sophisticated as a housefly or a mosquito."[70]

The bottom line is that when we look *down* at the tiniest parts of the living cell—the microcosm, in contrast to the macrocosm of the universe—we find the same mysteries we found when looking *up*. It seems highly unlikely that either could have arisen by chance. Both seem to have required massive fine-tuning, and the cell's enormously complex information processing seems suspiciously preprogrammed. Both, that is, show the glory of God in his creation. Glory in the heavens above and glory in the cells below.

Types?

Glory, yes. But what about *types* of the trinitarian God? Do we see anything from modern science that suggests there are messages left for regenerated

69. Barr, *Modern Physics and Ancient Faith*, 74–75.
70. Barr, *Modern Physics and Ancient Faith*, 110–11.

eyes to see and ears to hear? Messages saying more than simply "divine design," or that this is a *work* of God—saying, more specifically, anything of the *ways* of God?

Perhaps. Let me suggest a few.

First, God's works of creation show that he does things in ways that are literally unfathomable. We have heard all too often that "God is great" from Islamic terrorists about Allah, a false god. But Scripture says, "Great is YHWH [the LORD]" (Ps. 48:1). Too often we domesticate the God of Israel, imagining he is somehow a greater version of ourselves. But modern cosmology helps us correct our myopic anthropomorphisms. It has shown us that the Milky Way, which is only one of billions of galaxies, contains two hundred billion stars. The nearest star to us, in our part of this local galaxy, is Proxima Centauri, twenty-five trillion miles away. Light from that star thus takes four years to get to us. The stars on the other side of the galaxy are three hundred thousand trillion miles away, and their light takes seventy-five thousand years to reach us. Andromeda, another galaxy, is part of a small cluster of galaxies, of which our Milky Way is a part, called the *Local* (!) Group. Even though Andromeda is in our own Local Group, light from it takes three million years to get to us. And that's a galaxy that is nearer to us![71]

If God is the creator of all these galaxies, and they are *in* him (Acts 17:28), and he is Being itself (Exod. 3:14), *from* which these galaxies derive their minuscule being, just think how great this God is. He is the God of Israel *and* the God of all the galaxies, whose stars he has named (Ps. 147:4). If we cannot conceive the immensity of this universe, then we can conceive of God even less, for he is infinitely greater than the cosmos. He is the One *in* whom the cosmos resides. As the psalmist writes, "His greatness is unsearchable" (Ps. 145:3 ESV).

Scripture suggests two responses. The first has to do with us—awed appreciation that this infinite God cares about us in our infinitesimal (in comparison) littleness:

> When I look at your heavens, the work of your fingers,
> > the moon and the stars, which you have set in place,
> what is man that you are mindful of him,
> > and the son of man that you care for him? (Ps. 8:3–4 ESV)

The second response has to do with God—recognition of his infinite transcendence: "His greatness is unsearchable" (Ps. 145:3). The modern science

---

71. Giberson, *Wonder of the Universe*, 41–43.

we have seen in this chapter helps us appreciate how far beyond our understanding is God's greatness. If the vastness of the universe is greater than
we can get our minds around, how much greater is God, who is not another
being but Being itself, and so the infinite One in whom this near-infinite
cosmos dwells (Ps. 90:1–2). For this reason God's greatness is "unsearchable," beyond our ability to find it. Jonathan Edwards suggested that every
day in eternity we will be seeing more of God's greatness, and yet after millions of years of daily new discoveries, there will always be infinitely more
to discover.[72] It was this sort of recognition of God's mind-boggling *ways*
of creating that caused Job to throw himself onto the ground in repentance
and adoration (Job 42:6).

For a second type, think of quantum theory, which teaches us that electrons
are waves and not neat little balls. It is for this reason—that they behave as
waves and not simply particles—that uncertainty is part of their nature. And
this is not just a temporary stage until more complete scientific knowledge
arrives.[73] The wave-like electron can *never* be located precisely. As Heisenberg
showed, the closer one gets to the electron's location, the farther one gets
from its momentum or speed. And vice versa: the closer to the speed, the less
possible it is to determine the electron's location. Physicists tell us this is the
nature of the beast and always will be, that there never will be a time that
science will know both speed and location at the same time.[74] We can know
with a high degree of probability either the location or the speed, but never
the other at the same time with certainty.

We could say that this principle concerning electrons in the scientific world
is a *type* of faith in the spiritual world, for faith involves probability rather
than certainty. It walks without "sight" and is convicted of things "without
seeing" (2 Cor. 5:7; Heb. 11:1). It has "assurance" and so a kind of spiritual
certainty, but intellectual certainty is sometimes lacking. It can argue with a
high degree of probability, based on abundant historical evidence, that Jesus
rose from the dead, but it will never be able to prove this event to unbelievers
in a way that removes all doubt.

Yet here again science points to things in the world beyond science, for
philosophy of science tells us that the inability to remove all doubt is not un-
scientific. According to the great philosopher of science Karl Popper, to say
that something isn't proved is not nearly so strong as saying that it has been
proved incorrect. "Not proved" does not equal false. Popper even argued that

72. Jonathan Edwards, "Concerning the End for Which God Created the World," in *WJE*
8:443–44.
73. Giberson, *Wonder of the Universe*, 71.
74. Giberson, *Wonder of the Universe*, 71; Lewis and Barnes, *Fortunate Universe*, 185.

no scientific theory is ever proved by experiment because there can always be a new experiment that could possibly show different results.[75]

My point is that a scientific theory can be respected and accepted without being proved beyond doubt. As long as it is not proved incorrect, it can inspire confidence. Faith in the Christian God is similar. That it has never been proved scientifically is rather unimportant and even risible, for science cannot prove what is beyond its reach. Far more important is that this faith has never been proved false by science. And it never can be, for science uses nets with three-inch openings, as it were, and the things of religion slip through those three-inch openings.

A third type is sacramental. As we have seen, astrophysicists show us that light from distant stars takes decades and centuries and millennia to reach us. So the light we see from a *very* distant star can show us the star as it was thousands of years ago. Another way of putting this is to say that the past of the star comes into our present. This is a vivid astronomical analogue to what the New Testament suggests happens in the sacraments. Paul said that baptism joins believers to the death of Christ thousands of years ago (Rom. 6:3) and that the Eucharist is "a participation in the blood of Christ . . . [and] the body of Christ" (1 Cor. 10:16 ESV). Somehow the *past* of Christ's death and person come into the *present* of his disciples in the sacraments. In this way, then, light from the past of stars coming to our present shows us something of the ways God works with his people. He lifts them up into his eternity, where past and present are made one. In this case, astrophysics gives us a *type* of this way God works by showing us how the past can come into the present.

Finally, recent cosmology can help us see something of the moral nature of God. How could that be? Think of all the ways that the universe has been fine-tuned to allow for human beings to come to be. Christian faith tells us that it is the God of Israel, the Father of Jesus Christ, who superintended this cosmic process. It also tells us that we humans were created in his image (Gen. 1:27). So by looking at what sort of creatures this cosmic process has developed, we can say something about the God who created the process. Just as looking at a mathematical theorem tells us something about the mind of a mathematician, or seeing a beautiful building tells us something about the mind of the architect, so seeing the moral knowledge of human beings can tell us something about the God who made them in his image.

75. Ferguson, *Fire in the Equations*, 43. Einstein is said to have said nearly the same thing in a famous paraphrase: "No amount of experimentation can ever prove me right; a single experiment can prove me wrong." See Alice Calaprice, *The New Quotable Einstein* (Princeton: Princeton University Press, 2005), 291.

What is the moral knowledge that humans generally share? It is far from perfect, but generally they know that love is better than hatred and that to live for others is better than to live for themselves. Even if they don't live this way, almost all say it is the ideal way to live. They also know that love is a splendid ideal and that the ideal love is self-sacrificial. Every world religion— and arguably the religions shape the world's cultures—teaches these things. These facts alone suggest that the One who made human beings in his image is one who must value living for others by love and self-sacrifice. And while all world religions teach these principles, only the Christian God *embodies* them. Only the Son of God lived that self-sacrificial love concretely and to the end.

We have seen that modern cosmology shows that this universe was fine-tuned to allow for these moral humans to emerge. It is not a leap to conclude that an intelligent mind designed this fine-tuned universe and that this mind was the God who said he made humans in his image. It is another short step to infer that this fine-tuning was a series of signs or types that point to a moral God, since the human beings whom the fine-tuning developed are moral creatures. And while their morality points to the morality of the great world religions, it points *most* clearly to the Christian God, who put that morality into practice by living as a human being in the flesh. Human beings are the types or symbols that point to the *ways* that God lived in flesh as Jesus of Nazareth. In this way modern science contains types. It suggests that the universe was designed for the particular creatures who point to this very particular God.

5

Law

The Moral Argument

In the last four chapters we have focused primarily on types outside of the human self in the physical cosmos, at both the macro and micro levels. Now we will turn to human beings themselves and look within. We will look not at the physical body but at the immaterial soul. There we will see God's fingerprints—his types—planted in the conscience.

Most people know that the conscience is involved in both morality and religion. Yet in this time of history most have mistaken ideas about each. I saw this frequently during my years teaching undergraduates. To help them see these things a bit more clearly, I would often ask them two questions: Is it true that all the world religions teach basically the *same* things? Is it true that the moral traditions of the world teach wildly *different* things?

Most students said yes to each question. But they were wrong on both.

Do Major Religions Agree?

The fact of the matter is that the great world religions teach very different things. They give very different answers to the questions of whether there is a god, what that god is like, and how to get to that god. (I use "god" instead of "God" to distinguish between false gods and the only true God, the God of Israel who is the Father of Jesus Christ.)

For example, the Buddha said he didn't know whether there is a personal god and for all practical purposes was an atheist.[1] Brahman of the most respected philosophical tradition of Hindus was not a god but an impersonal principle, so philosophical Hindus are atheists.[2] Therefore major portions of the Buddhist and Hindu traditions are atheistic.[3] So is philosophical Daoism.[4] These are all major religions that happen to be atheistic. So on what is perhaps the most important question of all, whether there is a god, the world religions differ radically. Some say there is a god, and others say there is not.

Even those who say there is a god, such as popular Hinduism and Buddhism and the great Abrahamic religions, differ on the number and qualities of god. Popular Hindus and Buddhists tend to believe in many gods, even if most believe that one is chief among them. But each of those gods is different in its qualities from the other gods. Jews and Christians and Muslims agree that there is only one God but disagree on his qualities and how we reach him. Muslims, for example, say that God principally demands fear, while Christians say that God wants love above all else.[5] Muslims say our obedience is what gets us to Allah, while Christians say God provided his Son's obedience to get us to him.

So the world religions teach very different things about what is ultimate and how to reach it. What about the world's *moral* traditions?

Are the World's Moralities Wildly Different?

The first thing to realize is that every great moral system is founded on a religious tradition. The reason is that almost every great civilization has

1. See Richard Gombrich, *What the Buddha Thought* (London: Equinox, 2009), 60–74, esp. 72–73.

2. I refer here to Advaita Vedanta. By "atheist," I mean someone who does not believe there are any personal gods. These Hindus believe in a spiritual principle animating and driving what is real, but they reject the existence of any personal god.

3. By "major portions" I mean Theravada and Zen Buddhism, and Advaita and other Hindu philosophical schools. More popular forms such as Pure Land Buddhism and Hindu *bhakti* worship personal deities. At the same time, however, the nontheistic traditions are religious. I define "religion" as a set of answers to the most basic questions in life, such as where we and this world come from and how we are to live. These Buddhist and Hindu traditions have elegant answers to these religious questions, and so are rightly considered religious. For more on these distinctions, see Gerald McDermott, *World Religions: An Indispensable Introduction* (Nashville: Nelson, 2011); and Gerald McDermott, *Can Evangelicals Learn from World Religions? Jesus, Revelation, and Religious Traditions* (Downers Grove, IL: InterVarsity, 2000).

4. See McDermott, *World Religions*, chap. 4.

5. See Gerald McDermott and Harold Netland, *A Trinitarian Theology of Religions: An Evangelical Proposal* (New York: Oxford University Press, 2014), 60–72.

recognized that what we can see is grounded in what we cannot see—that there is a spiritual reality that sustains the material, and therefore morals come from the divine realm. The great ethical systems of Asia are rooted in the Asian religions. East Asian morality is founded on the teachings of Confucius, who spoke of honoring heaven by our lives on earth. South Asian morality comes from the Buddhist and Hindu religious traditions. In the West, where still a majority say they are Jewish and Christian, morality goes back to the Judeo-Christian tradition. Many of the minority who claim to be atheists or agnostics borrow from the moral legacy of the Judeo-Christian tradition, and others turn to secular humanism, which is its own religion, with answers to all the basic questions of life. Muslims all over the world appeal to Islam for its moral teachings.

Most people don't realize that most of these moral traditions teach the same basic principles, although they often interpret or apply them differently. For example, not one of the moralities rooted in the great religions teaches that it is good to be selfish or to lie or cheat or steal or murder. Every one of the great moral systems teaches that the best life is one that devotes itself to whatever is ultimate—either God or the gods or Brahman or the Dao or the teachings of the Buddha. Every one of these moral traditions says that it is better to live for the good of others and the community than for ourselves.

There are differences, of course. Muslims say a man can have up to four wives, while Jews and Christians say they are to have only one. Yet Muslims agree with Jews and Christians that marriage is sacred and its vows are not to be broken. Buddhists disagree with Jews and Christians on war; disciples of the Buddha say all killing is wrong, while Jews and most Christians believe in the possibility of a just war. But all three traditions agree that human life is sacred. They all agree that morality comes from what is ultimate and is not a human invention. None of the great religions, even those that don't believe in a personal god, thinks that morality is relative, without a transcendent source.

The similarities among these moral traditions need to be spelled out a bit to appreciate their extent. Jewish morality is nearly the same as Christian morality, and there are good reasons for this: Christians take 77 percent of their Bible from the Hebrew Scriptures, and Jesus and all twelve apostles were Jews. Jesus said he came not to abolish the Law and the Prophets but to fulfill them (Matt. 5:17). So it is no surprise that even those parts of Christian morality that are sometimes thought to be exclusively Christian—love for neighbor and love for enemy—come from the Jewish scriptures (Lev. 19:18; Exod. 23:4–5; Prov. 25:21). The Ten Commandments are from the Hebrew Bible, and all of Jesus's teachings in the Sermon on the Mount extend and internalize commandments taught in the Old Testament (Matt. 5:17–19; John 5:46; 1 Pet. 1:11).

We have seen that Muslim teaching on marriage is in substance different but in principle similar. The Islamic tradition holds to the other nine of the Ten Commandments, even if it refers to them with different words.[6]

The Buddha taught the Five Precepts: no sexual sin (no sex for Buddhist monks and none outside of heterosexual marriage for everyone else), no killing, no lying, no stealing, no intoxicants.[7] Hindus and Daoists hold to similar principles, all of which are variations of the Ten Commandments.

This is true even of what Christians call the First Table, the commandments specifically naming God. For example, in the First Commandment the God of Israel says, "You shall have no other gods before me" (Exod. 20:3; Deut. 5:7 ESV). Even nontheistic religions such as Theravada Buddhism and Hindu Advaita agree that nothing shall come before adherence to the Buddha's teachings or Brahman. The Second Commandment forbids taking the name of God in vain. Buddhists and Hindus agree that talk about the Buddha or Brahman should never devolve into careless jest or mockery.[8] Even the Third Commandment, urging the Sabbath to be kept holy, has its analogues in religions outside the Judeo-Christian tradition: Muslims have their weekly mosque services on Friday, while Buddhists, Hindus, and Shintoists have sacred days and times. Every great religion recognizes that human beings need to set aside regular times for contemplation of what is ultimate. This remarkable agreement between the Ten Commandments and the world's religio-moral traditions was noticed by historian John M. Cooper.

> The peoples of the world, however much they differ as to details of morality, hold universally, or with practical universality, to at least the following basic precepts. Respect the Supreme Being or the benevolent being or beings who take his place. Do not "blaspheme." Care for your children. Malicious murder or maiming, stealing, deliberate slander or "black" lying, when committed against friend or unoffending fellow clansman or tribesman, are reprehensible. Adultery proper is wrong, even though there be exceptional circumstances that permit or enjoin it and even though sexual relations among the unmarried may be viewed leniently. Incest is a heinous offense. This universal

---

6. See Frederick M. Denny, *An Introduction to Islam*, 2nd ed. (New York: Macmillan, 1994), 20.

7. "Five Precepts," https://en.wikipedia.org/wiki/Five_Precepts.

8. "Right Speech," *Access to Insight (BCBS edition)*, November 30, 2013, http://www.access toinsight.org/ptf/dhamma/sacca/sacca4/samma-vaca; Warren Lee Todd, *The Ethics of Śankara and Śāntideva: A Selfless Response to an Illusory World* (London: Routledge, 2016), 140–41.

moral code agrees rather closely with our own Decalogue taken in a strictly literal sense.[9]

Confucian Ethics

Confucius (551–479 BC), who, as we have seen, is regarded as the moral master for most of East Asia, taught that we can know what is right if we seek wisdom and that we should keep to the right even if it means deprivation or death. He is famous for teaching a negative version of the Golden Rule nearly five centuries before Jesus: "Do not do to others what you do not want others to do to you." He and his disciple Mencius advocated the moral life that looks neither to the right nor to the left but only straight ahead to the Way, their word for the perfect moral life. Those on the Way are happy with eating coarse rice and drinking only water if that is all that is available, for they are concerned not with profit but with what is right.[10] They seek neither a full belly nor a comfortable home; they are worried about staying on the Way rather than about poverty.[11] Sages cannot be led into excess when wealthy and honored, or deflected from their purposes when poor and obscure. Nor can they be made to compromise principle before superior force. Hence the virtuous never abandon righteousness (*yi*) in adversity, and they do not depart from the Way in success.[12] They refuse to remain in wealth or a prestigious position if either was gained in a wrong manner.[13] Even for one basketful of rice they will not bend. If it had been necessary to perpetrate one wrong deed or kill one innocent person in order to gain the empire, no virtuous person would consent to doing either.[14] True virtue (*te*) is unconcerned with what others think, recognizing that it is better to be disliked by bad people than to be liked by all. It is ready to give up even life itself if that is necessary to follow the way of benevolence.[15]

This little review of Confucian ethics shows the remarkable similarities in basic principles between East and West. It is another illustration of the commonalities among the most influential moral traditions in world history.

9. John M. Cooper, "The Relations between Religion and Morality in Primitive Culture," *Primitive Man* 4, no. 3 (July 1931): 31.

10. Confucius, *The Analects*, trans. and ed. by D. C. Lau (Harmondsworth, UK: Penguin, 1979), 7.16, 14.12, 16.10, 19.1.

11. Confucius, *Analects*, 1.14, 15.32.

12. *Mencius*, trans. and ed. by D. C. Lau (Harmondsworth, UK: Penguin, 1979), 3.B.2, 7.B.9.

13. Confucius, *Analects*, 4.5.

14. *Mencius*, 3.B.4, 2.A.2.

15. Confucius, *Analects*, 12.6, 13.24, 19.1.

I repeat what I said earlier: this does not mean agreement on application or interpretation of all these principles. But on the basic principles themselves—roughly corresponding to the Ten Commandments—there is extraordinary consensus. C. S. Lewis remarked that if we went to the British Museum (a library) to research the world's different moralities, after three days we would be bored.[16] For as we explored the moral teachings of the various civilizations, we would find the same basic axioms repeated over and over: one should live for the good of society and not for oneself, one should give oneself without spare to the divine, one should not violate marriage or promises or contracts or one's word or innocent human life or another's possessions.

Civil Law

It is not only the moral teachings of past and present civilizations, rooted in their religious traditions, that are so very much alike. We find similar commonalities in the *law* codes around the world today. Every nation's legal system contains laws against murder, theft, and perjury. Every country has laws on the books that regulate traffic to reduce accidents. Even if marriage is being redefined in the West, every civil code in East and West regulates divorce to protect marriage agreements and seeks to protect children who are produced by these marriages. In other words, every society's law code today uses something like the Second Table of the Ten Commandments to order its social life.

Many will object immediately that this similarity is illusory. Look at the Aztecs, who practiced human sacrifice, they will say, and at the Nazis, who thought it was their duty to kill Jews. Or the Soviets, who ruthlessly suppressed political difference and religious expression. Don't these examples prove the profound *differences* among the world's moral systems?

In interpretation and application, yes. But not in basic principles. For both Aztecs and Nazis still paid lip service to the principle that taking *innocent* life was wrong. Aztecs believed there were special times when the gods demanded an otherwise-innocent life, and Nazis redefined humanity by excluding Jews and arbitrarily assigning guilt to an entire people. Both societies were perverse in their understanding of humanity and innocence, yet both still held in strange ways to the principle that innocent life should be protected. The Soviet constitution guaranteed freedom of speech and religion, but its totalitarian political structure crushed all who dared use those freedoms. All three

16. This comment was in reference to Lewis's own study of the world's moralities enshrined in the classics of the great civilizations, which I will discuss shortly. Lewis pointed this out in "Illustrations of the *Tao*" at the back of *The Abolition of Man* (San Francisco: HarperOne, 2015).

societies were evil, not least because their practices contradicted their stated principles. They were gargantuan illustrations of the adage that hypocrisy is the tribute vice pays to virtue. Or as J. Budziszewski put it, "Rationalization is the homage paid by sin to guilty knowledge."[17]

Not Behavior but Belief about Behavior

Another objection to this commonality in moral thinking is that most people never live up to it. But such an observation misses the point. My point, and the point of moral philosophers who have noticed these commonalities for thousands of years, is not that people *behave* like this commonly, but that people commonly recognize that these are ways all human beings *ought* to behave. This is true across the world today and has been true back through history. For those who have assumed that morality is relative to endlessly varying social situations, and that ethical systems are merely human constructs that societies have used to keep order, this commonality is counterintuitive. It borders on the astonishing. For if morality were simply a social construction, it should vary in its core principles because societies have varied in size, wealth, geography, stability, religion, and nearly every other variable. Yet despite all this cultural diversity, the core moral principles have remained astonishingly similar. Lewis tabulated these similarities in the section entitled "Illustrations of the *Tao*" at the end of his classic volume *The Abolition of Man*. There he listed statements from moral and religious codes of both East and West on general beneficence (kindness to those in need), special beneficence (to family, parents, ancestors, children, and posterity), justice (against adultery, for honesty and justice in court), good faith and veracity, mercy to the unfortunate, discipline over one's body, and willingness to fight and die for truth and justice.[18]

Even today, postmoderns who say they don't believe in final truths tacitly recognize this same underlying code. Budziszewski wrote about Jonathan Glover, a British ethicist who insisted there is no God or God-given ethic and that we can—indeed must—make up our ethics as we go. He went so far as to say it might be right to kill someone who is not dying and wants to go on living, presumably if you are a physician and have decided that person's life is not worth living. A late abortion is permitted if the parents want a boy and the baby is a girl, or even if the pregnancy would interfere with a vacation abroad. Nevertheless, Glover objected to the holocausts

---

17. J. Budziszewski, *What We Can't Not Know: A Guide*, rev. ed. (San Francisco: Ignatius, 2011), 19.
18. Lewis, *Abolition of Man*, 83–101.

and gulags of the twentieth century, and particularly to the idea that there could be a God who ordained a world in which "babies are cut out of their mothers' wombs with daggers."[19] Budziszewski pointed to the irony of a man who could recommend a woman allowing a physician to cut her baby out of her own womb with a dagger while at the same time objecting to that happening to other babies and other mothers.[20] What made Glover object? Where did he suddenly get this idea that cutting a baby out of its mother's womb could be morally wrong? If morality originates with us and right and wrong depend on what we think suitable, why would other babies being cut out with a dagger be so bad? Budziszewski suggested that Glover knew all along, deep inside, what every one of us knows deep down but denies when it suits us—that there is a cosmic law of right and wrong, whether we admit it or not.

Natural Law

This cosmic law is, of course, the answer to the question of why this remarkable commonality in basic moral principles can be seen through much of history. It is what Christians have called "natural law," and it was explained best by Thomas Aquinas.

Thomas said that natural law is our participation in God's eternal law.[21] "Eternal law" is a general term for all the ways God rules the world in law-like fashion. Since the creation has many levels—from inanimate rocks and stars to animals that have rudimentary minds to human beings with souls—God's eternal law rules each level in a different way. At the lowest level of consciousness, where rocks and stars seem to have none, God rules them from the outside by physical forces like gravity and the cosmic constants we described in the last chapter. God rules organic things like plants and animals by their internal "entelechies," Aristotle's word for the inner drives that push them toward their purposes. Plants move toward full growth and beauty, and animals toward their roles in the ecosystem. Humans move toward their purposes from within, by cooperating with what reason tells them is to their good. When they follow this reason, they are following natural law, which is their participation in God's eternal law.[22]

19. Budziszewski, *What We Can't Not Know*, 12.
20. Budziszewski, *What We Can't Not Know*, 12–13.
21. Thomas Aquinas, *Summa theologiae* I-II, q. 94, art. 1.
22. John Lawrence Hill, *After the Natural Law: How the Classical Worldview Supports Our Modern Moral and Political Values* (San Francisco: Ignatius, 2016), 68–72.

It is called "natural" because humans are made in their nature to be able to grasp ethical principles. They are not born with these principles from the get-go. But when they are taught the equivalent of the Ten Commandments, they know instinctively these are right. Just as they don't know from birth that the whole is greater than the sum of its parts but understand when it is explained to them, so too they sense by their rational nature that killing an innocent person is wrong when it is told them.[23] So too for the other basic principles of natural law, such as the Golden Rule of fairness. Of course they don't typically *do* what is right, because of what Christians call the fall, which is the rejection by Adam and his descendants of God's authority over them. They have been broken in knowledge and behavior ever since. But even in that brokenness they have instinctual knowledge of both God and his law. As Paul wrote to the Romans, at the same time that human beings "did not honor him as God," nevertheless "they knew [him]" (1:21 ESV). And not only do humans know something of God in their fallenness, but they also can discern his natural law within them. For as Paul put it in this same Romans discourse, "The work of the law is written on their hearts" (2:15 ESV).

Most human beings, of course, don't hear the Ten Commandments in that form, since most of the world is neither Christian nor Jewish. And Muslims who have the same commandments hear them in different form in the Qur'an and Hadith. So in what form does the rest of the world hear these laws?

Seven Basic Goods

John Finnis, a leading proponent of the "new" natural law, said that the rest of the world hears natural law in the form of seven basic goods: life (living, health, procreation), knowledge, play, aesthetic experience, friendship or sociability, a plan of life for the moral good, and religion or holiness. Finnis meant that human beings in every culture recognize these things to be basic to human flourishing, and so goods to be esteemed. Nearly everyone, in other words, knows these are good things. They recognize that these are aims upon which to build a moral life. These aims are also roughly equivalent to the ideals taught by the Ten Commandments.[24]

Natural law has been criticized for supposing that all cultures have agreed on all these principles in the same form and that the variations of moral rules from culture to culture prove that natural law is an illusion. But Thomas never meant for natural law to be a list of detailed instructions for every situation.

23. Budziszewski, *What We Can't Not Know*, 25–27.
24. Hill, *After the Natural Law*, 81–82.

Instead it was intended to be a framework of general principles to be supplemented by sound practical thinking, conscience, and civil law tailored to the particularities of a given society. Thomas recognized that each society has different social and cultural circumstances and so will interpret each general principle of natural law in different particular ways.

Martin Luther King Jr. and Natural Law

Thomas also recognized that societies and not just individuals are sinful and blinded by prejudice, and so often they will violate natural law. When this happens in civil law, that law is no longer true law because it is not grounded in natural law. This was Martin Luther King Jr.'s powerful argument in his famous "Letter from Birmingham Jail." He invoked Thomas Aquinas and natural law. "How does one determine whether a law is just or unjust? A just law is a man-made code that squares with the moral law or the law of God. An unjust law is a code that is out of harmony with the moral law. To put it in the terms of St. Thomas Aquinas: An unjust law is a human law that is not rooted in eternal law and natural law. Any law that uplifts human personality is just. Any law that degrades human personality is unjust."[25]

King went on to say that when civil statutes violate natural law, they are "acts of violence rather than laws," and they do "not bind [us] in conscience."[26] His implication was that when a civil law violates natural law, the Christian is free or perhaps even obligated to engage in civil disobedience. You can see why Thomas's articulation of natural law has been appreciated not only by legal theorists and moral theologians but also by human rights activists to this day.

Slavery

But if human rights activists find occasion to use natural law, critics point to the history of the West for evidence of its impotence. One of its originators, Aristotle, they charge, held that slavery is natural. And while natural law has been around for more than two thousand years, slavery was not recognized by most to be "unnatural" until the nineteenth century. But in a new monograph Richard Helmholz argued that even before slavery was abolished, it was being undermined by natural law. At first, he reported, common law courts did not abolish slavery out of respect for the duly enacted positive laws of colonies and

25. Martin Luther King Jr., *Letter from Birmingham Jail* (n.p.: CreateSpace, 2017).
26. King, *Letter from Birmingham Jail*.

states that created the peculiar institution. Nevertheless, in cases such as *Somerset v. Stewart* (1772) and *Forbes v. Cochrane* (1824), English courts maintained that slavery had no part in the common law because it is contrary to reason and therefore held that a slave who set foot on English soil gained irrevocable freedom.[27]

This appeal to natural law did not end slavery by itself. But in later American decisions such as *Buckner v. Street* (1871), it provided the justification for refusing to compensate slave owners and dealers whose titles and contracts were abrogated by the Thirteenth Amendment. And although it did not itself abolish the institution of slavery, it was at the basis of the reasoned arguments of those who did, such as William Wilberforce and Abraham Lincoln.[28] Those are real accomplishments.

Protestant Objections

We have already addressed some of the most common objections that have been made to natural law—that it is proven illusory by moral differences in the world's cultures and that it has never made much of a difference to real moral struggles on the ground. We have seen that despite real differences in moral traditions and pervasive evil in history, there is a remarkable similarity in the professed ideals of moral traditions from East to West. We have also seen that natural law has played an important role in modern struggles against slavery and for civil rights.

Another objection has been advanced by Protestants. They argue that natural law is simply a Catholic artifact that does not take seriously the fallen condition of humanity. I have already shown that Thomas granted this fallen condition and that Paul argued for *both* that fallen condition *and* knowledge of God's law in every human heart. Perhaps the best answer to this objection is to show that the great Protestant Reformers who are famous for their emphasis on human fallenness also taught natural law. Here is Martin Luther: "Everyone must acknowledge that what the Natural Law says is right and true. . . . If men would only pay attention to it, they would have no need of books or of any other law. For they carry along with them in the depth of their hearts a living book which could give them quite adequate instruction about what they ought to do and not to do. . . . All nations share this common ordinary knowledge."[29]

---

27. Richard Helmholz, *Natural Law in Court: A History of Legal Theory in Practice* (Cambridge, MA: Harvard University Press, 2015), 108–9, 161–63, 214n63.

28. Helmholz, *Natural Law in Court*, 234n84, 238n138.

29. Martin Luther, WA 17/2:102; translated and quoted in Paul Althaus, *The Ethics of Martin Luther* (Philadelphia: Fortress, 1972), 26–27n12.

Calvin never developed a systematic theory of natural law, but he regularly used such expressions as "the law of nature," "nature says," "nature teaches," "the order of nature," "the sense of nature," "the sense of divinity" (*sensus divinitatis*), "the law of equity," "natural law," and "the law of the nations."[30] Stephen Grabill wrote that even though Calvin believed that man's natural endowments are corrupted by sin, he also believed they function competently in matters related to the earthly sphere such as politics, economics, and ethics. The (unregenerate) human conscience, he wrote, is able to provide knowledge of moral precepts.[31]

The Canons of Dort (1618–19), which are an important modern authority for much of the Protestant Reformed tradition, hold a similar view of natural law: "There remain, however, in man since the fall, the glimmerings of natural light, whereby he retains some knowledge of God, of natural things, and of the difference between good and evil, and shows some regard for virtue and for good outward behavior."[32]

Karl Barth and Natural Law

Protestant views of natural law did not vary considerably from Dort until the twentieth century when the powerful influence of Karl Barth made Protestants skeptical of natural revelation. Barth insisted there is no "point of contact" between natural and redeemed humanity. In his view the natural person can have no real knowledge of God's law; sin so thoroughly distorts the knowledge of the unredeemed that what they think is God's law is really something of an idol. For a fuller account of this position, see the appendix.

But not all twentieth-century Reformed thinkers agreed with Barth that natural man has no access to God's law. While Carl Henry rejected the term "natural law," he argued against Barth that there is indeed natural revelation and that this is precisely the point of contact between God and natural man. Henry wrote that this natural or general revelation "penetrates the very mind of man even in his revolt."[33] I would suggest, along with most of both the Catholic and Protestant traditions, that the form in which natural revelation penetrates the minds of people even in their revolt is natural law. It is this

30. Stephen J. Grabill, *Rediscovering the Natural Law in Reformed Theological Ethics* (Grand Rapids: Eerdmans, 2006), 15.

31. Grabill, *Rediscovering the Natural Law*, 96.

32. Canons of Dort, in *The Evangelical Creeds*, vol. 3 of *The Creeds of Christendom*, ed. Philip Schaff, 6th ed. (Grand Rapids: Baker, 1990), 588.

33. Carl Henry, *God Who Speaks and Shows: Preliminary Considerations*, vol. 1 of *God, Revelation, and Authority* (Waco: Word, 1976), 400; on point of contact, see 395–409.

deep awareness of basic moral principles that haunts postmodern humanity
in its anxieties and frustrations.

Seared Conscience

Of course many people today live as if they are blissfully unaware of the cosmic moral code. And at the conscious level this is true for many. Paul wrote
that often the conscience is "seared" by continual sin (1 Tim. 4:2). When
we repeatedly ignore our conscience by sinning against it, that voice within
grows quieter and quieter until eventually it is silenced. This can be true for
whole societies that have been propagandized against God's law by ideolo-
gies of race, sex, nation, and atheism. But all it takes is the arrival of crisis or
catastrophe and hearing from new voices of moral reason for the ears of the
soul to hear again the tones of divine obligation. Suddenly what had once
sounded ridiculous becomes plausible and even compelling.

Apostolic Assumptions

Today many Protestants are starting to see that natural law is more biblical
than they had imagined. Thomas Johnson, J. Daryl Charles, Carl Braaten,
Robert Benne, and Stephen Grabill are restoring to Protestant consciousness
a way of thinking about God's witness to the world that had been submerged
during the twentieth century.[34] They are reminding Protestants of Paul's
declarations that "God has not left himself without a witness" among the
pagans (Acts 14:17) and that those without God's written law know of God's
law nonetheless: "When Gentiles who have not the law do by nature things
required by the law, they are a law for themselves, even though they do not
have the law, since they show that the requirements of the law are written
on their hearts, their consciences also bearing witness, and their thoughts
now accusing, now even defending them" (Rom. 2:14–15).

That is the bright side. Those without the Bible know something of God
and his law nevertheless. The dark side is that according to the Bible, people

34. Thomas K. Johnson, *Natural Law Ethics: An Evangelical Proposal* (Bonn: Verlag für
Kultur und Wissenschaft, 2005); J. Daryl Charles, *Retrieving the Natural Law: A Return to
Moral First Things* (Grand Rapids: Eerdmans, 2008); Carl E. Braaten, "Natural Law in Theology
and Ethics," in *The Two Cities of God: The Church's Responsibility for the Earthly City*, ed.
Carl Braaten and Robert Jenson (Grand Rapids: Eerdmans, 1997); Robert Benne, *Ordinary
Saints: An Introduction to the Christian Life* (Minneapolis: Fortress, 2003), 68–74; Grabill,
Rediscovering the Natural Law.

tend to suppress that knowledge of God and his law. They pretend they don't know what they really do know. This pretension causes their minds to darken and to believe that what is wrong is right. They do the wrong and approve of others who do the same (Rom. 1:18–22). As the prophet Jeremiah wrote, the human heart is deceitful above all things. We don't understand ourselves (Jer. 17:9). So while people know these truths deep down, they often deny it. But even if their hearts are made of stone, God's carvings on those stones remain.[35]

The apostles assumed pagans had this knowledge of God's law. When they reasoned with Jews and God-fearing gentiles who had been attending the synagogue, they argued from the Scriptures. But when they reasoned with pagans, they began with the testimony of creation, with the gentiles' sense of the insufficiency of their gods or their sense of law written on their hearts.[36]

For example, when Paul addressed Greek thinkers on Mars Hill in Athens, his auditors were men and women who knew nothing about the Bible. Interestingly, Paul said not a word about justification or grace or salvation. Instead he spoke of judgment and the judge whose role was proved by his resurrection from the dead. Paul was appealing implicitly to knowledge of their guilt before the moral law, which he assumed was written on their hearts.

Vindication

This is the same Paul who wrote to the Romans and the Ephesians about the noetic consequences of sin. He knew that sin had darkened the minds of these Greek philosophers. But he also appealed to their consciences, sensing that they could still hear something of divine law registering there and the consequent charge of blame. As far as we know from Luke's telling of this encounter, Paul left his hearers with their guilt and his declaration that he knew who would judge them. Only *implicit* was the suggestion that there might be a way to avoid punishment by appealing to this judge. But like his teacher Jesus, who told parables without explaining them, he left his hearers with an unsolved problem. Like Jesus, he probably assumed that those with ears to hear would come after him with more questions. And some apparently did, for Luke wrote that at least four were converted through this evangelistic talk (Acts 17:34). Contrary to the conclusion of some scholars that this apologetic encounter failed, it succeeded remarkably. It vindicated Paul's

35. J. Budziszewski, *Written on the Heart: The Case for Natural Law* (Downers Grove, IL: IVP Academic, 1997), 184.

36. Budziszewski, *Written on the Heart*, 183.

assumption—and his inspired words in his letter to the Roman church—that pagans had God's law written on their hearts.

Conclusion

This chapter has shown another way that God's glory is embedded in his creation: his law is written on every human heart. Natural law is a set of God's fingerprints on the human soul. It is natural because it is in human nature, and it is law because it teaches us God's ways that obligate us. The requirements of this law are types pointing to the Triune God, showing us what his goodness means when it is lived by human beings and suggesting the perfect goodness that was seen in his Son Jesus.

In this day when Western societies have rejected the Judeo-Christian tradition in their courts and universities, it is imperative that Christians learn about and use the natural law tradition. It is no longer sufficient, if it ever was, to simply state what Scripture says. Too many ears in the public square are stopped against such declarations. But some are willing to hear appeals to what is reasonable and what can be accepted as rationally compelling. This approach will be important as we fight for justice in our societies. We will want to use natural law as we seek agreement that life in the womb should not be destroyed, that the sick should be cared for and comforted and not starved or pressured into suicide, that the poor should be able to send their children to schools of their own choice, that equal opportunity should be protected against racism, and that one should have the freedom to practice one's religion. That freedom includes being able to refrain from actions that violate one's conscience, such as providing food or flowers for a same-sex wedding. In debates on these and other moral issues, we won't get very far in the public square by quoting the Bible. But we might get a hearing by appealing to moral truths that nearly everyone knows.

6

History

Images of God in the Histories of Peoples

When Paul was in Athens talking to Greek philosophers, he observed that one of their poets got it right when he wrote, "In him we live and move and have our being" (Acts 17:28). In other words, not only is God *in* history, as every Christian can and indeed must say, but history is in *God*! Nothing is outside God, which means among other things that nothing can happen without his holding it in existence nanosecond by nanosecond. That does not mean there is no free will, but that even human and angelic choices are held up or permitted by God. Paul said something like this when he wrote elsewhere that "in [Messiah] all things hold together [*synestēken*]" (Col. 1:18). The upshot is that popular deism—the idea that history proceeds without God's intervention—is impossible for a biblical Christian. It also means that the idea that God moves only history's major actors, who in turn pull everyone else along, also falls short of Paul's claim.

What would this mean for a book on types in all of reality? Precisely this: that in the near-infinite confusion of history, we can recognize patterns, even if only dimly, amid the otherwise-inscrutable blur of events. Some of these patterns appear to be ways that God acts or directs in repeated ways and that point to his biblically revealed character.

The first thing that must be said about types in history is that they are recognizable patterns in human affairs that point toward their trinitarian author, and they are there by divine direction for that purpose among others.

Scripture tells us that God made known his *acts* to his people Israel, but his *ways* to Moses (Ps. 103:7). Moses apparently learned God's ways through the patterns or types revealed in his acts, informed by his words.

The second thing that should be added about history in general before we consider specific *types* in history is that history is both directed and fragile. By "fragile" I mean that nothing in history per se determines inexorably its future direction. It could go in any one of a variety of ways, with long-term consequences for the whole world. The great Cambridge University historian Herbert Butterfield wrote in his magisterial *Christianity and History* of the "unspeakable liquidity" of history. "Indeed, if Mr. Churchill had been ill or had lost heart in 1940[,] the mind must reel before the multitude of alternative courses that the world might have taken."[1] Hitler might have won, we would all be speaking German, and I would be afraid of writing something that might offend our new führer. So while we will see that history is full of types that point toward the end of history, their presence does not mean we can predict the *intermediate* future. Christ will win in the *end*, and the types point to that eventual victory, but our Lord has not told us of the twists and turns that will take place before the end.

Yet he *has* told us, according to Edwards and others, some of the patterns in those twists and turns, and those patterns are types. One of the most significant is the pattern of *revivals* directing the biggest twists and turns. According to Edwards, religious revivals and reformations are the principal engine of the historical drama, driving its sudden turns and, to some degree, its later twists.[2] Edwards pointed to major junctures in Israel's history as examples of this pattern or type. Covenant renewals—for example, under David, Hezekiah, and Josiah—were religious revivals that forever changed the history of redemption. The rise of the church in the first century was an enormous revival that eventually conquered the Roman Empire. Constantine's conversion was the leading edge of another revival in the fourth century that shaped medieval Europe. The Reformation was still another revival, the principal historical movement that gave shape to modern Europe. We can use this Edwardsean approach to history to argue, with some historians, that the Great Awakening was an American revival that helped precipitate the American Revolution.[3] Many historians would also agree that the Civil War

1. Herbert Butterfield, *Christianity and History* (New York: Scribner's, 1949), 111.
2. Jonathan Edwards, *A History of the Work of Redemption*, WJE 9:143, 195, 233, 422, 435–36, 449, 457, 460–61.
3. See, for example, Daniel N. Gullotta, "The Great Awakening and the American Revolution," *Journal of the American Revolution*, August 10, 2016, https://allthingsliberty.com/2016/08/great-awakening-american-revolution.

would not have occurred without the revival of the Second Great Awakening and the abolitionist movement that this awakening spawned. Hence the last two millennia bear witness to what can be called the historical type of revival producing revolutions of all sorts. This is a historical type pointing *back* to a biblical pattern of God's ways with his human creatures.

The National Covenant

In this first type we have been discussing—religious revivals producing deep changes in social and political history—I have assumed something that modern Christians don't usually assume—namely, that God deals with whole societies and not simply individuals. Let me try to make this claim plausible by introducing a concept that was long familiar to Christians before the modern era: the national covenant. This concept belongs to a long tradition going back to the early church—and the whole Bible, I would argue—that teaches that God deals with whole societies, not just individuals. Although this view is difficult to deny if you pay serious attention to the Bible, it has been a minority view since the Enlightenment and especially in this last century. Theologians, particularly since the 1960s, have tended to regard it as presumptuous and inevitably leading to idolatry of the nation. This way of thinking was heightened after the Vietnam War, which most intellectuals thought was a terrible mistake. They wondered where the idea came from that saw the United States as a "redeemer nation" whose mission it was to bring its political salvation (the American form of democracy) to the rest of the world.[4] Historians and theologians laid the blame at the feet of the Puritans, who came to the New World on what Perry Miller called an "errand into the wilderness." They came, he argued, for the purpose of reforming England and then the world, by being a "city on a hill" whose light would shine far and wide, transforming those who beheld its glory.[5]

The Puritans believed that God was judging England as a whole and was moving their little Puritan band to emigrate so that God could start a new, godly society under their direction. Were they right, that God deals with whole societies? The biblical authors seemed to think so. They portrayed God as blessing and chastising the nation of Israel, promising rewards for

4. Ernest Tuveson, *Redeemer Nation* (Chicago: University of Chicago Press, 1980). For the national-covenant tradition and its declension since the 1960s, see Gerald McDermott, *One Holy and Happy Society* (University Park: Pennsylvania State University Press, 1992), 11–36.

5. Perry Miller, *Errand into the Wilderness* (1956; repr., Cambridge, MA: Belknap Press, 2000).

its obedience to the covenant and punishments for unfaithfulness (Lev. 26 and Deut. 28). Edwards chronicled many of these ups and downs, and he argued that God deals with other societies as well. He quoted Proverbs 14:34 (ESV): "Righteousness exalts a nation, but sin is a reproach to *any* people." Look, he preached, at how God treated the whole world in Noah's day as a society that deserved punishment by a flood. Look at Sodom and Gomorrah, destroyed for their wickedness; Egypt, punished by the plagues; and Canaan, whose tribes were defeated and ousted because of their egregious sins.[6]

Edwards told his congregation—the largest outside Boston, in an eighteenth-century megachurch of a thousand souls—that in droughts and plagues and earthquakes God was chastising New England for its failures to live up to its national covenant.[7] According to this tradition, the national covenant had to do with this life only, not the next (that realm was administered by the covenant of grace). God is stricter in punishing a wicked *nation* in this world than a wicked person. After all, it is clear that wicked persons often prosper in this world. But nations as nations are punished only in *this* world. Often God endures their wickedness for a long time. But it is a biblical pattern, Edwards insisted, that when wickedness becomes open, unashamed, and pervasive, and when that nation's leadership endorses and defends perversity, then that nation is close to destruction.[8]

But first, said Edwards, God warns the nation of impending doom in a variety of ways. One is to permit other nations to threaten it with an attack of some kind. Edwards said this happened when various nations arrayed themselves against Judah in the first century before Rome finally destroyed Jerusalem in AD 70. Another is to bring lesser judgments before a great judgment. According to Edwards, this happened when Pharaoh was warned of his coming doom by the ten plagues. A third warning was judgment on a neighbor, such as when the captivity of the ten northern tribes in 721 BC was a warning to the southern tribes, who were captured a little more than a century later. Fourth, God sends messengers to warn, as he sent Noah, Jonah, and other prophets. A fifth kind of warning was God's sending a revival, such as the revivals under Josiah and Hezekiah before final destruction in 586 BC. Other revivals as warnings came under Jonah to Nineveh and under Jesus and the apostles before the fall of the city (Nineveh and then Jerusalem) just decades later.[9]

6. *WJE* 14:225; *WJE* 12:473; *WJE* 16:220.
7. McDermott, *One Holy and Happy Society*, 11–36.
8. See McDermott, *One Holy and Happy Society*, 29–34.
9. McDermott, *One Holy and Happy Society*, 29–34.

Notice the counterintuitive motif: revivals can be a sign of looming judgment. They can actually increase a nation's guilt if they bring only short-term religious excitement and not long-term repentance and reformation.

All of these patterns are historical types. That is, they are words in events, sent by God, to point to future events in biblical and postbiblical history. There is the major type consisting of revivals producing major sociopolitical changes and the minor types consisting of God warning of future judgment by threats of attack, lesser judgments, attacks on a neighbor, prophetic warnings, and revivals as warnings.

Recent Thinking on National Covenant[10]

So much for Edwards on historical types. Have more recent theologians seen types in history? The short answer is that even during the last century, some theologians and philosophers have argued that God's providence can be seen in a society, and in ways that undermine national self-righteousness.

The sociologist of religion Robert Bellah observed that "what Christians call the Old Testament is precisely the religious interpretation of the *history* of Israel." Then he asked, "Is it so clear that American analogizing from the Old (or New) Testament is necessarily religiously illegitimate? Why should the history of a people living two or three thousand years ago be religiously meaningful but the history of a people living in the last two or three hundred years be religiously meaningless?"[11]

Philosopher Leroy S. Rouner argued similarly that America has historical significance. He suggested that this "fact is largely lost at present because the left has fallen out of love with its homeland, and the right has celebrated it for mostly wrong reasons."[12] The great Lutheran theologian Wolfhart Pannenberg thought that the notion of national covenant had often accurately described the fortunes of a people relative to other peoples: "It would be unfair to belittle the obvious element of truth in this sense of historical destiny. The English revolution [for example] did indeed pioneer the political emancipation in the

10. This section is an adaptation of parts of my "Jonathan Edwards and the National Covenant: Was He Right?," in *The Legacy of Jonathan Edwards: American Religion and the Evangelical Tradition*, ed. D. G. Hart et al. (Grand Rapids: Baker Academic, 2003), 147–57. Used by permission.

11. Robert Bellah, quoted in *The Religious Situation in 1968*, ed. Donald R. Cutler (Boston: Beacon Press, 1968), 391 (emphasis added).

12. LeRoy S. Rouner, "To Be at Home: Civil Religion as Common Bond," in *Civil Religion and Political Theology*, ed. LeRoy S. Rouner (Notre Dame, IN: University of Notre Dame Press, 1986), 137.

Western world." Pannenberg added that the idea of a national covenant has explanatory power. The destruction of Germany in World War II, for instance, "may have been" a judgment on Germany's persecution and attempted annihilation of the Jewish people.[13]

H. Richard Niebuhr interpreted historical contingencies from a similar perspective. He suggested that the rise of Marxism was a judgment on the injustices and class-interests of "Christian" communities, and he interpreted dust storms on the American prairies in the 1930s as "signs of man's sinful exploitation of the soil."[14] Niebuhr's explanation of these interpretations by his doctrine of responsibility was remarkably analogous to Edwards's doctrines of divine sovereignty and national covenant. In all actions impinging upon the self, Niebuhr contended, God is acting. The responsible self must therefore respond to all actions as ways of responding to God's action. The same interpretation must be given to the events happening to a community.

> At the critical junctures in the history of Israel and of the early Christian community the decisive question men raised was not "What is the goal?" nor yet "What is the Law?" but "What is happening?" and then "What is the fitting response to what is happening?" When an Isaiah counsels his people, he does not remind them of the law they are required to obey nor yet of the goal toward which they are directed but calls to their attention the intentions of God present in hiddenness in the actions of Israel's enemies. The question he and his peers raise in every critical moment is about the interpretation of what is going on, whether what is happening be, immediately considered, a drought or the invasion of a foreign army, or the fall of a great empire.[15]

Pannenberg said that this idea of national covenant, which sees *God covenanting with whole nations*, undermines any potential idolatry by placing a nation under the judgment of God: "Christian theology should consider such a pledge [to a national covenant] to be of positive value, because it renders the policies of a nation accountable to the will of God as expressed in the Bible and places the nation under the judgment of God. . . . It [the nation] makes itself accountable to the terms of God's covenant."[16]

13. Wolfhart Pannenberg, *Human Nature, Election, and History* (Philadelphia: Westminster, 1977), 79, 104.

14. James Gustafson, introduction to H. Richard Niebuhr, *The Responsible Self: An Essay in Christian Moral Philosophy* (New York: Harper, 1963), 34–35.

15. Niebuhr, *Responsible Self*, 67.

16. Pannenberg, *Human Nature, Election, and History*, 81, 97. Interestingly, two American Lutheran ethicists also interpreted national crises as visitations of divine wrath. See Robert Benne and Philip Hefner, *Defining America: A Christian Critique of the American Dream* (Philadelphia: Fortress, 1974), 125–35.

Such accountability, Pannenberg suggested, enables those with spiritual eyes to see a range of types. One is the pattern of pervasive secularism and later judgment. This is the biblical motif of *God's withdrawal of his manifest presence from a society that has rejected him*: "When God seems absent not only from the world but from the hearts of human beings, this does not indicate, as a superficial evaluation would suggest, that perhaps he died. Rather, it foretells impending judgment over a world that alienated itself from the source of life."[17]

Another biblical pattern that is a recurring type in history is *war as divine judgment*. Abraham Lincoln was an earlier "public theologian" who believed in the national covenant and used it to find this type in American history. He famously referred to America as "the almost chosen people" and "the last, best hope of earth." In terms not unlike Edwards's invocation of the national covenant, Lincoln said in an 1863 proclamation of a general fast,

> We have been the recipients of the choicest bounties of Heaven. We have been preserved, these many years, in peace and prosperity. We have grown in numbers, wealth and power, as no other nation has ever grown. But we have forgotten God.
>
> We have forgotten the gracious hand which preserved us in peace, and multiplied, enriched and strengthened us; and we have vainly imagined, in the deceitfulness of our hearts, that all these blessings were produced by some superior wisdom and virtue of our own. Intoxicated with unbroken success, we have become too self-sufficient to feel the necessity of redeeming and preserving grace, too proud to pray to the God that made us! It behooves us then, to humble ourselves before the offended Power, to confess our national sins, and to pray for clemency and forgiveness.[18]

Like Edwards, Lincoln believed that God punishes a people corporately for its corporate sins. Lincoln applied this paradigm to the Civil War and concluded that it was just such a punishment. "And, insomuch as we know that, by His divine law, nations like individuals are subjected to punishments and chastisements in this world, may we not justly fear that the awful calamity of civil war, which now desolates the land, may be but a punishment, inflicted upon us, for our presumptuous sins, to the needful end of our national reformation as a whole People?"[19]

Two years later, in his oft-quoted Second Inaugural Address, Lincoln again referred to the war as a judgment of God. "If God wills that it [the Civil War]

---

17. Pannenberg, *Human Nature, Election, and History*, 93.

18. Abraham Lincoln, "Proclamation of a National Fast, March 30, 1863," in Roger Lundin and Mark A. Noll, *Voices from the Heart: Four Centuries of American Piety* (Grand Rapids: Eerdmans, 1987), 172.

19. Lincoln, "Proclamation of a National Fast," 172.

continue, until all the wealth piled by the bond-man's two hundred and fifty years of unrequited toil shall be sunk, and until every drop of blood drawn with the lash, shall be paid by another drawn with the sword, as was said three thousand years ago, so still it must be said 'the judgments of the Lord, are true and righteous altogether.'"[20] Lincoln not only believed that God deals with whole nations, but he also invoked the most common historical type—God punishing a society for its corporate sins.

What Are Some Historical Types?

In his Cambridge lectures Butterfield identified other discernible types in history. The first is what I would call *mediation in judgment*. God uses wicked nations to judge other wicked nations. God used wicked nations such as the Philistines, Assyrians, and Babylonians to judge sinful Israel. The lesson from that type is humility. Just as we would never call those nations righteous because they were God's servants in judgment, so too the British and Americans should not have concluded after World War II that they were righteous because God used them to destroy the wickedness of Nazism and Japanese imperialism. Of course there are degrees of righteousness, and that of 1940s America was superior to that of Japan or Germany at the time. But America had its own sins, such as racial segregation, and so could not claim to be righteous before God.

Judgment is *sometimes remedial*. That is another historical type. The exile in Babylon seems to have cured Israel of overt idolatry. Not every judgment renders its object null and void. Israel was judged by God in Babylon and emerged from the judgment with more steadfast faith before God. Butterfield made a similar judgment about the purgative effects of the fall of the Roman Empire in AD 410 and after. The fall of the empire "releas[ed] Europe for a new phase of human experience," which one might say brought a measure of good out of a corrupted empire.[21] In another example, Germany's radical departure from Nazism after its destruction and surrender in 1945 allowed for a postwar boom that continues to this day. While there was no extensive turn to God, there was a genuine national humility, lamenting its behavior in the preceding decade and before.

But Germany's destruction in World War II might represent yet another historical type, that of the sins of the fathers being visited on the third and

20. Lincoln, Second Inaugural Address (1865); quoted in Mark A. Noll, *One Nation under God? Political Faith and Political Action in America* (San Francisco: Harper & Row, 1988), 101.
21. Butterfield, *Christianity and History*, 61.

fourth and succeeding generations. Butterfield traced the genesis of Nazism to Frederick the Great's pursuit of militarism as a national ideal for eighteenth-century Prussia and to Bismarck's unification of Germany into a powerful European state. But he said the day of punishment was postponed for several generations because both Frederick and Bismarck "called a halt to a career of conquest, precisely because they had a curious awareness of the importance of the moral element in history."[22] In the latter stages of their lives they sought to maintain the peace of Europe.

Hitler had no such goal and committed the greatest historical sin, thinking himself to be a god. On this sort of leader, who worships the work of his own hands and says that the strength of his own right arm gave him the victory, "judgment in history falls heaviest." For "such a man by aping providence blasphemes God, and brings more rapid tragedy on the world and on himself, than the people who give half their lives to wine, women and song."[23] This is the most reliable type in history, that of the leader or people who in pride think they can displace the Deity. They or the generations following them are ultimately humbled or destroyed.

But Germany's destruction was not inevitable, according to Butterfield. If the German people had regarded their disastrous defeat in 1918 and the ruinous reparations imposed by the Versailles Treaty as God's judgments and had sought to discover what they had done to offend heaven, then good could have come from evil.[24] Redemption could have emerged from judgment. This is another type, the type of *redemption through repentance and faith*, that appeared in a limited and secular way after 1945.

The most interesting historical types involve Israel in postbiblical history. The first is that of the *remnant*. The prophets, and then Paul, distinguished between larger Israel and remnant Israel. Only the two southern tribes survived invasion and exile. Empires have come and gone in the last three thousand years, and many of them have killed Jews in the thousands and millions. But while the Assyrians and Babylonians and Romans and Nazis tried to destroy Israel, all those empires were destroyed instead. Israel alone remains. A Jewish remnant has always survived, with its culture, language, and religion intact. Every remnant that emerged after successive incarnations of Amalekites arose to exterminate Jews was a type of the holy remnant that is to come, Jesus's "little flock" that will join gentiles with a purified Israel in the new heaven and new earth (Luke 12:32; Rev. 7:4–8).

22. Butterfield, *Christianity and History*, 49.
23. Butterfield, *Christianity and History*, 60.
24. Butterfield, *Christianity and History*, 50.

Even more intriguing is the type of *vicarious suffering*. We all know that Isaiah's Suffering Servant is a *man* who will suffer for the sins of God's people (Isa. 53:1–12). But Isaiah also spoke of all *Israel* as the servant: "You Israel my servant" (41:8 ESV), "my servant Jacob and Israel my chosen" (45:4 ESV), "The LORD has redeemed his servant Jacob" (48:20 ESV), "You are my servant Israel in whom I will be glorified" (49:3 ESV). Butterfield proposed that this is a new kind of vicarious suffering. Israel suffers not because God is judging it at the hands of its persecutors, but because it is actually better than its persecutors and has a mission. Israel suffers as God's messenger "in order to expiate the sins of the Gentiles; she took their guilt and punishment upon herself, and accepted the consequences of their sins."[25]

If Butterfield's account is correct, it need not conflict with traditional Christian Christology and soteriology. For if Christ is the embodiment of his church because the church is his body, then he is also the embodiment of faithful Israelites who, before his coming, trusted in the Messiah who was prophesied. Jews who thought they would betray the God of their covenant if they joined the church and so stayed faithful to the synagogue might be among those Jesus had in mind when he said words spoken against the Son of Man could be forgiven (Matt. 12:32). Since Paul identified his own suffering with the Messiah's afflictions in Colossians 1:24, and since Jesus said that when the church was persecuted so was he (Acts 9:4), we could say that Jesus suffers not only when Christians suffer but also when faithful Israel suffers. Therefore if Jesus's suffering was vicarious for the sake of his body, all later vicarious suffering by his *body* points back to his suffering and participates in his, just as Paul said *his* suffering participated in the Messiah's afflictions by somehow "making up what was lacking" in them (Col. 1:24). If Paul's suffering somehow participated in the Messiah's sufferings, which expiate the sins of the gentiles, and if the Messiah as Suffering Servant is the embodiment of faithful Israel as suffering servant, then perhaps in a mysterious way faithful Israel's sufferings participate in the Messiah's redemption of the gentiles.

Martin Luther King Jr. did not believe, as far as I know, in an *ontological* connection—that is, at the level of being—between the suffering of his civil rights workers and the suffering of Jesus in his passion. But he certainly taught the power of vicarious suffering. When the editor of the *Christian Century* urged him in 1960 to describe his own sufferings, King wrote,

> I have known very few quiet days in the last few years. I have been arrested five times and [in] 1960 put in Alabama jails. My home has been bombed twice.

25. Butterfield, *Christianity and History*, 84.

A day seldom passes that my family and I are not the recipients of threats of death. I have been the victim of a near fatal stabbing. So in a real sense I have been battered by the storms of persecution. I must admit that at times I have felt that I could no longer bear such a heavy burden, and have been tempted to retreat to a more quiet and serene life.[26]

King was reluctant to detail his own sufferings because he didn't want to develop a martyr complex or make others think he was seeking sympathy. But he said these trials taught him "the value of unmerited suffering." They led him to think that suffering can bring transformation in himself and healing to "the people involved in the tragic situation." He became convinced that "unearned suffering is redemptive."[27] King was pointing to a profound historical type of vicarious suffering that benefits others, pointing back to and perhaps even ontologically connected to the antitype, Jesus's redemptive suffering in his life and death.

The last historical type in Butterfield's masterful account is the most pervasive throughout history and perhaps the most powerful: the *secret piety* of the unnumbered billions of faithful Christians who lived lives of beautiful faith by union with their Lord. This is a historical type because it can be seen in history—at least it could be seen by those who came close to these living saints—and it points to its antitype, Jesus the Jewish Messiah. The infinite varieties of faithfulness by God's saints point in typological fashion to the infinite aspects of the trinitarian God, the God of Israel. These saints were types in history pointing to, and teaching about, the living Triune God. Their faith, hope, and love pointed by life and word to the faithfulness and love of the trinitarian God. As Butterfield put it, these were the lights "that never went out" throughout the millennia of God's church on earth. Through the darkest periods of heresy and schism, priests and ministers were preaching the gospel week in and week out, "constantly reminding the farmer and the shopkeeper of charity and humility, persuading them to think for a moment about the great issues of life, and inducing them to confess their sins."[28] In every age the Lamb who takes away the sins of the world became known to millions through the everyday holiness of ordinary believers. In this way the church never failed to produce new historical types.

26. Martin Luther King Jr., "Suffering and Faith," *Christian Century*, April 27, 1960, 510; http://kingencyclopedia.stanford.edu/encyclopedia/documentsentry/suffering_and_faith.1.html.

27. King, "Suffering and Faith," 510.

28. Butterfield, *Christianity and History*, 131.

Discerning the Types

How, then, are we to discern? How can we know the difference between authentic types that *God* has placed in history and our imagined types that *we* ascribe naively to God?

First, we should always recall that just as the historical Jesus was often not recognized as Messiah, so today his footprints in the world—his historical types—usually go unrecognized. Not only are they hidden from the eyes of "the natural person" (1 Cor. 2:14), but even the regenerate often miss them.

Second, we should recognize that history is not only horizontal but also vertical. Because we distinguish Christian philosophy of history, which focuses on the linear, from ancient and Eastern philosophies, which tend toward the cyclical and circular, we can become *too* focused on the *telos* (the end goal). We imbibe the deist fallacy that history is simply a linear temporal continuum without ongoing participation in God's active providence. This is not only a metaphysical mistake but a failure to apply biblical theology to our philosophy of history. After all, Scripture says that we can "share Messiah's suffering" (1 Pet. 4:13) so that we can *now* "partake in the glory that is to be revealed" (5:1) and *now* "become partakers of the divine nature" (2 Pet. 1:4).[29] We can observe the linear story that is leading through twists and turns to the kingdom at the end of history, but we can also participate now in the eternal kingdom at every step of the way.

Another way of putting this twofold meaning of history is to see, with Butterfield, that every generation is equidistant from eternity. Every instant is eschatological. In that sense the purpose of life is not the future but the present, to participate in eternal life now. And one way of doing so is to see the types all around us, in nature and history, as present signs of the kingdom. History, then, is not so much a train traveling toward a destination—although of course in one sense it is—as it is like a symphony whose every *part* is to be enjoyed, not just the ending.[30] The architecture of the *whole* work, as Butterfield put it, can be experienced in every *part* of the work—or in our case, every moment of history.

For yet another analogy, think of the Chesapeake Bay Bridge-Tunnel. This amazing feat of engineering goes for twenty-three miles, and so do its travelers. Once on it, they cannot stop without getting hit from behind and thus withdrawing permanently from linear history. There are no exits or off-ramps until the end. That is how many Christians think of history: it will have no

---

29. See Matthew Levering, *Participatory Biblical Exegesis: A Theology of Biblical Interpretation* (Notre Dame, IN: University of Notre Dame Press, 2008), 1–7.

30. Butterfield, *Christianity and History*, 66, 121, 67.

final meaning or clarity until its end, and types are manmade and therefore unreliable at best, idolatrous at worst.

But imagine, if you can, the old Route 66 that was finished in 1926 and carried travelers for twenty-four hundred miles from Chicago to California. Drivers could stop almost wherever they wanted to enjoy the land or scenery, and they did. This is like history as we *should* imagine it, not merely linear but also participatory. It stops at every point to look up and around into eternity. Types are real and are all along the way.

But to get back to the question that opened this last section, how do we discern the true types? Two final rules. The first is the rule of written revelation. The types need to be suggested or authorized by God's written revelation in Scripture, just as God through words showed Moses his ways (Ps. 103:7). We have already discussed the scriptural precedents for what is admitted by almost all serious readers of the Bible—that *God dealt with Israel as a society* throughout both Testaments and that covenant renewals (*revivals*, if you will) in Israel's history had profound impact on the later development of Israel. The implication is that God still deals with whole societies and that God uses revivals to move the course of history. In fact, the God of the Bible testifies clearly to the first. He told Amos that he treated the Cushites (Ethiopians) and Philistines and Syrians as peoples in his sovereign stewardship of history (9:7), warned the people of Nineveh that he would destroy them unless they repented (Jon. 1:2),[31] and proclaimed judgment on whole nations because of their treatment of Israel (e.g., Zech. 12:2; Gen. 12:2–3; see also Isa. 43:9–10). The second notion, that God moves postbiblical history through revival, is not stated in the Bible but is plausible, given the examples I suggested earlier—if, for example, the Reformation and Great Awakening are considered to have been revivals. Both had indisputably massive impacts on so-called secular history.

I also laid out the biblical evidence for God's warning a people of future judgment through threats, lesser judgments, judgments on neighbors, messengers, and even revivals. For example, the revival that was the rise of the Jesus movement *within* Israel was a warning of the judgment that came in AD 70. Of course Jesus himself predicted the judgment (Matt. 24:2; Mark 13:2; Luke 21:6), but thinking of the early church as a revival within Judaism (we tend to forget how predominantly Jewish the early church was in its first generation)[32] helps us to understand how the revival that came to Nineveh under Jonah's preaching was also followed by judgment (after Nahum's prophecy).

---

31. Although repentance is not mentioned in Jonah's warnings (note 1:2; 3:4), it is implied when Nineveh indeed repented and God relented (3:10).

32. For example, that there were *myriades* ("tens of thousands") of Jews who followed Jesus as Messiah in Jerusalem (Acts 21:20).

There is considerable biblical testimony for the pattern or type of God's withdrawing from a people who reject him. In Jeremiah 11:14 God said he won't listen when Israel calls at a new time of trouble because of her recent refusals to listen to him. God told Ezekiel he would "withdraw" from Israel because it had defiled his sanctuary with detestable and abominable things (5:11). In Proverbs 1:24–29 God said he would not answer the prayers of those who have refused his calls and counsels.

We have already seen scriptural evidence for the types of mediation in judgment (God used Philistia, Assyria, Babylon, and Rome to judge Israel) and remedial judgment (Israel never committed blatant idolatry again after her exile in Babylon). Scripture makes clear the type or pattern of God redeeming a people who repent: "If my people who are called by my name humble themselves, and pray and seek my face and turn from their wicked ways, then I will hear from heaven and will forgive their sin and heal their land" (2 Chron. 7:14 ESV).

Also clear in Scripture are the historical types that God's faithful people are typically only a remnant who must endure the judgments that God sends to a whole people. Jeremiah, Ezekiel, Ezra, Nehemiah, and Daniel were faithful prophets and leaders who had to endure exile along with the rest of their people, even though they were not guilty of the idolatries that had precipitated the exile. Jesus spoke of his followers as a little flock, and Paul distinguished the faithful remnant of Israel from Israel generally (Luke 12:32; Rom. 9:7; 11:5, 11–12, 25) without relaxing his insistence that God still deals with Israel as a whole (Rom. 11:25–27).

The notion of vicarious suffering by the faithful for a larger people is also a biblical theme, as I wrote above, but admittedly more difficult to understand. The last historical type, the secret piety of the countless faithful whose lives point to the trinitarian God, is the most common type and easy to see in Scripture. Jesus said his followers would let their light shine by their good works, and those works would "glorify [their] Father in heaven" (Matt. 5:16). Paul wrote that true disciples would shine as "lights in the world" amid a "crooked and perverse generation," pointing to the Father of Jesus (Phil. 2:15). The Corinthian church, he wrote, would be his "letter of recommendation . . . to be known and read by all," testifying to the Messiah and his Father and Spirit (2 Cor. 3:2 ESV). Vibrant Christians are the most vivid historical types, showing the world the character of the true God.

These are some biblical evidences for the validity of these historical types. The second rule for discerning the types is that it is always safer to recognize judgment on our own ideas and works than on others. If we do venture the latter, we should beware of unwitting self-righteousness. For example, if we say the defeat of Islamic State of Iraq and Syria (ISIS) is a type of God's judgment of pride and blasphemy pointing to the final judgment, we must not presume that we are inherently better than members of ISIS. There is no doubt that the Christian faith (distinct from my apprehension of that faith) is infinitely superior to that of Islam, but my appropriation of that faith was a gift of God to this poor sinner. Right now my ideas are better than those of the ISIS fighter, and thankfully my inner character has been shaped to a degree by a Jewish stonemason. But I am what I am by the grace of God. And when I think of that ISIS soldier, I must remind myself that "there but for the grace of God go I."

7

Animals

The Zoological World Bursting with Signs

For as long as people have been reading the Bible, they have recognized that Scripture assigns symbolic value to animals. We are warned not to be as ignorant as mules (Ps. 32:9). Hosea speaks of doves as "silly and without sense" (7:11), but Genesis 1 and Matthew 3 suggest the dove as a symbol of the Holy Spirit, hovering over both the creation and our Lord's baptism. Perhaps this is why some have thought that the dove flying over the waters of the flood, when the earth was being remade, is a symbol of the new creation (Gen. 8:8–12).[1]

Sheep are the Bible's principal symbol for God's human creatures. They are sociable, easily led astray, vulnerable to predators, and desperately in need of direction (Isa. 53:6; Ezek. 34; Zeph. 3:3; Zech. 10:2; John 10:12). It might be the purity of their wool as a symbol for sinlessness that led God to command the Israelites to use a lamb as the twice-daily burnt offering and the annual Passover sacrifice (Exod. 12:5; 29:38–42; Isa. 1:18). It is no wonder that Jesus was "the Lamb of God who takes away the sin of the world" (John 1:29). He was the man—albeit the *God*-man—who represented all the positive attributes of sheep. He was obedient unto death, went like a sheep to the slaughter, and was innocent and without blemish (Phil. 2:8; Isa. 53:7; Heb. 4:15).[2]

---

1. James B. Jordan, *Through New Eyes: Developing a Biblical View of the World* (Eugene, OR: Wipf & Stock, 1999), 100.

2. *Dictionary of Biblical Imagery*, ed. Leland Ryken, James C. Wilhoit, and Tremper Longman III (Downers Grove, IL: InterVarsity, 1998), 27–28.

Goats in the Bible suggest the worldly-wise, who think they don't need God. For this reason they represent the damned whom Jesus sent to hell in his parable of the sheep and the goats (Matt. 25:31–46). It probably also explains the scape*goat* that was sent away to Azazel, who was likely the demonic prince of the wilderness (Lev. 16:9).[3]

Horses are symbols of war and power. Until the invention of the tank, they were major weapons of war, which is why kings of Israel were warned not to accumulate too many or to trust in them rather than God (Deut. 17:16; 1 Sam. 8:11). Pigs are symbols of uncleanness because they eat even the foulest substances and never lose their character even if they are prettied up. They always return to wallow in the mud (2 Pet. 2:22).[4]

Lions, for the biblical authors, are symbols of ferocity and power, and often signal approaching death. Therefore God and the devil are each represented as a lion (Hosea 13:7; 1 Pet. 5:8). Only Jesus is both a lion and a lamb (Rev. 5:5–6). Wolves are symbols of malicious and ruthless leaders who prey on God's flock (Matt. 7:15; 10:16). They can be religious or political leaders (John 10:12; Ezek. 22:27).[5]

The Closest Analogies

Animals appear throughout the Bible,[6] with profound typological meaning, because they are the closest of all the creation to human beings. Their analogies to humans are the most numerous. It is not stars or trees or rocks that have arms and legs and minds and feelings, but animals—at least some of them. In fact, the Bible even suggests that in some strange way some of them have a soul, not of course a human soul but a mysterious something that implies a kind of responsibility. For Scripture portrays animals as standing with human beings under capital punishment for murder (Gen. 9:5). Along with the people of Israel, their "livestock" were commanded to keep the Sabbath (Exod. 20:10; Deut. 5:14). Humans and animals (again, "livestock") alike were under the blessings and curses of the covenant (Lev. 26:22; Deut. 28:4). The firstborn of both belonged to God. In Nineveh both men and animals ("the herds and flocks") were told by God to repent, and they did (Jon. 3:7–10).[7]

3. *Dictionary of Biblical Imagery*, 28.
4. *Dictionary of Biblical Imagery*, 29.
5. *Dictionary of Biblical Imagery*, 30.
6. The Bible uses 180 words to refer to 70 distinct types (not species) of animals (*Dictionary of Biblical Imagery*, 26).
7. Jordan, *Through New Eyes*, 97–98.

Because of this analogy between human beings and certain of their animals, it was the latter that were used as sacrifices for sin. Five of their animals, those that were most valuable and most like their owners, stood in sacrifice as substitutes or representatives of their human owners.[8] The value of the sacrifice depended on the analogy—the resemblance of the animal to the human being. Indeed, we can say that the logic of the sacrificial system depended on the typological character of the animals used in it.[9]

Domestic and Wild, Clean and Unclean

In his masterful study of biblical typology, James Jordan observed that domestic animals in the Bible stood for Israel, God's domestic people. These were the animals that Israelites lived with every day—their cats, dogs, cattle, sheep, goats, and horses. They seemed more "human" than the wild boars and bears of the wilderness. For this reason, Jordan suggested, wild animals in the Bible represented gentiles. They were known by Jews to live by themselves in the "wilderness" of the world without the help of biblical revelation (100).

In the New Testament we can see a connection between unclean animals—most of which are wild—and gentiles: Peter's vision of "beasts of prey, reptiles, and birds of the air" (Acts 11:6) being lowered before him in a sheet. These unclean animals, Peter came to realize, represented gentiles (10:28). When he explained the vision to believers in Jerusalem, defending his table fellowship with gentiles, he related how God had told him "not to call profane what God has made clean" (11:9). In the next breath he said that "at that very moment" (11:10) three gentiles arrived and asked him to accompany them to visit a gentile centurion, which would involve eating together. Peter explained that "the Spirit told me to go with them and *not to make a distinction between them and us*" (Acts 11:12). He had previously assumed that it was "unlawful for a Jew to associate with or to visit a Gentile" (10:28), but as a result of this vision he learned, no doubt remembering the example of Rabbi Jesus, that he could have table fellowship with people represented by unclean animals—the gentiles. Jordan further observed that the "creeping" animals of the ground were thought to be unclean because they live in the dirt of the ground that was cursed after the fall (Gen. 3:14–17) (101–2).

8. Oxen, sheep, goats, doves, and pigeons. Although the last two were not too expensive, they were the most that the poor could afford.

9. Jordan, *Through New Eyes*, 98. In the next several paragraphs, page numbers in parentheses refer to *Through New Eyes*.

For millennia, rabbis and Christian exegetes have wondered what the rationale was behind the division between clean and unclean animals in Leviticus. Was there a rationally discernible principle that explained what seems irrational to us? Some have thought it was an ancient intuition of what was healthy and unhealthy. Yet some unclean animals such as lions and eagles are just as healthy as clean animals like goats, and there does not seem to have been any ancient reason for suspecting otherwise. Others have pointed to mythology and superstition, or association with disease such as flies and rodents.[10] Jordan advised that we go directly to the biblical explanation that clean animals have what the unclean do not (split hooves) and do something that the unclean do not (chew the cud) (101).

Therefore, Jordan argued, the key to this age-old puzzle lies in its typological meaning. The ground had been cursed because of the fall. For this reason pious men and women wore shoes so as not to soil their feet, and they took off their shoes or sandals only when the ground was holy. When they entered a house, they removed their shoes with their unclean dirt, and a good host would wash that unclean soil off their feet. All day while walking with shoes on unclean ground, they lifted their souls to heaven by meditating on God's words. Hence the clean animals are those that by analogy do the same: they wear shoes of split hooves, and they meditate by chewing the cud. Clean birds are those that are particular about where they put their feet. The unclean birds such as vultures will put their feet anywhere, even on rotting carcasses (101–2).

Hence the line between clean and unclean animals is best understood typologically. Animals are types of human beings in a huge variety of ways. One of them is the distinction in the First Testament between clean and unclean animals, signifying among other things God's providential distinction between Jews and gentiles (100).

God Speaks through Animals

If animals are analogies to human beings, we should not be surprised that many theologians in the last two thousand years have observed that God uses animals to speak to human beings. Not only directly in the way God used Balaam's ass, but also indirectly through types. The seventeenth-century Puritan Richard Baxter, for example, believed that "every Creature is a Letter, or Syllable, or Word, or Sentence, more or less, declaring the name and will of

---

10. *Dictionary of Biblical Imagery*, 27.

God."[11] Edwards agreed, arguing that "many things in brutes are analogous to what is to be observed in men" (*WJE* 11:85). To those who wondered why this was so, Edwards insisted that God "delights" in "teaching and instructing" us by "representing divine things" through all of his created works, including animals (*WJE* 11:67).

Baxter, Edwards, and others noted that the Bible teaches that God speaks through animals. Job urges us, "Ask the animals, and they will teach you. Ask the birds of the sky, and they will tell you" (Job 12:7). The author of Proverbs counsels, "Go to the ant, you sluggard, consider its ways and be wise" (Prov. 6:6). Jesus tells us, "Take a good look at [*or* fix your eyes upon] the birds of the air" (Matt. 6:26).

Jesus, Solomon, and Job seem to agree that there is wisdom in animals, put there by God typologically, that we can learn from. In another part of the Gospels Jesus warns us that he sends us out as sheep amid wolves, so we are to be as shrewd as serpents and as innocent as doves (Matt. 10:16). He presumes that we have already learned the traits of each of these animals and that we can apply what we know of them to gain wisdom in our lives of discipleship. So we are to learn from the serpent's shrewdness and the dove's innocence, the vulnerability of sheep and the cunning of wolves. All of these things we are to know and apply so that we might be wise.

No doubt Jesus knew the book of Proverbs; after all, Peter claimed that Jesus's Spirit inspired its author (1 Pet. 1:11). This author commended the wisdom of animals to us. Ants organize without a bureaucracy and plan ahead (Prov. 6:6–8; 30:24–25). Badgers are a people without power who somehow make their homes in rocks where they cannot be conquered (30:26). Locusts have no leader, but they still know how to keep order (30:27). Lizards are easily caught by the hand but are shrewd enough to live in kings' palaces (30:28). Lions teach us courage by the way they refuse to shrink from anyone (30:30). Even a strutting rooster and the he-goat teach us a "stately" way to conduct ourselves (30:29–31).

Far, far more can be said about biblical types that God has put in animals to teach us the ways of his kingdom. Consult the works in the footnote below for more on this fascinating subject.[12] In the remainder of this chapter we will

11. Richard Baxter, *A Christian Directory; or, A Body of Practical Divinity and Cases of Conscience* (London, 1825), 191; cited in Robert L. Boss, *Bright Shadows of Divine Things: The Devotional World of Jonathan Edwards* (n.p.: JE Society Press, 2017), 17.

12. G. S. Cansdale, *All the Animals of the Bible Lands* (Grand Rapids: Zondervan, 1970); E. Firmage, "Zoology," in *Anchor Bible Dictionary*, ed. David Noel Freedman, 6 vols. (New Haven: Yale University Press, 1992), 6:1109–67; B. L. Goddard, *Animals and Birds of the Bible* (Grand Rapids: Associated Publishers & Authors, n.d.); *Fauna and Flora of the Bible* (New York: United Bible Societies, 1972).

look more closely at two kinds of animals that are more familiar to most of us: birds and dogs. We will draw on the observations of several Christians who have studied birds and dogs for years.

Birds

Like many others in the history of Christian thought, Jonathan Edwards believed that birds represent "the inhabitants of heaven." For this reason, he thought, they are generally more beautiful than beasts and fish, and some have "gorgeous plumage." Also for this reason they create music, "sweetly praising their Creator" (*WJE* 11:84–85). While it is not pleasant music, the cockadoodling of the cock at dawn, so Edwards thought, is a type of preachers of the gospel, who wake up sinners from their sleep. This waking is also represented by the special singing of birds in the spring, which he saw as a type of an outpouring of the Spirit of God (*WJE* 11:92–93).

The British Anglican John Stott was a lifelong bird watcher, or as he would put it, an "orni-theologian."[13] Stott liked to quote Martin Luther on birds, from Luther's commentary on the Sermon on the Mount: "[God] is making the birds our schoolmasters and teachers. It is a great and abiding disgrace to us that in the Gospel a helpless sparrow should become a theologian and a preacher to the wisest of men. We have as many teachers and preachers as there are birds in the air. Their living example is an embarrassment to us[!]"[14]

In his marvelous book *The Birds, Our Teachers*, Stott wrote that storks in their annual migrations are examples to us of repentance. The prophet Jeremiah affirmed this point: "No one [in Judah] repents of his evil . . . . yet even the stork in the heavens knows her times" (8:6–7). Jeremiah was referring to the nearly half a million white storks that migrate over the Middle East every spring and summer between southern Africa and northern Europe, flying some eight thousand miles each way. They teach us to return to the God of Israel after we sin.[15]

Other species of birds teach typical lessons, according to Stott. Perhaps the best-known comes from Jesus's words about ravens. He famously told his disciples, "Consider the ravens, for they neither sow nor reap and they don't have a storehouse or barn. Yet God feeds them. You are worth far more than ravens!" (Luke 12:24).

---

13. John Stott, *The Birds, Our Teachers: Biblical Lessons from a Lifelong Bird-Watcher*, collector's ed. (Peabody, MA: Hendrickson, 2011), 10.

14. Martin Luther, *The Sermon on the Mount*, AE 21:197–98.

15. Stott, *Birds*, 18–19.

Jesus's point is that ravens teach us God's care for us. If God provides for them, and they are worth far less than we are, we should realize that he will provide for us too. Stott warned, though, that Jesus here forbids worry, not prudence. We are not to assume that we should not work for a living. Scripture teaches elsewhere that God feeds birds not directly but indirectly; they must forage for their food if they expect to be fed. "All [animals] look to you to give them their food in its season. You give it to them, and *they gather it up*" (Ps. 104:27–28).[16]

Hens are another kind of bird that point us to God's love. Jesus's lament over Jerusalem appealed to the love of a hen for her chicks: "Jerusalem, Jerusalem . . . how many times have I wanted to gather together your children, in the same way a hen gathers together her chicks under her wings" (Matt. 23:37). Jesus was drawing on a long Old Testament tradition that spoke of God's wings sheltering his people. In Deuteronomy God is said to have shielded and cared for his people "like an eagle that . . . hovers over its young, spreading out its wings, catching them, bearing them on its pinions" (32:10–11). Isaiah wrote that God would protect Jerusalem just like "birds hovering overhead" (Isa. 31:5). Psalms is full of references to God's people taking shelter under his wings: "Because you are my help, I sing in the shadow of your wings" (63:7); "I long to . . . take shelter in the shadow of your wings" (61:4); "I will take refuge in the shadow of your wings" (57:1); "Hide me in the shadow of your wings" (17:8 ESV); "Both high and low among men find refuge in the shadow of your wings" (36:7). Most of us are familiar with the promise of Psalm 91 to anyone who trusts in the Lord: "He will cover you with his feathers, and under his wings you will find refuge" (v. 4).[17] The point, repeated frequently, is that God will protect his people just as an eagle or hen protects its young with its wings. God loves his people, and he uses birds' wings as a symbol of that love.

If ravens and wings point us to God's love, sparrows direct our attention to our own self-worth. This is particularly important in a day when more and more people feel they are of little or no worth. Stott wrote that Jesus chose the most common and widely distributed of all land birds—"often regarded as useless and disposable"—and proclaimed that not a single sparrow "is forgotten by God" (Luke 12:6). He went on to say that no sparrow falls to the ground without God knowing about it (Matt. 10:29). So we should not be afraid, for we "are worth more than many sparrows" (10:31). Intriguingly, Jesus connected fear and self-worth, as if to say that fear will cause us to doubt

16. Stott, *Birds*, 12–16.
17. Stott, *Birds*, 70–71. Additional page references to Stott appear in parentheses throughout this section.

our value in God's eyes. In this way he suggested that the best antidote to low self-worth is to focus on God's estimation of us (33–38).

Pigeons, winked Stott, are the most pagan birds in the world. Of the twenty-seven orders of birds in the world (and there are nine thousand species), pigeons and doves belong to the only order that does not lift its head to drink. All other birds drink by gravity, and so after sipping water must lift their heads for the liquid to trickle down. Stott quoted a Ghanaian proverb: "Even a chicken, when it drinks, lifts its head to heaven to thank God for the water." Almost all birds, then, teach us gratitude to God when they drink water (41, 40).

Stott added that doves redeem their reputation by their honorable roles in the Bible (41). They were the first to announce the end of the flood by bringing Noah a fresh olive leaf (Gen. 8:11), represented the Holy Spirit at Jesus's baptism (Mark 1:10), and were called "innocent" by Jesus (Matt. 10:16). The Greek word used by Jesus literally means "unmixed" and so suggests purity of motive.

Perhaps the most characteristic feature of birds is their flight, even if some such as penguins cannot manage it. But the Bible associates bird flight with freedom: "Oh, that I had the wings of a dove! I would flee far away" (Ps. 55:8). Of course biblical freedom does not mean escaping problems, but being able to endure and even rise above them while enduring them. Rising above is its own kind of flight, and thus freedom.

Birds fly remarkable distances, and at a remarkable height and speed. Stott wrote that the European swift flies an average of five hundred miles every day, migrates annually to South Africa and back, and covers three million miles during one lifetime. A Rüppells griffon vulture was hit by a plane at thirty-seven thousand feet, more than seven miles high. Peregrine falcons are estimated to dive at somewhere between one hundred and two hundred miles an hour (52).

The most vivid image of freedom during stress comes from the wandering albatross, whose twelve-foot wingspan is the largest of any bird. It is famous for its ability to fly through the most ferocious storms, facing into the wind throughout. Because of a special lock on its wings, it can glide for weeks at a time, sleeping while in the air (52–53).

But the Bible's portrayal of the noblest of birds is the eagle. The author of Proverbs was "amazed" by "its way in the sky" (Prov. 30:18–19). Job said the eagle soars at God's command and builds his nest on high (Job 39:27). In what is one of the most majestic passages of Scripture, Isaiah compared those who wait on God—in other words, model believers—with an eagle. They will not faint or grow weary like young men, but will renew their strength.

"They shall mount up with wings like eagles" (Isa. 40:31 ESV). The picture is of the noble bird that does not rise by strenuously flapping its wings, but by catching God's winds and soaring effortlessly into the sky. This is the portrait of biblical freedom that the eagle provides: catching the updraft of the Spirit, which enables us to rise above suffering, even while enduring it. We live in the kingdom not by frantic self-effort but by relying on the Spirit of God. We catch his power and virtue and ride them, as on two wings, to God's purposes for us (56–57).

Stott discussed another noted feature of birds: their songs. He said that scientists have identified six different functions for their songs or calls: to advertise their presence and thereby assert their territory, to warn of danger from a predator, to threaten a rival, to keep contact with each other when traveling, to invite a mate, and to reassure the chicks they left back at the nest (80). But for most of us, the songs of birds communicate joy. When we get up just before dawn, it sounds like our neighborhood birds are rejoicing over the coming day or simply the fact that they are alive. The psalmist suggested that they are doing just this, praising God: "Praise the LORD! Praise the LORD from the heavens! Praise him . . . flying birds!" (Ps. 148:1, 10). Even if scientists do not acknowledge this function of birdsong, theologians have noted it for millennia. And we can add that the singing of birds is God's reminder to us to rejoice with our fellow creatures, the birds, that we get to enjoy this world and its Creator. They are another *type* given to us by God to teach us about himself and his kingdom.

Dogs

Scripture is far less positive about dogs than about birds. In the ancient Middle East dogs typically lived on the street, struggling for survival and eating at the dump.[18] They became biblical symbols of filth and paganism. When Jesus instructed his disciples not to give to dogs what is holy (Matt. 7:6), he meant not to throw holy things out, his language suggesting that in everyday thinking dogs were synonymous with garbage. In the Old Testament dogs were "de facto undertakers" who licked the blood of corpses (think of Naboth, Ahab, Jeroboam, Baasha, and Jezebel). Both Proverbs and Peter spoke of dogs returning to their vomit, likening them to unrepentant sinners (Prov. 26:11; 2 Pet. 2:22). "Dog" was the euphemism for male prostitutes in Deuteronomy (23:18) and Revelation (22:15) because of the position taken in male

18. *Dictionary of Biblical Imagery*, 29. The rest of this paragraph is indebted to the *Dictionary*.

intercourse. "Dog" was also used as an insult or term for extreme subservience (1 Sam. 17:43; 2 Kings 8:13). Paul went so far as to refer to Judaizers—Jewish Jesus-followers who insisted that gentiles had to become Jews in order to be first-class Christians—as dogs (Phil. 3:2). Needless to say, it was not a compliment.

Martin Luther suggested that dogs were not esteemed because they were so common. "The dog is the most faithful of animals and would be much esteemed were it not so common. Our Lord God has made his greatest gifts the commonest."[19] But even if dogs were not highly valued in the biblical period, they have been appreciated by Christians ever since, not least by Luther. Like many other Christians in church history, Luther found that dogs could teach him about God and his son, Jesus. Here is another word from the Reformer, this one in *Table Talk*, the record of his dinner conversations with students and guests. "When Luther's puppy happened to be at the table, looked for a morsel from his master, and watched with open mouth and motionless eyes, he [Luther] said, 'Oh, if I could only pray the way this dog watches the meat! All his thoughts are concentrated on the piece of meat. Otherwise he has no thought, wish or hope.'"[20] Luther took his dog to be a lesson in single-minded prayer.

Dave Burchett, dog-loving sports director for the Texas Rangers, found a host of other lessons waiting to be learned through his dogs. One was to be present with others in suffering, without feeling the need to theologize. When his wife Joni discovered she had cancer and everything looked threatening, his dog Hannah came near and stayed.

> Her intuitive evaluation of my emotions was uncanny. Hannah would come to me and nudge me as if to say, "I'm here." As she shifted her big brown eyes toward mine, her gaze communicated, "I don't know how to help, but I wish I could."
>
> There was incredible comfort in her presence.
>
> She was right. That was *all I needed*—presence. When Joni was sick with cancer, all we needed from friends and fellow followers of Jesus was caring presence.
>
> The theology of why bad things happen could wait.[21]

Researchers at Goldsmiths College in London discovered that dogs may respond to our emotions more than any other species, including our own.

---

19. Dave Burchett, *Stay: Lessons My Dogs Taught Me about Life, Loss, and Grace* (Carol Stream, IL: Tyndale, 2015), 23, in a quotation commonly attributed to Luther.

20. Martin Luther, *Table Talk*, AE 54:37–38.

21. Burchett, *Stay*, 20 (emphasis original).

Eighteen dogs were evaluated while their owner or an unfamiliar person pretended to cry, hummed, or carried on an ordinary conversation. The dogs did things that are consistent with what we would call empathy. They looked at, approached, and touched the people more when they were crying than when they hummed. None of the dogs came near when the people were talking normally. They approached the person crying even if that person was not their owner. One of the researchers concluded, "They were responding to the person's emotion, not their own needs, which is suggestive of empathetic-like comfort-offering behavior."[22]

Burchett likened this empathy to that of the Holy Spirit, who "rushes toward the crying of my soul." He cited Paul's words in Romans 8, "The Holy Spirit prays for us with groaning too deep for words" (v. 26). So dogs were a reminder to Burchett—perhaps a God-given type—of what the Holy Spirit does for us when we are hurting. They might even be instruments of the Spirit to comfort us when we are suffering.

Another lesson that his dogs taught Burchett was to live in the moment. When his dog Hannah came down with her own cancer, had surgery, and returned with a twelve-inch scar and prescription for chemotherapy, Burchett was reeling. He feared losing his beloved pet, his canine friend. But then his veterinarian changed his perspective with these words: "Hannah does not know that she is sick. Dogs have no fear of death, so they live in the moment. Enjoy each moment that you have [with her]."[23]

In the days ahead Burchett realized that his dog was teaching him the meaning of Jesus's words, "Don't worry about tomorrow, for tomorrow will have worries of its own" (Matt. 6:34). She was also helping him to understand what C. S. Lewis meant when he asked, "Where, except in the present, can the Eternal be met?"[24] We tend to live in the past and the future, finding it difficult to savor the present. Bad memories or fears for the future rob us of present joy. Dogs don't have that problem. As Burchett put it, they love life. They are on vacation every time you let them out the door.[25]

Dogs also illustrate absolute trust. For them, we (if we are their master/owner) are the center of their universe. We are the focus of their love and faith and trust. They serve us for scraps of food, and the same boring food day after day. But they are thrilled to get it every time. When we ask them to go with us, on a walk or in the car, they don't ask us where we are going.

22. Deborah M. Custance and Jennifer Mayer, "Empathetic-like Responding by Domestic Dogs (Canis Familiaris) to Distress in Humans," *Animal Cognition* 15 (May 2012): 851–59.
23. Burchett, *Stay*, 31.
24. C. S. Lewis, *Christian Reflections* (Grand Rapids: Eerdmans, 1967), 113.
25. Burchett, *Stay*, 187.

We don't have to beg or cajole. They jump with joy, trusting it will be fun.[26] There could hardly be a better model of what it means to trust and follow our Lord Jesus.

Dogs welcome their masters like few if any other animals. They jump up and wag their tail, rushing to our side when we walk in the door. They don't care a lick (Burchett's intended pun) about our wealth or looks or status. They are God's canine self-esteem boosters—not only when we get home but also any time we talk to them. As humorist Dave Barry put it, your dog thinks you're a genius. "You can say any fool thing to a dog, and the dog will give you this look that says, '. . . You're RIGHT! I NEVER would have thought of that!'"[27] What a picture of the way we ought to welcome and respect our loved ones, or our fellow members of the body of Christ! Burchett imagined how he should welcome his wife based on what he has learned from his dog.

> I [should] drop what I am doing to greet Joni, genuinely excited to see
> her.
> I show her physical affection without any ulterior motive.
> I am completely interested in her.
> I accept her mood, whatever it might be, without judgment.
> I listen to her frustrations without demanding to know how she could
> feel that way or offering countless "solutions."
> If she needs to talk, I am wholly present.
> If she cannot meet my needs, I am not angry or withdrawn.[28]

Of course Scripture does not tell us to welcome others as your dog has welcomed you. Instead it tells us to "welcome one another as *Christ* has welcomed you" (Rom. 15:7 ESV). But as I have been arguing throughout this book, God teaches us through his *creation* all sorts of things about life in his kingdom. And dogs are among his many creatures that teach us how to be, in this case, welcoming to our brothers and sisters in the body. They illustrate *types* of the welcoming character of Jesus.

That includes, perhaps most poignantly, forgiveness. Burchett suggested we take a little quiz to see who is most willing to forgive. Lock your spouse or significant other *and* your dog outside in the rain for thirty minutes. When you finally open the door, which one is glad to see you?[29]

---

26. Burchett, *Stay*, 75–83.
27. Dave Barry, "Earning a Collie Degree," *Miami Herald*, September 8, 1985; cited in Burchett, *Stay*, 121.
28. Burchett, *Stay*, 122.
29. Burchett, *Stay*, 108.

Burchett said he could do all sorts of unkind things to his dog and nothing would cause her to be unforgiving. He could ignore her or snap at her or refuse her nuzzles. But then when he called her name, she would still run to him with the abandon of love. She would never betray the least hint of unforgiveness or condemnation. I remember accidentally forgetting our dog Jaffa for most of a day. She was left inside our house without food or the chance to run outside. But when I came home, she rushed to me with her doggy smile, jumping up and down with joyous excitement. Not a trace of anger or resentment. She, like most dogs, was a model of forgiveness.

If we want to be happy, we need this lesson from dogs. University of Michigan psychologist Christopher Peterson found that of all the virtues "forgiveness is the behavior most strongly linked to happiness."[30] This comment should not surprise us. Jesus said that if we choose not to forgive others, God will not forgive us (Matt. 6:15). Paul commanded us to forgive "one another as God in Christ forgave you" (Eph. 4:32). If we do not forgive, then we are not reconciled with God, and our deepest connection with Love itself has been broken. With that connection severed, it is no wonder that we will have trouble finding the peace and joy necessary for true happiness. Dogs can help us forgive by showing how they forgive us—or to put it another way, by being *types* of forgiveness to us.

Dogs don't automatically demonstrate all these virtues, however. Like us, they need training. Elizabeth Haysom is a dog trainer at a prison in Virginia, incarcerated with a ninety-year sentence. She is now a dynamic Christian who inspires all who know her. Haysom said she sees many kingdom principles illustrated by the dogs with whom she works. One set of principles has to do with the way they learn obedience. "When training a dog, we build the behavior slowly step by step. We don't expect a dog to magically understand what 'stay' means. We build a *habit* of a good stay. And a good stay is one that holds through distractions (people, food, toys, other animals), distance (being out of sight), and duration (several minutes). Even the stay that holds through different trainers who have different meanings for the word."[31]

Haysom observed that we need to train in the virtues over months and years, and that it often must proceed step by step. Maturity never comes overnight. Christians will make mistakes and fail, just like dogs. But just as trainers don't let a dog quit, so too we should not let our failures excuse us from training in godly habits and attitudes.

30. Marilyn Elias, "Psychologists Now Know What Makes People Happy," *USA Today*, December 8, 2002, http://usatoday30.usatoday.com/news/health/2002-12-08-happy-main_x.htm.
31. Elizabeth Haysom, "Dog Notes," notebook loaned to me by the author.

Haysom has found that any dog can be trained, even those wounded by cruel masters. But they must be trained with love and a sense of partnership. Rather than using a choke collar and punishment, she teaches her dogs—many of whom came from abusive situations—rules and obedience with praise, massage, and food. But dog breeds are different, and different breeds have different skills and gifts. So while all dogs get tired and need rest, for example, they get that rest in different ways. One dog likes to take a break by chewing, another by chasing a ball, still another with a nap. Others are comforted by getting a good sniff of something nasty, or by putting their head in someone's lap. A good trainer watches a dog when it rests to see what it prefers. She will not condemn the dog for not wanting to nap if it gets its rest by chewing.[32]

So too, she observed, in the body we all have different gifts and inclinations. We should not condemn our brothers or sisters if they don't like what we like, or don't prefer our kind of spirituality. Differences in dog breeds and even among members of the same breed can help remind us to be forgiving and accepting of differences among members in the church. "Now there are varieties of gifts, but the same Spirit. . . . If the foot should say, 'Because I am not a hand, I do not belong to the body,' that would not make it any less a part of the body" (1 Cor. 12:4, 15 ESV). Just as good dog trainers recognize God-given diversity among dogs, so we should recognize that God has purposely made his people different. Rather than resent that fact when differences make us uncomfortable, we should celebrate it.

Haysom said that the most important cue she teaches a dog is the recall. "It can save the dog's life." By this she means the skill of coming when called, no matter what else is happening or what it costs. Just like people, dogs don't like to leave what they are doing. Whatever they are enjoying at the moment seems more important or fun than coming to the trainer. So Haysom uses rewards—the best food treats, the dog's favorite toy, romping fun, or even the chance to get back to what he was previously enjoying—to teach the dog that *coming to a command is always the best thing to be done*.[33]

This principle should sound familiar. Jesus said his sheep know his voice (John 10:3–5). They come to him when he calls, which means they obey, even when wandering in disobedience might seem more enjoyable. The obedience is all-important. It proves their love and is rewarded by both the Father and the Son. "Whoever has my commandments and keeps them, he it is who loves me. And he who loves me will be loved by my Father, and I will love him and manifest myself to him" (John 14:21 ESV).

32. Haysom, "Dog Notes."
33. Haysom, "Dog Notes."

As I wrote at the beginning of this section, Scripture does not have much positive to say about dogs. So I cannot claim with certainty that they illustrate God-given types shown clearly in Scripture. But what these last pages *have* shown is that dogs illustrate in remarkable ways a variety of Christian virtues to which God calls us. And since God is Lord of all, we can believe with some assurance that these traits are in dogs not by chance but because they have been put there by their Creator. He has filled his creation with *types*, and these are among them.

8

Sex

The Language of the Body

The sexual revolution of the 1960s and '70s promised freedom and bliss but brought pain and slavery instead. Women wake up crying with foggy memories of drunken hookups. Men are afraid to get married. They saw their parents' marriages collapse, and their own brains have become so conditioned by porn that they fear they won't be able to stay interested in one woman. Both men and women binge-drink to drown their guilt and pain—guilt from sex without love, and pain from broken relationships. Some feel shame because of abortion, others because of the STDs they live with. Most grew up in broken homes; those who have seen friends with parents who stayed together feel cheated because theirs didn't.

Often it is said that the sexual revolution made sex too important. Actually, the problem was that our culture didn't make it important enough. Rather than seeing physical love between a man and a woman as the profound mystery it is, pointing subtly to the meaning of the cosmos, it banalized it, reducing it to little more than a recreational exercise—or worse, simply the exchange of bodily fluids.

What Reason Shows Us

But there is hope. Reason has always hinted, often by whispering, that there is something profoundly meaningful in human sexuality. Other mammals reproduce by sexual coupling, but the mode of the human animal is different. Only human beings look each other in the eyes when they have sex. Only human beings joke and laugh during their "love-making." Only human beings feel shame when they learn they have been seen in coitus.

Then there is the physicality of human sex, which by itself cries out for interpretation. Why must the woman open her legs, as if to welcome? The welcome involves trust, for she has made herself vulnerable to a man, who is usually far stronger. Why does the man take off his clothes, opening himself to ridicule, if he does not trust the woman to welcome him? He exposes his most sensitive organ, which he knows the woman can harm if she chooses. He too must trust.

The two can avoid each other's eyes, but only by dodging what is more natural. This is the behavior of *persons* whose souls speak through the eyes. It is plain to those with eyes to see that these are not merely bodies exchanging pleasure, but that this is an action meant to exchange love. If there are no words of affection, one will often object. Their physical oneness calls out for tenderness. But why should it, if this is merely a physical or emotional release?

The man releases semen, a word that means "seed." He inserts his seed into the same canal that will deliver a baby—if the man and woman don't prevent the seed from joining the woman's egg. Clearly this act is designed to make a baby, even if the actors don't want it to.

Sex and Reproduction

More and more these days we hear that we should not want sex to be connected to reproduction. That would be presumptuous, we are told, because it would impose unnecessary meaning on a biological act that can be performed without fear of pregnancy. Besides, millions want to enjoy it without guilt. They don't want to burden themselves with the thought of children who would be unwanted, which is thought to be a fate worse than death. Far better to realize that sex need have nothing to do with reproduction, and that we can abort the unwanted babies that might be created by a slipup.

This way of thinking, common though it is, raises all sorts of questions. If we should not connect sex to babies, why does sex normally produce babies unless we intervene? If we should not have qualms about aborting the unwanted unborn, why not kill unwanted babies who are already born? And weren't some of us unwanted slipups by our parents? Should we have qualms about the possibility our parents could have aborted us?

Is Sexual Difference Merely Cultural?

This is not the place to answer the questions just posed. But the questions force us to consider the deeper questions about the meaning of sex that reason provokes. One of those deeper questions is why there is sexual difference in the first place. It is de rigueur to say that sexual difference is a cultural construction. Even if it is conceded that there are physical differences between the sexes, it is still asserted that gender differences are simply the product of culture. Boys, for example, prefer trucks and wrestling only because they have been raised to think that these are boyish or manly things to like. Girls prefer dolls only because some cultures have trained them to think they should do so. If children were raised in a different culture, boys might prefer dolls and girls might love trucks.

There's only one problem with this way of thinking: it is not true. To be more precise, a broad range of research shows there are profound differences between men and women, before and despite the influence of culture. For example, evolutionary biologists say that of all the differences between animals and humans, sexual differences are the most significant. They shape the voice, pelvic shape, hormones, brain organization, height, and strength.[1] The sexual difference is not only the most significant but the biggest. "Sex is easily the biggest difference within a species. Men and women, unlike blacks and whites, have different organs and body designs. The inferable difference in genomes between two people of visibly different races is one-hundredth of one percent. The gap between the sexes vastly exceeds that."[2]

Biologists add that sex differences, more than any other differences, are responsible for making life interesting. "If not for sex, much of what is flamboyant and beautiful in nature would not exist. Plants would not bloom. Birds would not sing. Deer would not sprout antlers."[3]

But it is in humans that sex differences are most numerous and striking. Let's start with their brains. Neuroscientist Larry Cahill reported that the differences between male and female brains are "marked, pervasive, and consistent."[4] The differences *between* the sexes are far greater than those

1. Glenn Wilson, *The Great Sex Divide: A Study of Male-Female Differences* (London: Peter Owen, 1989).

2. William Saletan, "Don't Worry Your Pretty Little Head," *Slate*, January 21, 2005, http://www.slate.com/articles/health_and_science/human_nature/2005/01/dont_worry_your_pretty_little_head.html.

3. Olivia Judson, *Dr. Tatiana's Sex Advice to All Creation* (London: Chatto & Windus, 2002), 1.

4. J. Budziszewski, *On the Meaning of Sex* (Wilmington, DE: ISI Books, 2012), 38. Budziszewski cites Larry Cahill, "Why Sex Matters for Neuroscience," *Nature Reviews: Neuroscience* 7 (2006): 477–84; Larry Cahill, "His Brain, Her Brain," *Scientific American* 292, no. 5 (2005): 40–47.

within each sex, contrary to an oft-repeated claim. The differences are not only in the ways the brain works but also in the ways it is structured and develops. All of this is true before culture has a chance to shape the brains of children. According to brain scientist Doreen Kimura, male-female brain differences start "so early in life that from the start the environment is acting on differently wired brains in boys and girls."[5]

The physical differences in the brain are many, from a larger CA1 region of the hippocampus in males and different ways neurotransmitters work between the sexes, to sex hormones and more connections in females between the right and left hemispheres. Chronic stress affects male and female brains differently. Brain diseases diverge between the sexes, as do the neurological aspects of addiction. These neurological differences between males and females mean that the neurological features of all of the following are different between the sexes: emotion, memory, vision, hearing, processing faces, pain perception, navigation, neurotransmitter levels, stress hormone action on the brain, and disease.[6]

Do these differences exist because of the different cultural roles that men and women have had to play? In a word, no. Researchers have found that sharp differences exist even after controlling for countries, educational levels, ages of respondents, and years in which the studies were conducted.[7] There *are* differences from culture to culture, but the opposite of what one would expect. Most of us would imagine that sex differences would be greater in poorer and less developed countries, where individuals are less free to break from tradition. But in fact sex roles are even more pronounced in richer and more developed countries. No one knows for sure why, though some have speculated that in poorer countries women sometimes feel compelled to take on traditionally masculine roles in order to support their families.[8]

In surveys conducted across a wide variety of cultures, women scored consistently higher on nurturing, tenderness, trustfulness, and anxiety. They tend to experience emotion more vividly and show more emotion in their faces. They are better able to decipher the emotions of others, are more susceptible to mood swings, and experience more depression. Men consistently scored higher in assertiveness, openness to new ideas, self-confidence, mechanical and spatial reasoning, and attention to physical attractiveness.[9]

5. Doreen Kimura, "Sex Differences in the Brain," *Scientific American* 267, no. 3 (1992): 119–25.
6. Budziszewski, *On the Meaning of Sex*, 39.
7. Budziszewski, *On the Meaning of Sex*, 46.
8. Paul T. Costa Jr. et al., "Gender Differences in Personality Traits across Cultures: Robust and Surprising Findings," *Journal of Personality and Social Psychology* 81, no. 2 (2001): 322–31.
9. Budziszewski, *On the Meaning of Sex*, 47–48.

Even when men and women share tasks such as household chores, they view them differently. When they practice the same virtues, they do so in different ways. So courage looks different in women than in men, and tenderness in women is different from that of men. Intriguingly, differences persist when they determine to resist the virtues. So while a man would kill a baby to get rid of it, women tend to deposit their babies in a dumpster or trash can. J. Budziszewski hypothesized that while the woman's act is not nurturing, "the inclination to nurturing has not been destroyed. . . . [She might imagine] her baby resting in the dumpster, quietly and painlessly slipping into a death that is something like sleep."[10]

The Meaning of Sex Differences

Some years ago Gilbert Meilaender provided a vivid picture of male-female differences from a Dave Barry column titled, "Listen Up, Jerks! Share Innermost Feelings with Her."

> We have some good friends Buzz and Libby, whom we see about twice a year. When we get together, Beth and Libby always wind up in a conversation, lasting several days, during which they discuss virtually every significant event that has occurred in their lives and the lives of those they care about, sharing their innermost feelings, analyzing and probing, inevitably coming to a deeper understanding of each other, and a strengthening of a cherished friendship. Whereas Buzz and I watch the play-offs.
>
> This is not to say Buzz and I don't share our feelings. Sometimes we get quite emotional.
>
> "That's not a FOUL?" one of us will say.
>
> Or: "You're telling me that's not a FOUL???"
>
> I don't mean to suggest that all we talk about is sports. We also discuss, openly and without shame, what kind of pizza we need to order. We have a fine time together, but we don't have heavy conversations, and sometimes, after the visit, I'm surprised to learn—from Beth, who learned it from Libby—that there has recently been some new wrinkle in Buzz's life, such as that he now has an artificial leg.[11]

Meilaender went on in this article to think about the meaning of sex differences. He is a Christian theologian who wonders what reason can tell

---

10. Budziszewski, *On the Meaning of Sex*, 51–52.

11. Gilbert Meilaender, "Men and Women—Can We Be Friends?," in *Wing to Wing, Oar to Oar: Readings on Courting and Marrying*, ed. Amy A. Kass and Leon R. Kass (Notre Dame, IN: University of Notre Dame Press, 2000), 145–46.

us about why God made us in two radically different ways. His answer was that sexual difference forces us to grow as persons because the opposite sex challenges us in ways our own sex does not. Friends of the same sex tend to think as we do, and so don't usually push us to be different. But those of the opposite sex, especially when we live with one of them (!), often see things very differently and challenge us to change. This can happen only in a close relationship. But because sexual attraction makes unmarried opposite-sex relationships unstable, it is usually only in a marriage—where sexual attraction can strengthen the relationship—that we can learn from the challenge, change, and grow.

Meilaender then asked, Why is this so? Why does God create his human creatures in this way, so that tension in marriage helps us to become better persons if we let it? His answer was that God is the great pedagogue, training us for heaven. "We are being prepared ultimately for that vast friendship which is heaven, in which we truly are taken beyond ourselves, and in which all share the love of God."[12]

Meilaender did not talk about *types*, but I will. We can interpret Meilaender to be showing us one way in which sexual difference is a *type* of the differences we find among people in all of life. Differences in this life are to be embraced in both the joys and stresses of friendship as they prepare us for the millions of friendships we will enjoy in the age to come.

We have not brought in biblical revelation yet. In a few pages we will, and from it we will go much deeper in our exploration of the meaning of sexual difference. But before we get there, let's use our reason to think about two more ways in which sexuality points us to God.

Thirst and *Erōs*

The first is the thirst that sexual fulfillment leaves lovers with. Paradoxically, even when sexual intercourse seems fulfilling to each partner, both are sometimes left with a thirst for more. If not more physical fulfillment, then more emotional and spiritual union with each other. William F. May wrote of the love that "asks for a continuance of love." Its lovemaking awakens "a further thirst even while it slakes. That is the grandeur and the misery of sexual love."[13] And even when the two feel united in love and spirit, the spiritually sensitive will sense there is still something missing. This is a deeper thirst for the ultimate

12. Meilaender, "Men and Women," 147–48.
13. William F. May, "Four Mischievous Theories of Sex," in Kass and Kass, *Wing to Wing, Oar to Oar*, 200.

love of God. "In the very union of the two, man and woman render themselves needier, which increases in them the thirst [for] the mystery" of God.[14] Reason shows us, reflecting on human experience, that sexual love, even when accompanied by emotional fulfillment, suggests the existence of a greater fulfillment.

The second sign in sexual difference that reason can discern is *erōs*. C. S. Lewis famously explained that this is not sexual desire but the desire for union with the beloved, even if union brings suffering. Oneness with my lover is more important than my happiness. This is the *erōs* of which Plato and, more recently, Allan Bloom wrote. It is not Christian *agapē*, because while *erōs* desires the beautiful, *agapē* loves even what is not beautiful. And *erōs* is a "wild and unruly" god that can become a demon if it is not submitted to *agapē*.[15] But even alone it is a *type*. For it points to love for God, which seeks union with him and not happiness. Of course happiness will come when we are united to God. But in the meantime we must seek God and not happiness, lest we confuse our desires with his and lose both him and happiness.

When Revelation Sheds Light

Reason has been helpful. We can see from it, but dimly, that sexual difference and sexual love point us to a future love and union that surpass the loves and friendships we now enjoy in broken and partly realized ways. But God's revelation sheds far more light on the meaning of sex, which is seen dimly in the *types* that God has embedded in this mysterious human experience.

Therefore Jesus told his hearers that they must go back to "the beginning" in order to understand marriage and sexuality. Only in God's revelation of the first man and woman, interpreted through Jesus's teaching and life, could the first disciples—and can we—see the full meaning of sex and love. "And Pharisees came to [Jesus], testing him and saying, 'Is it permissible for a man to divorce his wife for any reason?' When he answered, Jesus said, 'Have you not read that the Creator *from the beginning* made them male and female?' And he said [quoting the creation story], "'For this reason a man will leave his father and mother and be joined to his wife, and the two will be one flesh." So they are no longer two but one flesh. Therefore what God has joined together, let man not put asunder'" (Matt. 19:3–6).

So let us go, as Jesus says we should, back to the beginning. There we read that YHWH God said, "It is not good that the man [*adam*] should be alone.

14. Gerhard Müller, "An Opening to the Mystery of God," in *Not Just Good, but Beautiful*, ed. Steven Lopes and Helen Alvaré (Walden, NY: Plough, 2015), 13.
15. C. S. Lewis, "Eros," in *The Four Loves* (San Francisco: HarperOne, 2017), 117–48.

I will make for him a helper, as a counterpart" (Gen. 2:18). As many have observed over the millennia, this means that human beings cannot find themselves by themselves. We need the other—the sexually different other—to find our own meaning and essence. It is in my sexual difference, and by relating to a person who is sexually different, that I find who I am. It is "not good" for me to ignore my sexual difference or to live as if my sexuality makes no difference. I must "be" in some relation to what is sexually other in order for things to be "good."

Sexuality and the *Imago Dei*

The above passage from the second creation story (Gen. 2:4–25) has always been seen in conjunction with the first creation story (1:1–2:3), which says God made the first human beings *in* his image. I highlight the preposition because Scripture distinguishes between the Son of God, who *is* the image of God (Col. 1:15; Heb. 1:3), and human beings, who are made "*in* the image of God" (Gen. 1:27). We humans are both like God and unlike God, but Jesus *is* God: "When you see me, you see the Father" (John 14:9). "The Father and I are one" (10:30). "He was calling God his own Father, making himself equal with God" (5:18). "Thomas answered [Jesus], 'My Lord and my God!'" (20:28). In other words, we are not God but have been created by God with certain features that are from him and like him.

What are those features? Theologians have given several answers to this question, such as having a mind to think rationally and having the capacity to love others. The first creation story suggests that among the most important aspects of being in the divine image is *relating to someone who is fundamentally different*. Listen to the text: "And God created man [*adam*] in his own image. In the image of God he created him; male and female he created them" (Gen. 1:27).

Several things are implied. First, the image of God is both male and female, so we cannot know that image without knowing both sexes. Second, sexual difference is in some way intrinsic to the image of God. Third, God's image is seen in the relationship between man and woman. Therefore we can learn something about God by knowing how men and women are meant by God to relate.

Let's now look more carefully at the rest of the creation story, where Jesus told us to go understand the man-woman relationship. Here we will find more clues to *types* that God has planted within human sexuality. In Genesis 2 God tried to find a counterpart for Adam to remedy his *aloneness*, which God said was "not good." The text says that God brought every beast of the field and every bird of the heavens to Adam to name, which he did. But no "helper" was found who could serve as his "counterpart." Finally God created again, putting Adam to sleep and taking part of his side to fashion a woman. God "brought her to the man" (v. 22). Adam was thrilled: "Now at last there is bone of my bones and flesh of my flesh! She is rightly called *wo*man because she was taken from *man*" (v. 23).

Adam was thrilled not only, it seems, because the woman was beautiful and so similar to him. But now, unlike the animals he searched and named, she could *share* his joys because she seemed so much like him. In other words, he was excitedly grateful that God had given him a great *gift*. In answer to his loneliness and frustration from not finding a counterpart, God had again created from nothing—while using Adam's own bones and flesh—a similar-but-different person with whom he could work and enjoy the garden.

Sexual Difference as Gift

Adam's excitement and joy suggested that he realized God had done what he did not have to do—remedy Adam's need by *giving* what he did not have and does not deserve. The author implied here and earlier (in 1:26, where God created Adam in freedom out of nothing) that every one of us has been "brought" to life as a gift to ourselves and others, just as God "brought" the woman to Adam as a gift. Life itself is a gift, and to have a spouse is to have a similar-but-different person *brought* to us by a *giving* God. The existence of others who are sexually different is a manifestation of *grace*—that God created us by a gift and created others who are similar-but-different as gifts. God is a *giving* God, and sexual difference is a clear sign of that giving.

Irreducible Unity of Body and Soul

Also important in Adam's cry of exultation is the link between the body and the soul. By Adam's joyous words about *her* but expressed through bones and flesh, he showed us that the person was the irreducible union of body and soul: "Now at last there is bone of my bones and flesh of my flesh!" As Pope John Paul II expressed it, the body "reveals a living soul."[16] Budziszewski observed that the body may be a sign, but it is far more than a sign. It does

---

16. John Paul II, *Man and Woman He Created Them: A Theology of the Body*, trans. Michael Waldstein (Boston: Pauline Books, 2006), 183 (14.4). On John Paul's theology of the body, see Eduardo J. Echeverria, *In the Beginning: A Theology of the Body* (Eugene, OR: Pickwick, 2011).

not just stand for a soul but *embodies* the soul. This is why sex is the joining not merely of bodies but of souls and *persons*. It is also why the meeting of persons in sex has profound meaning. It points, as we have just seen, to the gracious giving of God but also to our own identity as persons who are to relate to other similar-but-different persons. Since sex has been taken nearly universally as an expression of *love*—at least before the recent postmodern turn reduced it to impersonal pleasure—it suggests by its own action, now informed by biblical revelation, that we are designed for *loving* relationships with other persons who are different from us.

The Language of the Body

After recording Adam's delight, the author of Genesis told how it relates to marriage. "Therefore a man leaves behind his father and his mother and cleaves to his wife, and the two have become one flesh" (2:24).

By giving us this definition of marriage immediately after telling us of the creation of the similar-but-different body-soul unions called man and woman, the author suggested that man and woman are made for marriage. Furthermore, sexual difference was created expressly for the purpose of two becoming one, that is, for marriage. As John Paul II famously put it, "The language of the body is nuptial." Bodies were made by God to join souls to one another in marriage, and—we shall get to this—to point them to marriage to God himself. By "language of the body" the pope meant that sexual difference was designed for *union* of persons who are different. All the things that make a man and woman different, not least their sexual organs, are intended to unite the one to the other. And that union of love is meant to create new love and new life. The male reproductive organ is designed to enter the female body, and by that entrance man and woman became a new organism that bears fruit—not only in love but in children.

Imagine a visitor from Mars. After a while on the green planet watching movies and studying anatomy textbooks, this observer would notice that the male and female sexual organs fit together. The Martian would also notice that when a man and woman come together in this way, a new degree of love is often expressed and created, and children come into being. He would conclude from the way these human bodies are made and work that they must have been designed for love and fruitfulness. This is part of what is meant by "the language of the body."

But the Martian without access to God's revelation would not know what else the body's language is saying—that the body-soul union of persons is made for a loving relationship with God. Only by reading the Bible or hearing from the church would the Martian connect the dots—that the love and fruitfulness of which the body speaks is a *type* pointing to love to God that also bears fruit.

This is how Jews and Christians have read the Song of Songs for millennia. The bride and her beloved have mostly been taken as *types* for God's people in their love affair with God. Of course on a literal level the poem is about the love, often sexual, between two human lovers. But Israel and the church have typically read it at a deeper level, showing the God of Israel passionately pursuing his human bride, Israel and then the church. Or in a way that joins the two, believers have seen the erotic relationship as a *type* of God's love for his people. Paul made this *type* explicit in Ephesians 5, where he wrote that the Genesis 2:24 definition of marriage, which we have just seen, is a "mystery" that "refers to Messiah and the church" (v. 32).

Naked and Unashamed

The last statement in the second creation story is almost as mysterious as Paul's claim. "And the two of them, the man and his wife, were naked and unashamed" (Gen. 2:25). Most of us feel a certain embarrassment when we are naked in the presence of others—say, in a medical exam. Psychiatrists report that it is common for people to dream of being naked in public and feeling great anxiety because of it. It is significant that this part of revelation comes from ancient Israel, where nakedness was taboo (Gen. 3:7; Ezek. 16:7–8). So what could it mean?

John Paul argued that this part of the creation story shows humanity's "original innocence" before the fall. Before sin, the man could regard the woman, even in glorious nudity, as a subject and not an object. He could see her as a beautiful person and not just as a prize for his own pleasure. He could enjoy her inner beauty without lusting after her outer beauty. Likewise, the woman could view the man as an intriguing person with whom she could share a relationship with God and the creation, not as her own possession to be used for her own sake. She viewed him as a gift from God with whom she could help tend and rule the garden for God's glory. The two could enjoy what Martin Buber called an I-Thou relationship, where they could see each other as equals deserving full mutual respect.[17] They remained distinct persons who were irreducibly different but shared communion in love.

17. Martin Buber, *I and Thou*, trans. Walter Kaufmann (New York: Touchstone, 1971).

This picture of prefall innocence is "a distant echo" that we hear in our conscience when we consider what the man-woman relationship ought to be. It signals the radical gift-giving of ourselves to our spouse in marriage, in the context of which sex is without shame. When we give totally of ourselves to our spouse, we commit forever. It is no coincidence that the fruit of such total giving of body and soul—children—requires a mother and father committed to each other for life. The best social science has drawn this conclusion.[18] It also makes sense if sex is God's creation for love and procreation. God *would* have structured human persons so that sex not only produced love and children but also reinforced a lifelong nurturing environment framed by the different parenting skills of men and women. If sex is a *type* of self-giving love for others and God, one would expect God to use it to nurture the children created by it. It is another curious phenomenon that we say sex at its best is "making love" by a man and woman permanently committed to each other, and that their sexual intercourse really does "make" love, that is, increase their love for each other. This increased love then further nurtures their children.

When by God's grace married believers are able to experience nakedness without shame, they are seeing the visible sign of the invisible mystery.[19] The mystery is self-giving love that is perfectly seen in the Messiah's life and death. There we see the freedom to live for others and not ourselves, the freedom of self-offering that has as its *type* man and woman giving themselves to each other in sexual love.

What Sex Shows Us about God

I have been arguing that sex points to self-giving to another person who is irreducibly different and that it suggests the total and permanent gift of self that we saw in Jesus's gift to the people of God. But can we get more specific about what it is about *God* that sex tells us?

I suggest five things are intimated about God through sex: intimacy with truth, coinherence, Trinity, the marital union between Christ and his church, and the nature of life in heaven. First, *intimacy*. The Swiss theologian Hans

18. Ana Samuel, "The Kids Aren't All Right: New Family Structures and the 'No Differences' Claim," *Public Discourse*, June 14, 2012, http://www.thepublicdiscourse.com/2012/06/5640; Kristin Anderson Moore, Susan M. Jekielek, and Carol Emig, "Marriage from a Child's Perspective: How Does Family Structure Affect Children, and What Can We Do about It?," *Child Research Brief*, June 2002, https://www.childtrends.org/wp-content/uploads/2013/03/MarriageRB602.pdf.

19. Christopher C. Roberts, *Creation and Covenant: The Significance of Sexual Difference in the Moral Theology of Marriage* (New York: T&T Clark, 2007), 235.

Urs von Balthasar once observed that the only analogy that nature provides to intimacy with truth is the union of the sexes.[20] In other words, the Judeo-Christian tradition teaches that ultimate reality is finally about persons and love because this cosmos was created by a personal, loving God. The Christian side of that tradition says that Truth is not a principle but a person and that that person walked the earth in ancient Palestine. His disciple Paul taught that human intimacy in marriage is a divinely provided image (or *type*) of that person's union with his church (Eph. 5:25–33). So intimacy in marriage is an analogy to—or *type* of—intimacy with the divine person who is truth incarnate. Knowing the Truth is not only intellectual but also personal and affective.

Second, *coinherence*, which means one person sharing being with another. Jesus prayed to his Father, "I . . . ask . . . that they [his disciples] may all be one even as we are one, I in them and you in me, that they might be perfected into one" (John 17:20–23). The model, in a way we cannot fully understand, is Jesus's oneness with the Father. He said he is in the Father and the Father is in him. They are distinct persons who share one being. Even though we believers are separate beings one from another, somehow we can share the being he shares with the Father, and they (the Father and Son) can share our being. Jesus said that if we love him by keeping his word, then his Father will love us and, along with the Son, will come to us, and the Two will make their home with us (John 14:23). In a way similar to the Father and Son coinhering in us, we can somehow coinhere with other believers: "that they may be one even as we are one" (17:11). The coinherence of the Father and the Son is different because they are two persons in one divine being, and we believers are separate beings. Yet Jesus said there is nevertheless some similarity in the way we share being.

The similarity is best seen in the oneness of marital sexual union, where "the two become one" (Gen. 2:24; Matt. 19:5). A husband and wife are two beings who share oneness at a deep level, not just physical but personal and spiritual, and perhaps ontological—that is, at some level of being. This is seen most clearly when their union creates a child—they join their persons into one unit that produces a third being. As Budziszewski put it, at that point they become one organism in which two persons reside, and from that organism a third person arises.[21]

Robert Capon wrote of how this coinherence in marriage points to the communion of persons not only in God but also in heaven. "The meeting in

---

20. Hans Urs von Balthasar, *Prayer* (New York: Sheed & Ward, 1961), 64.
21. Budziszewski, *On the Meaning of Sex*, 87.

bed is not the end. Its greatness lies in the ends that it serves. And the greatest of them all is not the meeting of lover and beloved, of Dante and Beatrice, but the meeting of the whole Body of the Coinherence, the entrance of man into the City of God."[22] Sex gives us a glimpse of the union of persons we see in the Father and the Son and the ultimate communion of persons in the new heaven and earth.

The coinherence of the Father and the Son brings us to the *Trinity*, for it is only by the Spirit that the Father dwells in the Son and the Son in the Father. John 16:15 (ESV) epitomizes this coinherence of the Three: "All that the Father has is mine; therefore I said that he [the Spirit] will take what is mine and declare it to you." The Father gives all of himself to the Son; the Spirit takes that "all" and gives it to believers. When the Spirit brings someone to God, it is only by his taking from the Son what the Father has given to the Son. New spiritual life comes by the mutual work of all three persons in the Trinity, and the sexual union of a man and woman points to that Trinity.

The father-mother-child threesome produced by sexual union—three coming from one organism—is a *type* of the divine Three in One. Just as sexual love is only by persons being in relation, so the Trinity shows that God is a being in relation. His being *is* relation. The theology of the body speaks a language of the body that is all about relation—one body made for loving union with the other, and that loving union creating a third. Once it is created, there is an eternal relation of three in one.

If a child uniting a man and woman is a visible type of the Trinity, there is a more subtle type of the Trinity in the love between a man and a woman. That threesome—man, woman, and the love between them—is analogous to the Father and Son, who share the Spirit, who is the love between them. As Budziszewski put it, "Don't the husband, the wife, and the living love between them provide a flashing glimpse of how Three might be infinitely One?"[23]

Sexual union contains a fourth type, that which images our *Messiah's love for his church*. Paul made this meaning absolutely explicit in Ephesians 5. After telling husbands to love their wives, in the same breath he said they are to do so just as Christ loved the church and gave himself up for her (v. 27). Then he returned to husbands, telling them again to love their wives, but this time as much as they love their *bodies* and themselves (v. 28). Then once more he reverted to Christ and the church, reminding his readers that Christ nourishes

---

22. Robert Capon, "Bed and Board: Liturgies of Home," in Kass and Kass, *Wing to Wing, Oar to Oar*, 603.

23. Budziszewski, *On the Meaning of Sex*, 144.

and cares for his church "because we are limbs of *his* body" (v. 30). Just as men care for their bodies, so the Messiah cares for his.

At that point Paul pulled out the Bible's original definition of marriage and used it in an astonishing way. He went to the same Genesis 2:24 passage that Jesus used to take the Pharisees back to "the beginning" of the first marriage (Matt. 19:3–12; Mark 10:1–12). But while Jesus used this passage to explain human marriage, Paul used it to suggest that the *divine* marriage is the prototype of all human marriages. "'For this reason a man leaves behind his father and mother and cleaves to his wife, and the two become one flesh.' This is a great mystery. But I tell you that it is about Messiah and the church. This applies to all of you. So let each so love his own wife as himself, and let the wife respect her husband" (Eph. 5:31–33).

What Paul suggested in this remarkable coupling of human and divine marriage is that the original marriage is between the Messiah and his people, and that all human marriages are patterned on this divine marriage. Another way of putting it is to say that human marital love is a *type* that points to the divine antitype of the Messiah's marriage to his people. Not only are we to learn about Christ and the church from human marital unions, but we are also to get instruction from the divine marriage to apply to our human marriages. The learning goes both ways.

Augustine connected human sexual union and the divine marriage in a graphic way that will surprise most of us. "Like a bridegroom Christ went forth from his chamber, he went out with a presage of his nuptials into the field of the world. He came to the marriage bed of the cross, and there, in mounting it, he consummated his marriage. And where he perceived the sighs of the creature, he lovingly gave himself up in place of his bride, and he joined himself to the woman forever."[24] We might never before have imagined a connection between sex and the cross, but there you have it. The greatest of the fathers made that connection because he followed Paul in seeing marital union as a *type* of Christ's love for his church.

The fifth and last way that human sexuality points to God is its intimation of *heaven*. We have already heard Meilaender's suggestion that challenges from the opposite sex help to prepare us for the infinitely diverse friendships we will have in heaven. But while Meilaender focused on sexual difference on earth, Augustine believed that sexual difference makes a difference in *heaven*. It will not be used for physical sex, for that will not take place there. And it does not affect the reason, for whereas men and women will retain their sexual

---

24. Augustine, *Sermo Suppositus* 120, 8; quoted in Patrick Coffin, *Sex au naturel: What It Is and Why It's Good for Your Marriage* (Steubenville, OH: Emmaus Road, 2010), 58–59.

differences in heaven, their capacities to reason will not be different. The image of God pertains to "the spirit of [a human person's] mind," where "there is no sex."[25] Instead, for Augustine, the different sexes will have different ways of worshiping God in heaven, and those differences will enrich our worship. "[In heaven the sexual parts of a woman, but also of a man] will then be exempt from sexual intercourse and childbearing, but the female parts will nonetheless remain in being, accommodated not to the old uses, but to a new beauty, which, so far from inciting lust, which no longer exists, will move us to praise the wisdom and clemency of God."[26]

Augustine was saying that sexual difference will be redeemed in heaven. Somehow it will cause us to see God's beauty in new ways, and our praise will be that much more joyful. So for Augustine, sexual difference in this life is a type pointing to different joys in heaven.

A Testimony

Much of this chapter has been abstract. Here is a little testimony from a couple who learned from John Paul's theology of the body and used it in their marriage.

> When Alecia and I got engaged, we both were committed to a marriage that would last a lifetime and that would be grounded in faith. We both wanted lots of babies.
>
> Providentially, each of us had learned about John Paul's theology of the body just before our first date. Once we got engaged, it helped us understand the commitments we had made, but in beautiful ways. It showed us that our bodies were made to fit each other, and that they give us opportunity to image God and participate in the love of the Trinity. It reminded us that our married life was not to be about us or our happiness and fulfillment; instead, it was to be about fulfilling God's universal call to love and holiness by offering a gift of ourselves to our spouse first and then to children who might result from that gift of self.
>
> Now we have four children, and we have experienced what this theology promised. To put it simply, this view of the body's language has shown us that hugging and kissing help us become who God made us to be. Loving each other with our bodies, open to new life, is all about God working in us, making us more fully human, and bringing us to greater life and love in him.[27]

25. Augustine, *On the Trinity: Books 8–15*, trans. Stephen McKenna and Gareth Matthews (Cambridge: Cambridge University Press, 2002), 12.7.12.

26. Augustine, *City of God*, trans. R. W. Dyson (Cambridge: Cambridge University Press, 1998), 22.17.

27. John and Alecia Acquaviva, email to author, June 2, 2017, used by permission.

What about Singles?

This couple's testimony might suggest that life and love can be experienced with intensity only in marriage. That is not what they intended, and neither is it what I mean to suggest. But what *about* singles? Do virgins and celibates miss out on the spiritual joys of sex? Do they have less knowledge of God because they cannot enjoy all the types we have discussed in this chapter?

The short answer is no. In fact, they understand perhaps better than the married what it means for the body to be "spousal." This is the word for the meaning of the body used by John Paul, who was also celibate. By this he meant that the body's sexuality gives it a language that speaks the words, "This body is meant for marriage." And the marriage that the body is primarily designed for is the marriage we have just discussed, that between Christ and his church, which is *his* body. Single believers who embrace the language of their bodies already participate in that "nuptial" meaning by giving themselves in love to their heavenly bridegroom, Jesus the Messiah. They show those of us who are married the true meaning of our own bodies and the meaning of our own marriages.

What does this kind of life look like? Angelo Cardinal Scola argued that it requires "detachment" from one's "egoistical satisfaction." It treats the other person as a mysterious other who deserves to be affirmed in his or her destiny—that is, the life God intends for that person. This is what he called "Christian virginity." It is "the manner of love characteristic of Jesus Christ, which all Christians, even spouses, are therefore called to live." It is true love. It looks on one's spouse detached from all selfish desire. "If I am incapable of gazing upon the one I say I love so as to see her as she really is, in her metaphysical reality which may not correspond to what I think, want, or make her out to be, then there will never be true love."[28]

This "Christian virginity" is therefore available by the Holy Spirit to both married and single believers. It is the purity of love within marriage, and it is the love for Jesus their Husband that enables singles to taste the joy of the *marriage* supper of the Lamb.

28. Angelo Scola, *The Nuptial Mystery*, trans. Michelle K. Borras (Grand Rapids: Eerdmans, 2005), 269–70.

9

Sports

Its Agonies and Ecstasies

You can try too hard to find types in sports. For example, there are those who think Babe Ruth was mystically prophesied in Luke's Gospel: "This will be a sign to you: You will find a babe wrapped in bands of cloth and lying in a manger" (Luke 2:12). After all, the Babe was often in rumpled clothes lying to his manager.[1] Other sports fans draw comfort from the Bible's recognition that "for everything there is a season" (Eccles. 3:1 ESV).

Baseball seems to have inspired the most attention to its supposedly *typical* (containing theological types) character. Think of its holy trinities: three outs per inning, three strikes per batter, three outfielders, three-squared players (nine), three-squared innings per game, three-cubed outs per team per game (twenty-seven). All its fixed dimensions are divisible by three: the pitcher's rubber (twenty-four inches by six inches), the pitcher's mound (fifteen inches high) in the center of a circle whose diameter is eighteen feet and that stands sixty feet, six inches from home plate, and the base paths, which are ninety feet long.[2]

Some point to the fact that (major league) baseball is relatively error-free and therefore suggests the new earth, where there will be no sin. Or that its

1. Gary Graf, *And God Said, "Play Ball!" Amusing and Thought-Provoking Parallels between the Bible and Baseball* (Liguori, MO: Liguori Publications, 2005), 31.
2. Doug Hornig, *The Boys of October: How the 1975 Boston Red Sox Embodied Baseball's Ideals—and Restored Our Spirits* (Chicago: Contemporary Books, 2003), 5.

relative freedom from violence is a foretaste of the time when the lion will lie down with the lamb. In a Lutheran theology of sports—which, like its tradition, highlights our sinfulness—we are reminded that the very best players fail to reach base safely seven times out of ten, thus proving the universal need for justification.

Boston Red Sox fans might be the worst examples of those who try too hard to find theological types in sports. (True confession: I am a Sox fan.) In the 2004 American League Championship Series the Yankees were ahead three games to none, and in the fourth game were leading the Red Sox, 4–3, in the bottom of the ninth inning. Their legendary closer Mariano Rivera was on the mound, having already retired the heart of the Red Sox batting order in the previous inning with apparent ease. VIP Yankee fans left early to beat the crowds. John Sexton told a friend who was a minority Yankee owner, "If you go, you will reverse the Curse."

By that he meant the curse that Sox fans believed hung over their team since 1919, when they traded Ruth to the Yankees. Sexton recalled that he also thought of the biblical warning, "Pride goes before the fall" (Prov. 16:18).

Sexton's friend left, and the rest is history. Boston won that game and the next three, and then went on to win the 2004 World Series. The curse was broken.[3]

Sports in the Bible?

I trust you recognize that what I have written so far has been tongue-in-cheek. But is there anything serious and straightforward that can be said about the Bible and sports? Can we even go so far as to talk about theological types that might exist in sports pointing us to the Triune God? Let's see.

Sports are marginal to the Bible, but they are there nonetheless. The apostle Paul did not discuss sports directly, but he used them for analogies to the Christian life. In his letters to the church at Corinth, he wrote about a runner and a boxer. In his first letter Paul used ten separate items from a sports-specific vocabulary, including "athlete," "runner," "boxer," "beating the air," and "disqualified."[4] In 2 Timothy he referred to a wrestler (2:5).[5]

Paul was probably inspired by the Isthmian Games, the great athletic festival held every two years at Corinth. The winner's prize at those games was

3. John Sexton, *Baseball as a Road to God: Seeing beyond the Game* (New York: Gotham Books, 2013), 12–13.

4. Robert Ellis, *The Games People Play: Theology, Religion, and Sport* (Eugene, OR: Wipf & Stock, 2014), 132.

5. Ellis, *Games People Play*, 132. On Paul's metaphors, see James Hoffman, *Good Game: Christianity and the Culture of Sports* (Waco: Baylor University Press, 2010).

a wreath made of withered celery, which seems to be what Paul meant by his "perishable wreath" in 1 Corinthians 9:25. Another connection to these games for Paul was the tents in which many visitors stayed. He was a tentmaker and probably profited from the city's needs during at least one set of these games (in either AD 49 or 51).[6]

Some have wondered how Paul, a Hellenistic Jew, could have attended games that were often dedicated to pagan deities. But while Jerusalem Jews were typically opposed to all Greek games, Hellenized Jews like Paul were less so. Philo of Alexandria attended wrestling contests. At Miletus, just across the Aegean Sea from Corinth, Jews had specially reserved seats for their games.[7] But even if Paul did not participate in the games, he probably knew of them, might have attended them, and likely profited from their need for tents.

What *Are* Sports?

So Paul seems to have recognized sports' popular appeal, and therefore their usefulness for images that could communicate things about the kingdom of God. But before we think about what sports can communicate, we need to be sure we know what we mean by sports. What are they?

Whatever they are, they are immensely popular, perhaps even more than in Paul's day. Over one billion people watch the (soccer) World Cup final every four years. Half of the American public watches the Super Bowl each year. There must be a special appeal in sports, because we don't get that many people to watch the best farmers plow or the best builders put up a house.

We might add, parenthetically, that American sports have become immensely popular partly because of their colorful characters. Baseball's Yogi Berra, for example, amused millions with his unwitting humor: "It's tough to make predictions, especially about the future." "Ninety percent of the game is half-mental." Casey Stengel was another baseball legend who charmed the masses with his banter. Once in spring training, for instance, he instructed his team, "All right, everybody line up alphabetically according to your height."[8]

Sports are popular and always have been. Not only were they familiar to apostles like Paul, but the church's members have always been drawn to them. Back in the fourth century, when the Roman Empire was newly Christian, there was fierce competition in chariot racing, and the competition was

6. Ellis, *Games People Play*, 136.
7. Ellis, *Games People Play*, 136.
8. Graf, *And God Said*, 128–29.

partly theological. One team was called the Blues, who argued that God is a
Trinity. Another team, the Greens, didn't think Jesus had two natures.[9] Both
might have appealed for legitimacy to language that Paul took from chariot
racing in his letter to the Philippians: "Brothers, I myself do not think I have
arrived. But this one thing I do, forgetting the things that are behind me and
straining forward toward what is ahead, I press on toward the goal for the
prize" (3:13–14).

Christian engagement with sports has been messy. They "have been opposed and denounced at regular intervals from pulpits, Councils and imperial
thrones" because of the danger of idolatry—turning them into a god—and
sins that lurk around them such as gambling and drunkenness.[10] But because
of their popularity among Christians, the church has often tried to use them
for its own purposes. Christian leaders have found missionary and sometimes
even soteriological rationales for them,[11] even if often "there was little more
than a recognition that games are better for the masses than drinking and
fighting."[12]

Recently, theologians have tried to go deeper, probing the nature of sports.
Lincoln Harvey regarded athletic games as "liturgies of nonnecessity." "Liturgy" comes from a Greek word meaning "work of the people." Harvey said
sports consist of an *ordered* work so that, like the ordered prayers in religious
liturgy, they are a public ritual. And like any other public ritual, they proceed
under the guidance of rules.[13]

Sports are nonnecessary because we don't need them to live. The word
itself suggests this. Sport is a form of "disport," which comes from the Latin
portare ("to carry") and *dis* ("apart"). That is, sports carry us apart from our
necessary activities. They are superfluous and nonproductive for the absolute
needs of life. They create nothing necessary to us. As Harvey put it, they are
"a gratuitous waste." They are *for* nothing but themselves.[14]

Don't get me wrong. They are wonderful in all sorts of ways, also helpful
to us in ways we will soon discuss. But their only meaning is internal. There
is nothing outside of them that requires their existence. They can *provide*
meaning to us, but only after we have submitted to their rules. They exist
within a parallel universe, with their own space and rules and time. Yet they

---

9. Lincoln Harvey, *A Brief Theology of Sport* (Eugene, OR: Cascade, 2014), 32–33.

10. Harvey, *Brief Theology of Sport*, 56.

11. Here Harvey (*Brief Theology of Sport*, 54) cites Thomas Hughes's *The Manliness of Christ* (1880), in which Jesus's athleticism is a model for emulation.

12. Harvey, *Brief Theology of Sport*, 54.

13. Harvey, *Brief Theology of Sport*, 101.

14. Harvey, *Brief Theology of Sport*, 68. On the meaning of "sport," 65; for this paragraph, 62–72.

are generally free from the serious business of life. They can *suggest* ultimate things, but in themselves they are not ultimately significant.[15]

This means that the Liverpool Football Club manager Bill Shankley, while accurately expressing the way some people treat sports, was a bit off the mark: "Some people believe football [soccer] is a matter of life and death. I'm very disappointed by that attitude. I can assure you, it is much, much more important than that."[16]

Shankley risked treating sports as an idol. The Dutch historian Johan Huizinga thought sports were very important but not matters of life and death. Instead, they are about who we are. He argued that they are a form of *play* that is both fun and free. By free he meant that they express what is fundamental to us as human beings—our freedom as rational creatures. Other animals also play, but we play far more, and our play is creative in a way the play of the animals is not. Our play is integral to our culture, so much so that our species can be called *homo ludens*—the primate that plays. Francis of Assisi was the embodiment of life as play, and joyful play at that. He called himself a fool for Christ, and he loved all the animals except the ants. Why not ants? He thought they work too much and don't know how to have fun![17]

Types in Sports

If sports are about fun and play that express something about who we are, are they imprinted with types pointing to God? Scripture is not clear on this point. But if there are signs within them pointing to God, they are not primarily about moral lessons. It is true that sports can teach us moral lessons about handling success and failure, overcoming adversity, getting along with teammates, working toward a common goal, using talents, the brevity of success, friendship, and even love.[18]

But if sports are imprinted with images of the divine, they are different from morality tales. And they are not particularly easy to discern. It may be impossible to prove their existence to someone who is skeptical of divine images existing anywhere outside the Bible. As Thomas Aquinas said of rational arguments for God's existence, to one who has faith they are unnecessary, and to one without faith none will satisfy. But for those who are open to seeing

15. Harvey, *Brief Theology of Sport*, 66–69.
16. Quoted in Ellis, *Games People Play*, 5.
17. On play, see Ellis, *Games People Play*, 2–4, 125–29; on Francis, see Harvey, *Brief Theology of Sport*, 72n3.
18. Graf, *And God Said*, 53–54.

God's footprints in the world, images that point to life in the Triune God can be seen in sports just as in nature. Let me suggest eight such images.

1. Sports are *free creations*. This is an elaboration of Huizinga's free play. We human beings create sports freely, which means we make up the rules for each sport. We adjust those rules when we play at home or in the neighborhood because we are free to do so. In a similar way, God was free to create or not. He was a perfectly happy Trinity of persons, a joyous society of Three that had no need for more fellowship or love. Nothing required God to create a world beyond himself or to create this world as opposed to some other world. He was and is free, and so are we. The sports that we devise show that freedom in a special way.[19]

If sports are free, they are also creative. Each sport is the creation of a new world of its own, with its own laws and leaders and stars. God is the only one who creates out of nothing. Our creations, including sports, are subcreations because they use ideas and things that God originally gave to us. But since they bring into existence something that was not there before, they are images of things in God's creation that he brought out of nothing.

2. Sports are *unnecessary*. They don't have to be. Unless we are in the business of sports, they are unnecessary to our existence, illustrations of the "inescapable lightness of being."[20] Scripture suggests that we are held in existence moment by moment only by God's continuing will. Consider the image from Jonathan Edwards's famous sermon "Sinners in the Hands of an Angry God" of a spider hanging by a silky thread over an open flame. Only God's goodness keeps that spider out of the reach of the flame, preventing its destruction. We are like that spider, kept from destruction every nanosecond only by God's love.

If these things are true, and Scripture suggests they are, then sin is our insistence on our necessity. It is our choice to live as if we were independent of God. It is denial of our contingency, our refusal to admit that we live only by grace. It is taking ourselves too seriously, thinking we are more than we are—imagining we exist by our own choices rather than God's choice to continue to sustain us nanosecond by nanosecond.

If we choose this way of thinking, then our sports will be distorted. We will take *them* too seriously. They won't be fun anymore because we will have taken what are unnecessary and considered them necessary. We will have treated sports as essential to life rather than as beautiful but nonessential gifts. After all, there are other ways to relax and enjoy drama, such as watching a good

19. Harvey, *Brief Theology of Sport*, 79, 108.
20. Harvey, *Brief Theology of Sport*, 81, 108.

movie. And we can stay fit by other means like weight lifting or jogging. Sports are a kind of celebration of life, a way to enhance life. The minute we turn them into the purpose of life, we have transformed a gift into a demon. But if we do sports with what Doug Webster called "intensity without ultimacy," we can dive headfirst into games with "holy indifference."[21] It's a passion for play but commitment to God alone.

3. *God plays*, so sports show us something of the divine character when we see them as play. More than a few theologians have noted a playful aspect in God's joy. Proverbs tells us that the wisdom of God during the works of creation "was daily God's delight, *playing* (or *sporting*) before him at all times" (Prov. 8:30). The early church father Gregory of Nazianzus wrote that "the sublime Word plays in all kinds of forms, judging His world as He wishes, on this side and on that."[22] Modern theologian Romano Guardini observed that in the Proverbs 8 passage "the Son 'plays' before the Father." This, he said, is characteristic of the highest beings, the most stunning examples of which are the flaming cherubim of Ezekiel 1. They moved this way and that for no human purpose, but simply to follow the Spirit for the glory of God. In this way they became "a living song before Him."[23] Guardini said we can see this quality best in the creativity of an artist and the play of a child. Neither has a purpose for what he or she does other than the sheer joy of doing it. They are expressing what they were created by God to be and do.[24] You hear this joy in Olympic runner Eric Liddell's words in the movie *Chariots of Fire*: "When I run, I feel His [God's] pleasure." The artist, the child, and Liddell suggest that joy comes in the doing—the play—which has no social purpose outside the play. The play is the thing, and nothing else matters.

Scripture tells us in Ecclesiastes that different kinds of play were made for us by God: music and the human form (2:8), food and drink (2:24; 9:7), laughter and dancing (3:4), love and lovemaking (3:5, 8), relaxing (4:6; 5:12), material prosperity (5:19; 7:12–13), wine (9:7), and one's spouse (9:9).[25]

Zechariah wrote that play is integral to the new heaven and new earth: "And the plazas of the city will be full of boys and girls playing in those broad

21. Doug Webster, "Intensity without Ultimacy: A Christian Perspective on Sports," *The Other Journal: An Intersection of Theology and Culture*, March 21, 2016, https://theotherjournal .com/2016/03/21/intensity-without-ultimacy-christian-perspective-sports.

22. Quoted by Maximus the Confessor in his *Ambiguum* 71, in Maximos, *The Ambigua*, vol. 2, ed. and trans. Nicholas Constas (Cambridge, MA: Harvard University Press, 2014), 313.

23. Romano Guardini, *The Spirit of the Liturgy*, trans. Ada Lane (London: Sheed & Ward, 1935), 97–98.

24. Guardini, *Spirit of the Liturgy*, 98–105.

25. Ellis, *Games People Play*, 146.

places" (Zech. 8:5). Sports at their best remind us of a future time and world of play.

4. Sports are *unproductive*. They don't produce profit for most of us. In fact, they often drain us of money. Furthermore, they don't help us get on in the world. Unless, that is, we stay healthy by participating in them and we gain emotional release. Those benefits are important, but they are not direct or tangible gains. Also, spectator sports can bring a boatload of disappointment. Yet for all of these ways in which sports do not produce, they sometimes deliver a measure of joy.

We can say something similar for worship. It doesn't produce anything directly, nor does it help us advance in the world, at least not in any direct way. It is the celebration of God and his goodness. It is also joy, to the degree that we enter into its fullness. It is a joy that the world will never experience and cannot comprehend. Outsiders will always ask, "Why this waste?" (Matt. 26:8 ESV). Even insiders will sometimes wonder. The time and effort, and often money, that are given to worship seem wasteful to those who do not see the beauty of holiness. To them it will always seem unproductive and therefore wasteful.

Worship, however, *does* produce one thing, which is something the world cannot measure—God's glory. We cannot say the same for sports, of course. God might be glorified by individuals turning to him during or because of a game, but there is nothing intrinsic in sports that brings him glory in the way that worship does. In that sense, sports are particularly unproductive. But at the same time they are perhaps a dim image of this other devotion that can seem so wasteful.

5. Sports are *discomfiting*. I have followed the Boston Red Sox for more than five decades, fairly religiously until several years ago, when one season's team got fat and lazy. Or so it seemed to this fan, who had been inspired most years by what he took to be hustle and grit.

For most of those decades I was dispirited by defeat and elated in victory, but almost always more by the former. Until 2004 the Red Sox were among the most legendary losers in professional sports. But that's a good thing. Sports, even at their best, are not supposed to comfort us perpetually. After all, they're about winning and losing, and for every winner there must be a loser. Or in some sports like track, many losers. If they are honest and not corrupted, they reflect real life, where things are often unfair and there is plenty of loss.

Here there is some similarity to true religion. C. S. Lewis wrote, "[I don't] go to religion to make me happy. I always knew a bottle of port would do that. If you want a religion to make you feel comfortable, I certainly don't recommend Christianity."[26] Sports, like faith in the trinitarian God of Israel, often make us feel discomfited, out of sorts. They rub us the wrong way because they challenge our preferences. If they did not, they would not be the real article. Either the sport would be fixed, or the religion would be idolatrous.

6. Sports have *their own time*. The world of work and advancement keeps one time, and the world of sports another. Think of a steamy August evening when it is 8:00 p.m. at a restaurant in Chicago's North Side, but in the baseball game at Wrigley Field it is the middle of the third inning. That's the only time that matters for the game. If one team has a big inning, the third inning might not end until 9:00 p.m. Then the relevant time would not be 9:00 but the end of the third inning. Similarly, the church has its own time. At the restaurant it is two hours to closing, at the ballpark it's one-third the way through the game, but for the church it is time for evening prayer. The time of year is also different. In baseball it is near the end of the season, in business it is slow season because people are on vacation, and in the church it is the middle of Ordinary Time, or Pentecost season.[27]

If sports, like God's kingdom, have their own times, they also share a sense of timelessness. All serious fans and players remember occasions when time seemed to stand still because of the drama or intensity of the game. They lose track of the clock and seem to be lifted out of linear time. This is what happens when we are transfixed by the beauty of a piece of music or art. It also happens in worship when we are so captured by the beauty of God or the gratuity of grace that we forget who and what we are. It is akin to what happens in the Eucharist when we are lifted into sacramental time, when we are joined to Jesus at Calvary and the resurrection. The time of Jesus back then becomes fused with our time today. At those times we might recognize that the occasional sense of timelessness in sport is an analogue or image of what happens in the sacrament.

7. In sports there are *winners and losers*. We all know it doesn't matter in the big scheme of things whether the Nationals win the pennant or whether Tiger Woods will ever win another tournament. So to pray for our favorite team might be putting God to a test, which we are commanded by Jesus not to do (Matt. 4:7). As Robert Benne asked, "Why should God care who wins in an athletic contest?"[28] After all, the Bible suggests that losing is often better than winning for developing character (2 Cor. 12:9–10).

26. C. S. Lewis, "Answers to Questions on Christianity," in *God in the Dock* (San Francisco: HarperCollins, 2014), 48.
27. Ellis, *Games People Play*, 151–60.
28. Robert Benne, "Does God Favor the Yankees?," unpublished paper loaned by the author.

Yet the *idea* of winning is biblical. The fathers had it right when they said that a nondispensable aspect of Jesus's atonement was his *victory* over Satan and his dark powers. We can see this dynamic in the Gospels when Jesus "set his face to go to Jerusalem" (Luke 9:51 ESV). He headed resolutely toward the city that "kills the prophets and stones those who are sent to it" (13:34 ESV). He was determined to do battle. He set his own time for conflict, when he was ready to fight demons and disease and death by confronting the prince of darkness himself. His aim was to *conquer* the devil and all his works (Matt. 12:28; Acts 10:38; Heb. 2:14–15).

The upshot is that there are losers—not only the devil and his minions but all those who side with them. Not everyone will get a ribbon for participating in life. Some will be winners, and some losers. Sports make no final difference in eternity, but they are signs that point to what does. The winning and losing we see in our games are signs of what lies ahead, and therefore what *is* ultimate.

8. Sports are *occasions for gratitude*. James Nuechterlein wrote he was weary of "deep-think interpretations that impose on sports events a burden of meaning they cannot bear."[29] For Nuechterlein, sport is simply a grace—a minor grace—that relieves the weight of life. It reminds us not to take ourselves too seriously by its "absurd elevation of the trivial." The games we watch and play offer us "a pleasurable interlude in life" for which we don't need to repent but for which we should be grateful. The apostle Paul wrote that the most basic sin is ingratitude: "Although they knew God, they did not glorify him as God or give thanks" (Rom. 1:21). If we give thanks for sports and the ways they give us a respite from the burdens of life, we are on our way to knowing our Creator and how to live under him. As Brian Bolt put it, "When we do sports well, we nurture love [for the game] as a spectacular gift and remind ourselves of the giver of all good things."[30]

But Are They Types?

Of all the realms we have considered so far—nature, modern science, natural law, history, animals, sexuality, and sports—the last has the weakest support for displaying types. That is why I have used the word "images" in the above paragraphs, not "types." There is little doubt that we can find images or reflections in sports that remind us of things in God's kingdom, but Scripture

29. James Nuechterlein, "The Weird World of Sports," *First Things*, June 1998, https://www.firstthings.com/article/1998/06/001-the-weird-world-of-sports.

30. Brian Bolt, quoted in Webster, "Christian Perspective."

says precious little about the world of games. Only in jest would we argue that the Preacher had sports in mind when he wrote, "For everything there is a season" (Eccles. 3:1 ESV). The only one of the eight images above that might qualify as biblically endorsed is play, which, as we have seen, could be called a divine activity. In that sense all play—including the play of sports—might be the surfacing of a God-like predilection, a sign that we were made in the image of the One who is delight. If sports are not God-planted *types* in the creation—and there is no clear biblical reason to say that they are—they are images or signs that we were created by a God who plays.

10

World Religions

So Similar and Yet So Different

Are people outside the Judeo-Christian tradition totally ignorant of God? Not according to the authors of Scripture. The Bible casts its light on a wide array of people outside Israel and the church who had some knowledge of the true God. Even the wicked were not without some knowledge of God and his ways. The pagan prophet Balaam, for example, whom the New Testament condemned for leading Israel into idolatry and immorality (2 Pet. 2:15; Jude 11), prophesied truly about the future of God's chosen people (Num. 24). Pharaoh's magicians recognized "the finger of God" after the plague of gnats (Exod. 8:19). Pharaoh himself confessed several times that he had sinned against YHWH, thus showing some knowledge of sin, even if his repentance was insincere (9:27; 10:16). People in the Bible can be wicked and clearly outside God's kingdom but at the same time know something of God or his ways.

Pagans in the Bible with Some Knowledge of God

Then there are Bible characters whose spiritual status is unclear but who clearly had some knowledge of God. The Syrian general Naaman, who was healed of leprosy by YHWH, confessed that as a result he learned "there is no God in all the earth except in Israel" (2 Kings 5:15). Nebuchadnezzar said something similar about the God of Israel after Daniel interpreted his dream, and then again after the three young Jews survived the fiery furnace. When he regained his sanity after mental illness, he testified to the God of Israel as the "king of heaven" (Dan. 2:46–47; 3:28; 4:34–37). When Darius saw that Daniel emerged alive after a night with hungry lions, he commanded all the people of the earth to "tremble and fear before the God of Daniel" (6:26 ESV).

Other people in the Bible were outside Israel but seemed to know the true God. Melchizedek was a Canaanite priest who blessed Abraham in the name of "El Elyon, Creator of heaven and earth." Abraham responded by hailing "YHWH, El Elyon, Creator of heaven and earth," thus implying that Melchizedek and Abraham worshiped the same God (Gen. 14:19, 22). The author of Hebrews seemed to think so, for he wrote that Melchizedek's blessing of Abraham showed "beyond dispute" that Melchizedek was Abraham's "superior." He added that Melchizedek resembled "the Son of God" because he "continues a priest forever" (Heb. 7:7, 3 ESV).[1]

The Canaanite prostitute Rahab heard from afar of the God of Israel and decided to cast her lot with the people of that God (Josh. 2:10–11). We can infer from the story that Rahab and her family joined the people of Israel and came to embrace the revelation that YHWH made to the Israel of her day.

Hiram the king of Tyre was more ambiguous. He told Solomon that he could see that Solomon's God YHWH was the One who "made heaven and earth" (2 Chron. 2:12). We don't know whether Hiram committed himself to YHWH. If not, he was like Naaman, Nebuchadnezzar, and Darius, who were pagans with some knowledge of the God of Israel.

We have evidence for other pagans with true religious knowledge in the New Testament. When he preached to pagan philosophers in Athens, Paul quoted two pagan poets (Epimenides and Aratus, sixth and third centuries BC) as if to say they had knowledge of God, even if broken and imperfect: "'In him we live and move and have our being'; as even some of your own poets have said, 'For we too are his offspring'" (Acts 17:28). Paul was affirming the accuracy of these poets' words. He was not saying they were saved—not by a long shot—but he was clearly suggesting that they knew some true things about God and his ways with people.

1. Daniel Strange argued that Melchizedek and other so-called holy pagans gained their knowledge of the true God by special revelation from YHWH and usually came into contact with Israel or the church. Perhaps so, but in the case of Melchizedek we do not know this from the text. Moreover, one thinks of Job, who seemed to have had no contact with Israel, thus rendering less than conclusive Strange's suggestion that Old Testament saints "were never pagans but confessed Christ albeit in an embryonic way." Daniel Strange, *The Possibility of Salvation among the Unevangelized: An Analysis of Inclusivism in Recent Evangelical Theology* (Eugene, OR: Wipf & Stock, 2002), 179–89, 195.

If the Bible shows *individual* pagans with some true knowledge of God, what about truth in the world religions? We already saw in chapter 5 that most of the great religions agree on the principles behind the Ten Commandments and that Confucian ethics bear remarkable similarities to Judeo-Christian principles. Are there also religious truths in the great religions—truths about God and his ways of saving us?

Buddhist Similarities

Christians are familiar with the biblical admonition not to confuse our own thoughts and words with those of God: "My thoughts are not your thoughts, and my ways are not your ways, YHWH declares. As high as the heavens are above the earth, so too my ways are higher than your ways, and my thoughts than your thoughts" (Isa. 55:8–9). Surprisingly, we find a similar warning in Buddhism. Siddhārtha Gautama Buddha (ca. 448–386 BC) and his successors stressed that ultimate reality lies far beyond our ideas about it. They said that, compared with our thinking and talking about reality, actual reality is "empty." It cannot be filled with our concepts and images, for every human thought and picture is limited by space and time, whereas ultimate reality is unlimited. So there is no one-to-one correspondence between our thinking and what really is.[2]

Thomas Aquinas agreed. God's "essence," he wrote, "is above everything that the mind is capable of apprehending in this life." All of our thinking about God is "not confined by the meaning of our word but goes beyond it." Therefore, our knowledge of God "is not a knowledge of his essence, but a knowledge that is dark and mirrored, and from afar."[3]

2. For some representative primary texts that illustrate this doctrine, see "Essence of the Wisdom Sutra," in *Buddhism: A Religion of Infinite Compassion; Selections from Buddhist Literature*, ed. Clarence H. Hamilton (Indianapolis: Bobbs-Merrill, 1952), 113–15; Paul Reps, ed., *Zen Flesh, Zen Bones: A Collection of Zen and Pre-Zen Writings* (New York: Doubleday, n.d.), esp. nos. 21, 36, 42 in "101 Zen Stories" and nos. 1, 5, 23 in "The Gateless Gate"; and *The Platform Sutra of the Sixth Patriarch: The Text of the Tun-Huang Manuscript*, trans. Philip B. Yampolsky (New York: Columbia University Press, 1967). For a more general introduction to both early and later Buddhist writings, see E. A. Burtt, ed., *The Teachings of the Compassionate Buddha: Early Discourses, the Dhammapada, and Later Basic Writings* (New York: Signet Classics, 1955). For secondary overviews of Buddhist thought, see A. L. Herman, *An Introduction to Buddhist Thought: A Philosophic History of Indian Buddhism* (Lanham, MD: University Press of America, 1983); and Kenneth Ch'en, *Buddhism in China: A Historical Survey* (Princeton: Princeton University Press, 1964).

3. Thomas Aquinas, *Summa theologica*, trans. Domican Fathers, 5 vols., rev. ed. 1920 (Notre Dame, IN: Christian Classics, 1981), I, q. 12, art. 13, ad 1; q. 13, art. 5; Aquinas, *Commentary on the Gospel of St. John* 1:18 (no. 211). Thomas did not deny personal knowledge of God in Christ that is intimate, but he insisted that it was still "through a glass, darkly" (1 Cor. 13:12 KJV).

Most Christian theologians have agreed with Thomas on this point.[4] They have also agreed that we and this world are radically dependent on God. Philosophers use the word *contingent* for things that do not have their own independent existence but depend on something else to *be*. This too is a concept that overlaps with Buddhist thinking. Buddhists talk about *dependent origination*, which for them means that nothing exists on its own with independent substance, but that everything depends on every other thing. There is an infinite network of causation, apart from which no one thing exists. Nothing is without cause, and the cause of each thing is the infinite concatenation of all other things.

Christians believe that "in Christ" all things in reality are "held together" (Col. 1:17). This means that nothing subsists on its own by itself, and if not for Christ, not only the cosmos but also each thing would cease to exist. Jonathan Edwards interpreted this statement to mean that each thing at each moment exists only by God's thinking that thing at that moment by means of his eternal Word (Christ). Each thing or person or event is therefore an instance of God's communication. As the American colonial thinker Samuel Johnson put it, "Things are God's words in print." The Buddha was for all practical purposes an atheist and so did not believe in a divine cause for things. But he did agree with Edwards and other Christian theologians that there is no independent substance and that everything depends for its existence on a vast web of relations.[5]

Finally, later developments in Buddhism taught something similar to Christian grace. The Buddha did not teach this idea, but a later Pure Land school of Mahayana Buddhism preached not only that we can do nothing good on our own but also that we need divine aid to accomplish anything worthwhile. Shinran (1173–1262) was the Japanese founder of Jodo-Shin-shu (Pure Land True Sect). He said that we should reject all "ways of effort" if we want to be saved from endless rebirths and that we must rely on "the power of the other." By this he meant the power of Amida Buddha, a later buddha who, unlike the original Buddha, was regarded by Shinran as a deity dispensing

    4. See, for example, William C. Placher, *The Domestication of Transcendence* (Philadelphia: Westminster John Knox, 1996), 31.
    5. Samuel Johnson, *Technologia sive technometria*, in *Samuel Johnson, President of King's College: His Career and Writings*, ed. Herbert Schneider and Carol Schneider, 4 vols. (New York: Columbia University Press, 1929), 2:67; Jonathan Edwards, "Of Atoms," in *Scientific and Philosophical Writings* (New Haven: Yale University Press, 1980), 215. On Edwards's ontology, see Stephen H. Daniel, *The Philosophy of Jonathan Edwards: A Study in Divine Semiotics* (Bloomington: Indiana University Press, 1994), esp. chap. 3. On the Buddha's view of substance and relation, see Raimundo Pannikar, *The Silence of God: The Answer of the Buddha*, trans. Robert R. Barr (Maryknoll, NY: Orbis, 1989), 23, 28, 55–56.

helps. Amida Buddha would bring to his Pure Land (a kind of heaven) all those who put their faith in him.

Shinran's description of inner selfishness sounds like the apostle Paul or Augustine:

> In their outward seeming are all men diligent and truth speaking,
> But in their souls are greed and anger and unjust deceitfulness.
> And in their flesh do lying and cunning triumph.[6]

Shinran recognized, in a way similar to that of Isaiah in his description of our righteous deeds as "filthy rags" (Isa. 64:6), that even his outer goodness was tainted within: "Even my righteous deeds, being mingled with this poison, must be named the deeds of deceitfulness. . . . I, whose mind is filled with cunning and deceit as the poison of reptiles, am impotent to practice righteous deeds."[7] He hoped for divine mercy, using words that sound strangely like Martin Luther's.

> There is no mercy in my soul. The good of my fellow man is not dear
>   in mine eyes.
> If it were not for the Ark of Mercy,
> The divine promise of the Infinite Wisdom,
> How should I cross the Ocean of Misery?[8]

We will see that Buddhist ideas of dependence and grace are different from their Christian counterparts in profound ways. But it is nevertheless arresting to see these surface similarities, and we may well wonder why they are there.

Daoist Similarities

Most readers know little about Daoism, though some might remember the Dao De Jing from its popularity among hippies in the 1960s and '70s. This is the text from the fourth century BC that, along with the Zhuang-zi, is at the roots of philosophical Daoism, which is different from religious Daoism.[9] One reason that hippies fifty years ago found these texts captivating is the

---

6. Shinran's Confession, in Hamilton, *Buddhism*, 141–42.
7. Shinran's Confession, 141–42.
8. Shinran's Confession, 141–42.
9. Religious Daoists believe in gods with saving power, sinful human nature, and redemption from guilt and sin by prayer, penance, and alchemy. They seek immortality. But philosophical Daoists are atheists who do not believe in life after death. Nevertheless, they believe in a hidden reality that they call the Dao, which animates the cosmos. See chap. 7 in Gerald McDermott,

same reason they found the New Testament so compelling. Both teach the paradoxical nature of reality, that, among other paradoxes, strength often comes through weakness. The Old Testament tells the story of God telling Gideon he had to become weaker before God would use him. And in the New Testament Paul told the story of his "thorn in the flesh," where it was only through his weakness that he could experience the power of Christ (2 Cor. 12:9–10). The most stunning illustration of this paradox, however, is the cross of Jesus. It was through the humiliating agony of crucifixion that God brought salvation to the world.

Daoists do not recognize the cross of Christ, nor do they usually believe the Bible is inspired. But they agree that the Dao—their word for the ultimate power that moves all of reality—works through weakness and in furtive ways. The Dao De Jing asserts that by a "mysterious power" there is a "producing without possessing, doing without presuming, growing without domineering."[10] Even when it seems there is no plan, things appear to happen according to purpose. "The Way is always uncontrived, yet there's nothing it doesn't do. . . . By not wanting, there is calm, and the world will straighten itself. . . . Higher virtue is uncontrived, and there is no way to contrive it. . . . Nobility is rooted in humility, loftiness is based on lowliness. That is why noble people refer to themselves as alone, lacking and unworthy."[11]

Strangely, things seem to arise out of nothing: "When the potter's wheel makes a pot, the use of the pot is precisely where there is nothing. When you open doors and windows for a room, it is where there is nothing that they are useful to a room."[12]

So if we want to go higher in life, the best way is to lower ourselves: "The reason why rivers and seas can be lords of the hundred valleys is that they lower themselves to them well. . . . So when sages wish to rise above people, they lower themselves in their speech. When they want to precede people, they go after them in status. . . . Because they do not contend, no one in the world can contend with them."[13]

The reverse is also true. Those who are strong and presumptuous often fail: "Should you want to weaken something, you must deliberately let it grow strong. Should you want to eliminate something, you must deliberately allow it to flourish." The Dao De Jing observes that "those who assert themselves

---

Can Evangelicals Learn from World Religions? Jesus, Revelation, and Religious Traditions (Downers Grove, IL: InterVarsity, 2000).

   10. Thomas Cleary, trans., The Essential Tao (San Francisco: HarperSanFrancisco, 1993), 10.
   11. Cleary, Essential Tao, 37.
   12. Cleary, Essential Tao, 11.
   13. Cleary, Essential Tao, 66.

are not illustrious; those who glorify themselves have no merit, those who are proud of themselves do not last."[14] The text concludes with words nearly identical to Paul's in 2 Corinthians 12:10: "Weakness overcomes strength."[15]

Muslim Similarities

While most of this book's readers might know little of Buddhism and even less of Daoism, many have learned at least a modicum about Islam in the decades since 2001. We have heard perhaps more than we want to know about radical or jihadist Islam. Many might not know, however, that Islam is similar to Christianity in a number of ways. For example, Muslims agree with Christians that there is only one God and that he is a person. This statement might sound obvious and not worth mentioning to some. But a good part of the Hindu world is polytheistic, and large parts of the Buddhist, Daoist, and Hindu worlds are monistic or nondual, which means they believe that all is one, and therefore there cannot be a personal god. For if all is one, there are no final distinctions. No distinctions, say, between you and this book you are reading. Therefore no distinction between a supposed god and the world. And if there are no distinctions between god and the world, then that "god" cannot be a person, for a person is distinct from all that is outside that person. For this reason philosophical Hindus, Buddhists, and Daoists do not speak of ultimate reality as a "he" or a "she." Those words would imply a person with mind, will, and emotions. Instead, for them ultimate reality is *im*personal. If anything, reality is "it." Or better, simply all that is.

So for Muslims to say that God is a person distinguishes their religion from other great religions, and it is another point where they agree with Christians. They also agree with Christians that God is moral. This too might at first seem not worth mentioning, but all monistic religions (i.e., those that say that all is one) reject the notion that ultimate reality is moral. Even the Buddha, who had lots to say about the moral life (as we saw in chap. 5), referred to the moral life as a provisional raft that can be left behind once we attain our final goal of nirvana. So ultimate reality is *not* moral. In nirvana we will see, Buddha would say, that there is no final difference between good and evil.

Muslims disagree, as do Christians. We believe that good and evil are not simply temporary arrangements that evaporate once we reach eternity, but that they are rooted in God's eternal reality: good is defined by God's being and will, and evil is departure from God and his will.

14. Cleary, *Essential Tao*, 35, 24.
15. Cited in Lin Yutang, *From Pagan to Christian* (London: Beinemann, 1960), 125.

So Islam shares some profound agreements with Christianity, and they are not to be taken for granted: there is a God, and this God is personal and moral. Muslims also agree that the Bible is the Word of God and that Jesus is the Word of God! I will show in just a few pages that there are critical limitations to both of those Muslim beliefs, but they are intriguing nonetheless.

So are a range of other shared convictions. In a day when we regularly hear about jihadist Islamists killing innocents, it is important that we know we share commonalities with Muslims who reject this militant form of Islam.

1. *The need for forgiveness.* Muslims deny the Christian doctrine that grace from God is wholly unmerited. But the Qur'an insists that all human beings need forgiveness.[16] The text repeats incessantly that Allah is "forgiving, merciful," and "ever relenting" (e.g., 3:31; 4:100, 106; 110:3). It even claims that Allah is "the best of forgivers" (7:155). According to an important Muslim commentator, "Man's nature is weak, and he may have to return again and again for mercy. So long as he does it sincerely, Allah is Oft-returning, Most Merciful." This Muslim theologian went on to suggest that our weakness requires divine help: "For His grace helps out the sinner's shortcomings."[17] In several places in the Qur'an readers are urged to ask forgiveness lest they be consumed by the fires of hell: "Our Lord, truly we believe, so forgive us our sins, and shield us from the punishment of the Fire" (3:16).[18]

Muslims put more trust in their own obedience to save them than Christians do. But the Pelagian character of Islam is sometimes exaggerated. The scholar of Islam Valerie J. Hoffman pointed to the popular hadith (an alleged saying of the Prophet) that compares the family of the Prophet to Noah's ark. Only by clinging to that family will a person be saved from the flood of God's judgment. In other words, Muslims' salvation comes more from that family's obedience than from their own.[19] Hoffman added, "Despite what Christians say about Muslims, Muslims don't believe God will simply stack good deeds against bad—in fact, such a perspective is very frightening to Muslims, who

16. For this section I am using Seyyed Hossein Nasr, ed., *The Study Quran* (New York: HarperOne, 2015).

17. *The Holy Qur'an: English Translation of the Meanings and Commentary,* ed. The Presidency of Islamic Researches (Medina: King Fahd Holy Qur'an Printing Complex, 1991?), 2:38n.

18. See also 3:160: "If God helps you, none shall overcome you. And if he forsakes you, who then can help you thereafter? And in God let the believers trust."

19. See Valerie J. Hoffman-Ladd, "Devotion to the Prophet and His Family in Contemporary Egyptian Sufism," *International Journal of Middle East Studies* 24 (1992): 615–37; Valerie J. Hoffman, *Sufism, Mystics, and Saints in Modern Egypt* (Columbia: University of South Carolina Press, 1995).

are well aware of their faults. They tend to place their hope in God's mercy and the Prophet's intercession for them."[20]

Even if Muslims deny the Christian doctrine of original sin, the tradition does not have an optimistic view of human nature. Humans are seen to be involved in "wrongdoing" and "ungrateful" (Qur'an 14:34). Allah himself seems exasperated: "May man perish! How ungrateful is he!" (80:17). In their pride, men ascribe their good fortune to their own merits rather than God's grace: "When harm befalls man, he calls upon Us. Then, when We confer upon him a blessing from Us, he says, 'I was only given it because of knowledge'" (39:49).

2. *Redemptive suffering.* Most Muslims believe we must suffer and atone for our own sins. Yet there is a tradition among the 20 percent of Muslims who are Shiites (those who believe that Muhammad's son-in-law Ali, not Abu Bakr, should have been Muhammad's first successor) that the sufferings of the assassinated Husayn, Muhammad's grandson, were a "ransom for his people, for Mankind."[21] However different from Jesus's redemptive suffering (e.g., he was a sinless God-man, but Husayn was a sinful man), it is a point of contact that Christians might use when trying to explain Jesus to a Shiite.

3. *Submission to God.* Christians believe we must submit to God because Scripture commands it (James 4:7). But while adoration and love for God are the heart of Christian discipleship, submission is primary for Muslims. In fact, "submission" is the literal meaning of the word "Islam." The Qur'an tells its readers that submission is the essence of all true religion (3:19). Many Muslims obey in order to earn paradise, but they are told to obey regardless of their personal desires. One is not to bend the knee because it will make the Muslim feel good or bring worldly benefit, but only because God is God. Muslims proclaim that God alone is great, and that all of us will have to face him at his fearful judgment seat. Therefore it makes sense, they believe, to submit every detail of our lives to him by obeying his commands. To give preference to anything else—money, family, success, sensual pleasure—is to commit the ultimate sin of *shirk*, idolatry. If our sins are more than our obedience, then we will face searing wind and boiling water in hell.

In one sense, Islam is Christianity without grace. It is law without redemption. But even if as a whole it is finally a false and destructive religion, its parts can be seen as distortions of what is true in Christianity. One of those distorted but partly true parts is its insistence that we are to *submit* before the awesome Ruler of the cosmos, whether it seems helpful to us personally or not.

---

20. From my correspondence with Professor Hoffman, 1999.

21. Hamadi ibn Abdullah al-Buhri, *Utenzi wa Sayedina Huseni*; quoted in John L. Esposito, *Islam: The Straight Path*, 3rd ed. (New York: Oxford University Press, 1998), 112.

4. *Creation as a theater of God's glory*. Another one of those distorted but true parts is Islam's celebration of creation as full of "signs" of God's glory. In other words, even Muhammad recognized the types in nature. The Qur'an claims that the mere existence of the heavens and earth are signs of God. So are the daily changes of night and day, rain that takes brown earth and makes it green, the multiplicity of animals, lightning that produces both fear and hope, and stars that guide us through the darkness. Muhammad marveled at the winds and storms with their showers. All of these beautiful "signs" are for the "intelligent" to learn that God rules the world and will call us before his judgment (2:163–64; 6:97; 30:22–25, 48).

Human culture is also full of signs from God: ships that are carried by winds from God and agriculture, which shows God's bounty and rule. God's acts of providence in history are other signs (30:23, 46; 31:31). For example, God had mercy on humanity by saving Noah's family while sending just judgment to the rest of humankind. Even languages are divine signs: their beauty and complexity show an intelligent Designer (30:22; 33:41).

The most striking sign of all is the human person. Just as Paul said in Romans 2:14–15, a person's conscience is a testimony to God's moral law and our responsibility to comply. The varied complexions of our skins and our sleep are also signs (Qur'an 30:23; 90:10; 91:7–8).

Yet despite the world's being filled with signs, most people refuse to acknowledge them or listen to their testimony. Because of pride and perversity, they turn to various forms of *shirk* (idolatry). They will reap the fires of hell because they turn away from God's clear proofs of his reality (3:21; 7:36, 177; 30:10; 31:7, 32; 33:10, 46).

5. *Regular and theocentric prayer*. Like Christians, Muslims are told to pray regularly. But while Christians are told to "pray without ceasing" (1 Thess. 5:17) and most churches encourage believers to pray at least daily, Muslims are given more specific instructions. The two greatest Islamic communities, Sunnis and Shiites, instruct their followers to pray five times every day: early morning, noon, midafternoon, sunset, and evening. At each of those times Muslims recite several set prayers of worship, praise, and gratitude. They repeat the first sura (chapter) of the Qur'an, which praises Allah as creator and sustainer, gracious and merciful, master of the day of judgment, and then ask for help to follow the "straight path." Only at the end do Muslims say a short prayer for their own personal needs.[22]

There are similarities here to the Lord's Prayer given us by Jesus. The emphasis is not on our personal needs (though we ask for our daily bread

22. Frederick M. Denny, *An Introduction to Islam* (New York: Macmillan, 1985), 105–11.

and forgiveness of our sins) but on God's praise and glory. By using this set prayer, we are reminded that the Christian tradition has prayers that are usually richer than what we can compose on our own, and that a balanced prayer life contains praise and thanksgiving as well as petition.

6. *Charity to the poor.* Christians are reminded of our obligation to help the poor in nearly every book of the Bible, from Genesis to Revelation. A similar emphasis appears in the Qur'an. Almsgiving, which in the Islamic tradition is usually directed to other Muslims, is one of the duties that defines righteousness. "Piety is he who believes in God, the Last Day, the angels, the Book, and the prophets; and who gives wealth, despite loving it, to kinsfolk, orphans, the indigent, the traveler, beggars, and for [the ransom of] slaves" (2:177). The unrighteous are condemned for not caring for orphans, who in premodern society were without the primary social security of family (89:17–18). Like the epistle of James (1:27), the Qur'an defines true religion as helping the poor, so the one without religion is he who "drives away the orphan, and does not urge feeding the indigent. So woe unto the praying who are heedless of their prayers, those who strive to be seen, yet refuse small kindnesses" (107:1–7).

Helping the poor is so important that it is part of social discipline. The person who fails to fulfill an oath must expiate his sin by "the feeding of ten indigent people with the equivalent of that which you feed your own family, or clothing them, or freeing a slave" (5:89). Inattention to the poor is a reason for condemnation to hell. Some will be asked, "What led you into *Saqar* [hellfire]?" They say, "We were not among those who prayed; nor did we feed the indigent, and we engaged in vain discourse with those who do the same, and we denied the Day of Judgment, until certainty came upon us" (74:42–47).

Just as in the Bible, the Qur'an warns its readers that almsgiving must not be for external show. This will only "annul" one's charity. But if you keep your alms secret, this will "acquit you of some of your evil deeds" (2:264, 271).

Differences within the Similarities

You might have noticed my pausing at several points to say that there are differences within these similarities. While there are sometimes remarkable correspondences on the surface—such as these six emphases in Islam that can also be found in the Christian Scriptures—there are deeper differences. I will explain each of the above three religions in turn.

First, Buddhism. On the whole it has a vastly different view of ultimate reality, the human person, and the world. The Buddha said that he was no more than a man and that we are to be lamps unto ourselves. Later Buddhist traditions treated the Buddha as a god, but the original Siddhārtha Gautama Buddha said there is no creator or redeemer who can help us. While Jesus stressed moral corruption as the root of sin (Mark 7:20–23), the Buddha said that desire—for sensual gratification and one's ego—is the cause of all suffering. The way to overcome suffering is *knowledge* of the Buddha's teachings. The difference between the Buddha and Jesus is starkly illustrated by their most common images: a smiling Buddha seated on a lotus blossom and a suffering Jesus nailed to a cross. The upshot is that in Buddhism devotees are taught how to escape suffering, but Christians see in Jesus a way to conquer suffering by embracing it.

I have alluded to the different ways that Buddhists and Christians regard ethics. For Buddhists the moral life is a temporary stage on the journey to a realm where good and evil no longer exist. For Christians, however, good and evil are part of the eternal fabric of reality because they are rooted in the eternal God and opposition to him.

I will touch briefly on three other Buddhist-Christian differences. First, Buddhists see this life in history as a vale of tears: in the Dhammapada they read that "there is no misery like physical existence."[23] This life is an endless cycle of life, death, and rebirth in which desire causes endless suffering. Their only hope is to escape the wearisome cycle by breaking ties with ordinary existence and its routines such as family life and sexuality.

A second difference is that Buddhists who are devoted to the original teachings of the Buddha believe that only male monks (who are unmarried) can achieve nirvana, and so if they are married they must achieve enough merit in this life to be reborn as a male monk. Family and sexuality are therefore impediments to one's spiritual goals in this world of misery. Jesus agreed with the Buddha that there is suffering but added that there is joy *in him* in the midst of suffering. He never denounced sexual intercourse and family but in fact spoke of it as the ordinary life in which salvation is to be lived out (Mark 10:1–9; Matt. 19:3–9). The single life is one way to follow him, but it is not the way for the majority, and it is not the higher way (Matt. 19:10–12; 1 Cor. 7:1–9).

Third, grace in the Buddhist Pure Land tradition is different from biblical grace. The Pure Land Buddha confers grace freely but without suffering, while Jesus imparts grace at infinite cost to himself. Shinran's grace comes from the universal Buddha nature, which Pure Land teaches is inherent in

23. Thomas Cleary, ed., *Dhammapada: Sayings of the Buddha* (New York: Bantam, 1995), 15.6.

all beings: we are saved by self-abandonment, but we can do that only be-cause "self-abandonment is a shining forth of our inner Buddha-nature."[24] For Christians, however, grace comes from a Creator God who is fundamentally distinct from his creation, and it comes to us creatures whose inner nature is fallen and ungodly. These same differences, by the way, apply to the way grace works in Hindu *bhakti*, which teaches that Krishna and other deities can liberate from *samsara* (the cycle of death and rebirth) those who put their trust in their (Hindu) god. Krishna and the other Hindu saviors do so without cost to themselves.

So there are important similarities between the Buddhist and Christian ways, but there are deep differences as well. For philosophical Daoism we see the same pattern, and the profound difference turns again on suffering. Both Lao-Zi and Zhuang-zi teach a kind of stoical wisdom that suggests that the way to minimize and perhaps escape suffering is to resign oneself to the vicissitudes of life. Ultimate reality for them is impersonal, and the way to gain peace amid the Dao's ups and downs is to accommodate ourselves to its ways and trust that they will eventually work for the best. In contrast, Jesus said the cosmos is personal because it was created by an infinite-personal God. This God did not stand at a distance and watch us suffer but endured the ultimate suffering of death. By that endurance he conquered it, and now he invites us to be taken up into himself and his victory.

Philosophical Daoist teachers point to the paradox that weakness is a subtle strength, but only Scripture teaches *why* this is so. The Bible says it is about a personal God—not an abstract order called Dao—humbling the arrogant and showing all the world its absolute dependence on him. God allowed calamity to come upon Israel at the apex of its glory in the reigns of David and Solomon. David committed both adultery and murder, and Solomon worshiped idols. Civil war and kingdom division resulted. The early church finally triumphed over the Roman Empire when Constantine converted and became emperor. But then the heresy of Arianism roiled the church for nearly a century. According to Edwards, this paradox of strength leading to weakness was allowed by God to humble his people and show that he alone has the glory.

'Tis often God's manner to bring some grievous calamity on his saints, es-pecially when they have received the greatest lights and joys, and have been most exalted with smiles of heaven upon them, as Jacob was made lame when admitted to so extraordinary a privilege as wrestling with God, and overcom-ing him, and so obtaining the blessing. . . . Sometimes extraordinary light and

24. Paul Williams, *Mahayana Buddhism: The Doctrinal Foundations*, 2nd ed. (New York: Routledge, 2009), 262–63.

comfort is given to fit for great calamities, and sometimes for death, which God brings soon after such things. So when God gives his own people great temporal prosperity, he is wont to bring with it some calamity to [e]clipse it, to keep them [from] being exalted in their prosperity and trusting in it.[25]

Scripture also explains the paradox of weakness producing strength. Paul wrote of his thorn in the flesh, which was probably a physical illness of the eyes that started in Galatia fourteen years before he wrote his second letter to Corinth (Gal. 4:13–15). He said it brought him contempt and scorn and was a "messenger from Satan" (2 Cor. 12:7). He prayed three times for God to remove it, but God did not. After the third prayer Christ Jesus explained why: "My grace is enough for you, because my power is perfected through weakness" (v. 9a). Apparently God wanted Paul to go deeper, to experience more of the Messiah's powerful reality, but God also knew it would not happen if Paul were released from his illness. True strength would come only through weakness. There is something about our success and strength that prevents us from experiencing the power of God. So Paul decided, "I will boast in my weaknesses, so that the power of the Messiah will live in me" (v. 9b).

Then there is Islam. Here too the similarities rest on foundational differences. Muslims hold Jesus in high esteem by citing the Qur'an's references to him as "Messiah," "word from God," "a Spirit from God," and the son of Mary, who was "strengthened with the Holy Spirit" (2:87; 3:45; 4:171; 5:75). They teach the virgin birth (Mary is said by Muslims to have been the purest woman in all creation; 3:42, 47) and accept the historicity of all the gospel miracles but one—Jesus's resurrection.

But Muslims deny Jesus's death on the cross and do not define his messianic role the way Christians do (3:55; 4:157).[26] While they say the Bible is the Word of God (2:136), they believe it has been corrupted. Jews, they claim, took the message intended for all nations and made of themselves the chosen nation. Christians took Jesus as the greatest of all prophets before Muhammad and turned him into a God whose suffering atones for all human beings. The reality is, they argue, that we must be responsible for our own sins. To call Jesus God's Son is to imply that God had sex, which is blasphemous.[27]

25. Jonathan Edwards, *Notes on Scripture* (New Haven: Yale University Press, 1998), 292.

26. While the qur'anic text says that the Jews did not kill or crucify Jesus, some Muslims concede that Jesus did in fact die and may have been crucified—but not by Jews. See, for example, the Egyptian Muhammad 'Abd al-Latif (Ibn al-Khatib), *Ahdah al-tafasir* (Cairo: Al-Matba'a 'l-Misriyya li Awlad Ibn al-Khatib, n.d.), commentary on 3:54.

27. See, for example, *Holy Qur'an*, 2.116n: "It is a derogation from the glory of Allah—in fact it is blasphemy—to say that Allah begets sons, like a man or an animal. The Christian doctrine is here emphatically repudiated. If words have any meaning, it would mean an attribution

As I wrote earlier in the chapter, both Muslims and Christians deny polytheism and affirm that God is one and personal and moral. Yet the oneness of the Christian God is also threefold. This trinitarian identity of God is emphatically rejected by Muslims. So is the way that Christians describe God's personal nature as love in its essence (1 John 4:16). Muslims say God cannot be love because to say that is to ascribe a human concept to Allah, who is utterly transcendent and removed from all human categories and conceptions. Besides, for the Islamic tradition the fundamental relation between God and his human creatures is justice. "The constant reference is to God as sovereign Lord (*Rabb*), and man as his servant or slave."[28] The Qur'an never commands its readers to love Allah or to love one's neighbor, and it rejects Jesus's teaching to love our enemies.[29] In the Christian Scriptures, in contrast, the principal theme is love between God and his human creatures: he loves them, and they are to love him (Deut. 6:4–5; Matt. 22:34–38). And they are to love their neighbors and their enemies (Matt. 5:43–48).

So the God of Islam is significantly different from the God of the Christian Scriptures. One puts far more emphasis on justice with next to no mention of love, and the other stresses love without neglecting justice. Furthermore, while both are said to be all-powerful, their power is sketched in vastly different ways. Allah commands power from atop the cosmos, while the God of Israel shows the power that descends to the world of suffering and weakness, embraces death, and triumphs over it.

Where Did Those Similarities Come From?

If the world religions are fundamentally different in what they say about God and salvation, we are still left with the question of why there are similarities in the first place. We wonder about the striking agreements in moral teachings and the remarkable parallels we have seen in the religions we discussed in the previous pages. Where did these parallels come from?

Let's start with where they did *not* come from. Insofar as parallels are parts of the religions' answers to the question of how to resolve the human

---

to Allah of a material nature, and of the lower animal functions of sex." Interestingly, the qur'anic description of Jesus's conception depicts God (or an angel) blowing the Spirit into Mary's vaginal canal (21:91; 66:12)—about as crassly physical as what they (falsely) imagine Christians to teach.

28. Norman Anderson, *God's Law and God's Love* (London: Collins, 1980), 98.

29. For more on this detail, see Gerald McDermott and Harold Netland, *A Trinitarian Theology of Religions: An Evangelical Proposal* (New York: Oxford University Press, 2014), 60–72.

predicament, none of these were by direct revelation from the God of Israel. God is Truth and does not contradict his own revelation of salvation as told by the Bible. If Buddhists believe that the basic human predicament is suffering because we are trapped in *samsara* and that liberation comes by devotion to the Buddha's teachings, then every Buddhist principle, even if it is parallel to a Christian principle, is distorted by its setting in the Buddhist framework of liberation from *samsara*. To use another example, even if Muslims are right to say that God is one and not none or many, their testimony to divine oneness is distorted by their denial of the Three within the One. Therefore these parallels within other religions are limited and do not come by direct revelation from the Triune God, who alone is Truth.

But we don't have to stop with a negative statement. We can speak positively of three possible sources for these parallels or similarities, and each is *related* to God's revelation of himself. The first is *reflection on God's general revelation*. In this book we have discussed repeatedly God's revelation of his beauty and design in nature at large (Ps. 19 and Rom. 1) and of his moral law in every human heart (Rom. 2). Paul told the crowds at Lystra that "God did not leave himself without witness" but showed his goodness by giving people all over the world food and gladness (Acts 14:17). This general witness can help explain why many of the world religions speak of a creator, life after death, and moral principles like the Ten Commandments. It also helps us understand why all of the religions say this world is badly spoiled and why many assert that we humans have broken its basic laws and must do something to make up for our wrongs. Reflection on this general revelation might explain the Confucian "negative golden rule": do not do to others what you do not want done to yourself. Five hundred years before Jesus taught the positive form of this in his Golden Rule, Confucius was articulating what Thomas called "natural law," the human recognition of God's eternal law.[30] Reflection on general revelation also helps explain why all the great religions have recognized marriage as the lifelong bond between a man and woman best suited for procreation and child-rearing. They used God's gift of reason to reflect on our moral nature, the needs of society and children, and marriage's mysterious sanctity.

A second source is the *prisca theologia* (Latin for "ancient theology"), a long Christian tradition that attributed truth in the religions to contact with Noah's sons—who were the founders of the nations (Gen. 10)—and to contact with later Israel. There is little historical evidence for much of this idea, but its basic thesis should not be rejected out of hand. We know that Christianity

---

30. Thomas Aquinas, *Summa theologiae* I-II, qq. 90–106. See chap. 5 above.

was most likely planted in India in the first century AD and that missionaries continued work there in the second and third centuries.[31] It is plausible that Christian ideas influenced developments in Buddhism and Hinduism such as grace in Buddhist Pure Land and Hindu *bhakti*. At the very least, we know that all three religions lived side by side for centuries. Later, it is clear, Christianity influenced modern Hindu schools of thought such as the Brahma Samaj and the Ramakrishna movement.[32] Furthermore, there is plenty of evidence that Islam arose as a response to both Judaism and Christianity. Muhammad was a trader who had many contacts with Jews and Christians.[33]

Third, religions could have been *influenced by the Logos, the eternal Word*. Justin Martyr (d. ca. 165) pointed to John's statement at the beginning of his gospel, "[The Logos] was the true light that enlightens every man" (John 1:9). Justin argued that every thinker who teaches truth got that truth from the One who is the Truth (John 14:6). Drawing on the parable of the sower and the seed, Justin proclaimed that philosophers and religious teachers "spoke well in proportion to the share [they] had of the seminal [i.e., seed-like] divine Logos." They mixed truth with error "because they did not know the whole Logos, which is Christ, [and so] they often contradicted themselves." If they did not *possess* the Logos, they were not saved. But if they shared in *part* of his truth, they communicated things that were true nonetheless—just as all human beings have access to God's law written on their hearts even if they do not worship God.[34] This influence could account for some of what is true in the world religions.

But Are These Types?

Now we return to the subject of this book: types, or divinely planted images of the Triune God. If these remarkable similarities in the world religions communicate true things about the God of Israel, but only at one level, were they really planted there by God? If they are planted within religions that

31. Samuel Hugh Moffett, *A History of Christianity in Asia*, vol. 1, *Beginnings to 1500* (San Francisco: HarperSanFrancisco, 1992), 25–39. See also Robert Eric Frykenberg, *Christianity in India: From Beginnings to the Present* (Oxford: Oxford University Press, 2008), 91–115.

32. Robert D. Baird and Alfred Bloom, *Indian and Far Eastern Religious Traditions* (New York: Harper & Row, 1971), 107–14; see also Arvind Sharma, ed., *Neo-Hindu Views of Christianity* (Leiden: Brill, 1988).

33. Richard Bell, *The Origin of Islam in Its Christian Environment* (1926; repr., Oxford: Routledge, 1968); Abraham Katsch, *Judaism in Islam*, 3rd ed. (Lakewood, NJ: Intellectbooks, 2009).

34. Justin Martyr, *Second Apology*, in *The Fathers of the Church: A New Translation*, vol. 6, trans. Thomas B. Falls (Washington, DC: Catholic University of America Press, 1948), §§10, 13.

on the whole tell false stories, how could they have been put there by God? How can something placed or allowed by God be partly true and partly false?

C. S. Lewis wrote of "good dreams" and "great stories" scattered throughout the myths of the world that God planted or permitted in order to point people to the "true myth" of the Jewish Messiah Jesus.[35] Jonathan Edwards wrote about God planting types of true religion in false religions. God outwitted the devil, he suggested, by using diabolical religion to impart religious truth. Two shocking examples were pagan idolatry and human sacrifice. The first, Edwards said, prepared pagans for the Christian doctrine of incarnation, the notion that God inhabits matter and even a human person. The second helped pagans understand that God could sacrifice the man Jesus to save the world (WJE 13:391–92). All religions at some point practiced sacrifice, Edwards argued, not by the light of nature but by God's express commandment immediately after he revealed the covenant of grace. God clothed the first couple with skins taken from animals sacrificed by God, which taught them the necessity of propitiation—an offering to appease God's anger at sin—and hinted at the eventual propitiation of Christ's sacrifice (WJE 9:134–36). In these ways, according to Edwards, God used abominable practices in false religions as teaching devices for pagans. Non-Christian religions could therefore contain types that point to Christian truths.[36]

The Old Testament suggests that God permits what is less than best when his human creatures are stubborn and reject his will. God told his people that he hates divorce (Mal. 2:16). But Jesus said that Moses permitted divorce "because of the hardness of your hearts . . . but from the beginning it was not so" (Matt. 19:8). Rather than abandoning his people because of their recalcitrance, God worked with them over time by education and discipline, and eventually sent Jesus to recall them to his original plan for marriage.

But is this a bad analogy? After all, the "less than best" was in the true religion of Judaism (Jesus was a Jew teaching his fellow Jews) and not a religion like Buddhism or Islam that mixes truth with error. Yet the church fathers believed that God nevertheless sowed seeds of truth in religious systems that were finally false. They believed that religions outside the Judeo-Christian tradition were inspired by fallen angels and therefore were rife with distortions and falsehood. It was only because these angels had once been good and brought their memory of the truth with them that admixtures of

35. C. S. Lewis, *Mere Christianity* (New York: Macmillan, 1967), book 2, chap. 3; C. S. Lewis, *Miracles* (London: Bles, 1947), chap. 14; C. S. Lewis, *The Problem of Pain* (New York: Macmillan, 1962), chap. 6.
36. For more on Edwards and other religions, see Michael McClymond and Gerald McDermott, *The Theology of Jonathan Edwards* (New York: Oxford University Press, 2013), 580–98.

truth were scattered among the falsehoods. God permitted these mixtures, they believed, to help prepare whole cultures (not to mention individuals) for eventually receiving the gospel. For example, the truth of God's law that is distorted within the religions' pervasive legalism is used by God to teach respect for his law. This emphasis can help them see Christ as the fulfillment of God's law and show them that law cannot give them the perfection they need to live in God's presence.[37]

To make this point practical, let's consider Buddhists, Hindus, and Muslims. Pure Land Buddhists and Hindu *bhaktas* already know something of grace, the idea that divine power can deliver them from a realm of eternal frustration. God might have permitted this distorted image—a type, if you will—to help them see the vast superiority of Christ's grace, where absolute holiness and infinite sacrifice are lacking in their own religions. So too Muslims are told that God is closer to them than their jugular vein (Qur'an 50:16), but most of the other portraits of Allah in the Qur'an put him at near-infinite distance from them. When they read of Jesus calling his disciples "friends" and promising them repeated experiences of his own love and the Father's love, they are astounded by the intimacy of this God (John 14:21–23; 15:15). God might have permitted the hint of closeness in the Muslim holy book to draw Muslims to the stunning intimacy of Jesus and the Father with their people.

Shiite Islam might have drawn its notion of redemptive suffering from early Muslim contacts with Christians.[38] But no matter how it originated, God has used this idea of redemptive suffering to show Shiites the greater beauty of Jesus's redemptive suffering. Muslims around the world are coming to faith in Jesus as God because of dreams, visions, and witness from others.[39] The Shiites among them are seeing that their previous understanding of redemptive suffering—perhaps a type—helped prepare them to accept Jesus as their suffering redeemer.

I close this chapter with one more word about types in the world religions. The messianic types in the Old Testament were rarely identified by the Old Testament authors, and even more rarely explained. Yet Jesus expected his disciples and even his opponents to recognize them, as we saw at the end of chapter 2. So we should not expect all types outside the Bible to be identified explicitly inside the Bible. But if they are indeed types, their meaning must

37. For more on the fathers and world religions, see Gerald McDermott, *God's Rivals: Why Has God Allowed Different Religions?* (Downers Grove, IL: IVP Academic, 2007), chaps. 5–8.
38. Bell, *Origin of Islam*, 190–216.
39. See, for example, David H. Greenlee, ed., *Straight Path to the Narrow Way: Journeys of Faith* (Downers Grove, IL: InterVarsity, 2012).

fall within the range of the clear teachings of Scripture and orthodox theological tradition. So if the parallels in the world religions are really types put there by God, they are not true in themselves (because of their location in a false religion) but only to the extent that they point to their corrections as taught by Christian orthodoxy.

It helps to recall that the God of the Bible wants the peoples of the world to know him. This is true as much in the Old Testament as the New. In the story of the exodus of the Jews from Egypt, YHWH said that he would harden Pharaoh's heart so that "the Egyptians [would] know that [he was] the LORD" (Exod. 14:4). In Isaiah 37 King Hezekiah prayed that YHWH would save Judah from capture by the Assyrians "so that all the kingdoms of the earth may know that [he] alone [is] the LORD" (v. 20). The prophet Ezekiel declared that through YHWH's chastisements Israel's pagan neighbors would learn that he alone is God: the Ammonites, Moabites, Philistines, residents of Tyre and Sidon, and the Egyptians (Ezek. 25:5, 11, 17; 26:6; 28:23; 29:6, 8, 16; 30:19, 26; 32:15). YHWH told Israel's enemy Gog that YHWH would use him to invade Israel so that, he said, "the nations may know me, when through you, O Gog, I display my holiness before their eyes" (Ezek. 38:16).

It also helps to remember that Jesus pointed to pagans as examples of faith. He told the people of Nazareth that they should think like the widow at (pagan Phoenician) Zarephath and Naaman the (pagan) Syrian, whom God chose to feed and heal rather than the other "widows in Israel in the time of Elijah" and the "many lepers in Israel in the time of the prophet Elisha" (Luke 4:24–27). Jesus "marveled" at the faith of the (gentile) centurion who sought healing for his slave: "Not even in Israel have I found such faith" (Luke 7:9 ESV). Jesus celebrated the faith of the (gentile) Canaanite woman, recommended the moral behavior of the (non-Jewish) Good Samaritan, and pointed out that "a foreigner" was the only leper to "return and give praise to God" (Matt. 15:21–28; Luke 10:25–37; 17:18 ESV).

My point is not that pagan faith is better than Jewish or Christian faith. Scripture clearly rejects that proposition. Each of these pagans probably had imperfect faith, some thinking of him as little more than a healer or prophet. They needed to spend time with Jesus and the apostles to have their faith grow to maturity, just as any pagan does today. But insofar as their initial ideas about God were partly wrong and partly right, needing correction by Jesus and the early church, they showed the same pattern we have found in the world religions. God used their early imperfect faith, as he might use these similarities—types—in this chapter, to lead to faith in the trinitarian God of Israel.

11

A New World

Believing Is Seeing

One has heard those heavenly announcements, by which, in the words of the Prophet, the glory of God is declared, and, travelling through creation, has been led to the apprehension of a Master of the creation; he has taken the true Wisdom for his teacher, that Wisdom which the spectacle of the Universe suggests; and when he observed the beauty of this material sunlight he had grasped by analogy the beauty of the real sunlight; he saw in the solid firmness of this earth the unchangeableness of its Creator; when he perceived the immensity of the heavens he was led on the road towards the vast Infinity of that Power which encompasses the Universe; when he saw the rays of the sun reaching from such sublimities even to ourselves he began to believe, by the means of such phenomena, that the activities of the Divine Intelligence did not fail to descend from the heights of Deity even to each one of us; for if a single luminary can occupy everything alike that lies beneath it with the force of light, and, more than that, can, while lending itself to all who can use it, still remain self-centred and undissipated, how much more shall the Creator of that luminary become all in all, as the Apostle speaks, and come into each with such a measure of Himself as each subject of His influence can receive! Nay, look only at an ear of grain, at the germinating of some plant, at a ripe bunch of grapes, at the beauty of early autumn, whether in fruit or flower, at the grass springing unbidden, at the mountain reaching up with its summit to the height of the ether, at the springs on its slopes bursting from those swelling breasts, and running in rivers through the glens, at the sea receiving those streams from every direction and yet remaining within its limits, with waves edged by the stretches of beach and never stepping beyond those fixed boundaries of continent: look at these and such-like sights, and how can the eye of reason fail to find in them all that our education for Realities requires?

Gregory of Nyssa, On Infants' Early Deaths

The beauty of the world can be found in its sweet mutual agreements, both between things in the world, and between the world and the Supreme Being. The sweetest and most stunning beauty in the world of nature is its resemblance to spiritual beauties—since material things are only images and shadows of spiritual beings, and spiritual beauties are infinitely greater than material beauties. So the more that something in nature is an image of spiritual beauty, the more charming it appears to us. This spiritual beauty that nature suggests is greater than anything human beings can produce.

Think of the planets moving around the sun. Their orbits suggest their trust, dependence on, and acknowledgment of the sun, by whose power they are made happy, bright, and beautiful. The sun gives the planets authority, as it were, to control their own moons revolving around themselves. The sun is therefore an image of majesty, power, glory, and goodness in the midst of the solar system—as well as being an image of these things among creatures and plants here on earth.

The harmonies of shapes and motions throughout the natural world cannot be numbered, but each one of this infinite number points to the spiritual beauty that consists in sweet harmony and agreement. For example, the gentle motions of trees and lilies are designed by God to represent calmness, gentleness, and benevolence in the heavenly realm. But they also seem to speak in their own way. The fields and woods seem to rejoice, and the birds appear to soar with delight. The fields are full of every grace imaginable when the sun shines serenely and without disturbance upon them. At these times, every graceful and beautiful disposition of mind is suggested—such as the gratitude and love of a being toward its creator, preserver, kind benefactor, and fountain of happiness.

On a calm and placid day we have a picture of a holy and virtuous soul. And the light of such a day—indeed of any day—contains an infinite number of similar beauties. In each of its infinite shades and colors are complex harmonies and proportions that are images of sweet mutual consents between creature and Creator.

Jonathan Edwards, "The Beauty of the World"

That cushiony moss, that coldness and sound and dancing light were no doubt very minor blessings compared with "the means of grace and the hope of glory." But then they were manifest. So far as they were concerned, sight had replaced faith. They were not the hope of glory, but an exposition of the glory itself.

C. S. Lewis, Letters to Malcolm: Chiefly on Prayer

Having my eyes opened to seeing types in all the Scriptures has opened my awareness further still to see types in the all the world. I now realize that God has filled his whole creation with types. When I go on my daily runs, I can't help but see the blue sky and white clouds as types of Christ's purity and holiness. When I hear peals of thunder, I hear God's voice of judgment against sin and injustice. When I read the front page of the newspaper and see wickedness punished or goodness rewarded, I see types of God's judgment and faithfulness. When I gaze at the bare, gnarled tree in my front yard on a dark winter's day, I see the terrible beauty of the tree of the Cross of Christ planted by God for salvation. When I officiate at a wedding, I see not just a man and a woman being joined in marriage but Christ married to his Bride, the Church, by the giving of his life for Her. God has filled the world with types.

Mark Graham, Lutheran pastor, letter to author

The four epigraphs here are four testimonies of believers—one from the early church, one from the eighteenth century, one from the twentieth, and one from today. Each writer had his eye opened to the glory of the Lord in all of reality. Each one could see that God has planted his types not just inside the Bible but out in the world, and that their beauty and meaning were manifest to those with eyes to see.

These four testimonies give us a peek at what it is like to see all the world as full of God-implanted images. In this final chapter I will elaborate a bit more on what all this would mean for readers of various sorts. First I will sketch a bit of what it would be like to go through the rhythms of daily life with this approach to the world about us. Then I will discuss the implications of the preceding chapters for Christian believers. I will conclude with brief reflections on how this might help the church in the public square and how it might help seekers think through their seeking.

Types in the Day's Rhythms

Here and there in this book I have suggested that God has built into our daily lives certain rhythms that have meaning in and of themselves. Let me gather a few of these rhythms together.[1]

The first thing to notice is that these rhythms are many, and they are *constantly changing*. Night gives way to day, which passes again into night. The weather moves from cold to hot, calm to stormy, brighter to darker, and vice

---

1. Most of these draw in some manner from Edwards's reflections in "Images of Divine Things," in *WJE* 11:51–153.

versa. These constant changes in light and darkness, weather and climate, are types of God's providence toward us as he regularly sends us changes in life, affliction following prosperity and then back again. Changes of day and night, weather and seasons, are types of the changes in life that God sends our way.

During the dawn before the *morning*, the stars gradually vanish as light on the horizon first appears and then brightens. This is a type of the gradual disappearance of pagan darkness as the light of the gospel spread through the first millennium of Christianity, not to mention the gradual way that the leaven of Christ takes a whole lifetime to brighten the soul. When the sun starts to peek above the horizon and raises the world with it—getting people out of bed and bringing all the world back to life after a night of sleep—it is a type of Christ rising from the grave and raising all the church with him to newness of life. Because of Jesus's new life at his resurrection, believers joined to him have been born again to a living hope, with a new happiness and light. His resurrection was the firstfruit that gave them new life and will one day raise their bodies from the dead when he returns at the end of history. The sunrise is a type of all of this.

Daytime is controlled by the *sun*. Even when there are violent winds, the sun's beams are not scattered. In this way the sun is a type of God's love, which is steady toward us, no matter how violent the storms of affliction around us. The sun still shines even when clouds obscure it, just as we know God loves us even when we can't feel that love. But just as clouds and rain are necessary for the earth to prosper, Scripture tells us that God uses affliction to prosper our souls. The devastating heat of the sun, which can kill those who are not prepared for it, is a type of the wrath of the Lamb (Rev. 6:16), which will destroy those who resist him.

A pleasant *day* amid blue sky, green fields, and pretty flowers is an image of God's goodness, grace, and love. The rich blue of the sky is a sign of the purity of the saints in heaven: just as that blue is unfading beyond the vagaries of weather below, the beauty and glory of heavenly things never diminish.

As we *walk* around, we are reminded of two things. First, we are made to walk with feet on the earth, posture erect, and our face toward the sky—showing that we are made to have heaven in our eyes and the earth underfoot. Second, in order to keep walking we must breathe continuously. Just as our breath maintains our physical life, so the Spirit of God maintains the life of our souls. "My life is but a breath," which God can take away in an instant (Job 7:7). We are "a mist that appears for a little while and then vanishes . . . [as] the Lord wills" (James 4:14–15).

Eating is rich in types. Our bread is a type of the "heavenly manna" that is Christ (John 6:35). Our drink is a type of the "living water . . . welling up to eternal life" (4:10, 14 ESV). The fact that we need to eat three times a day tells us that we need to come back to Christ to get spiritually fed throughout the day. Cooked food is a type of our need to suffer to become holy (Heb. 5:8; 12:10), just as food needs to suffer boiling and pressing to become tasty.

Our need to *purge ourselves* of wastes throughout the day is a type of two things. First, we all are sinners and have inner corruption that needs to be eliminated, and second, we need to confess our sins regularly to God and to others (Prov. 28:13; James 5:16).

In the *evening* we take off our clothes for bed. Many people wear pajamas or a nightgown in case they must get up suddenly, but some do not. This is a type of what happens when people fall into a spiritual sleep, neglecting the things of God. They are warned by Scripture that Jesus "is coming like a thief" in the night. They should "stay awake [and] *keep their garments on* so they don't go about naked and become exposed!" (Rev. 16:15).

The *night* is a time for thieves and robbers (Obad. 5; Rev. 16:15). It is also a time "when all the beasts of the forest creep about," and the "young lions" come out from their lairs to "roar for their prey" (Ps. 104:20–21 ESV), just as the devil "prowls around like a roaring lion seeking someone to devour" (1 Pet. 5:8 ESV). Paul associated the night with sinful activities and urged believers to walk by day: "The night is far gone; the day is at hand. So let us cast off the works of darkness and put on the armor of light" (Rom. 13:12).

God shortens the daytime in winter and lengthens the night, just as he says he will shorten the days of tribulation for the sake of his church (Mark 13:20). But during the night throughout the year God gives light by the moon and the stars. This is a type of God's support for his saints in their days of trouble; he will never leave them in total darkness without encouragement and light during their dark nights of the soul.

The *moon* is a type of earthly glory that is always changing. Just as the moon never stops waxing and waning and at points is even extinguished until at length its brightness can again light up the night, so too our prosperity goes up and down. Like the moon, it waxes and wanes. Sometimes we fail utterly in the world, and then at other times—often inexplicably—everything we touch turns to gold.

The *stars* have a special typical value. By their movements through the heavens they influence planets like ours, and thus our lives—but of course all under God's providence. This is similar to the ways that Scripture suggests God uses the angels to order parts of his kingdom.[2]

2. See James B. Jordan, *Through New Eyes: Developing a Biblical View of the World* (Eugene, OR: Wipf & Stock, 1999).

But more vivid are the stars as types of the eternality of God's kingdom. Although astrophysicists tell us the stars move, from our vantage point they are immoveable, even in their movements across the sky through the years. The latter are predictable because they are so regular. In other words, the regularity of their motion is immoveable. This is a type of the kingdom of the Father that he delegates to the lordship of the Son. It is immoveable and forever (Luke 1:33; Rev. 11:15). Everything else is in flux, but God and his kingdom are forever. When we gaze at the stars at night, this is one of the things they are telling us (Ps. 19:1–3).

How a Typological View of Reality Can Help Believers

As I said at the beginning of this book, two sets of arguments are being made today that discourage believers from thinking that God has anything to do with *nature*. On the one hand, secularists and atheists try to convince us that this world is either a predictable machine or a cold and alien universe. They suggest that it is merely an arena in which we struggle for survival or an economy for the exploitation of the proletariat or the stage for inner psychological conflict. On the other hand, some within the church tell believers that the realm of nature is fundamentally removed from the realm of grace. We can see God's hand at work in the latter but not in the former. Or they tell us that the beauty of God is so estranged from beauty in this world that the two beauties have nothing to do with each other. Others want to tell us that, even if there were revelations of God in nature, they are inevitably misunderstood and so not revelations at the end of the day. We can know God by looking at Jesus and the Bible, but there is nothing of God in nature or the world that we can discern clearly.

This book rejects that counsel of despair. It has argued that the modern church has lost the historic church's vision of God's glory in nature (chap. 3). Of course this is a fallen world, and we are fallen creatures. We see through a glass darkly, and sin often mars our vision. But God has revealed his glory in all the worlds we inhabit. There is truth about him in all those worlds that we and others can perceive—because he has radiated his glory into those worlds. Unbelievers cannot know enough of the glory to be saved. For that, they need the special revelation of Jesus Christ. But they can know something of God and his glory, as Psalm 19 and Romans 1 testify. And believers can see far more of the glory because they wear the right spectacles (as Calvin put it).[3] They see the beauty of God in the face of Jesus Christ, and they can

---

3. John Calvin, *Institutes of the Christian Religion*, ed. John T. McNeill, trans. Ford Lewis Battles (Philadelphia: Westminster, 1960), 1.6.1.

use that vision to see and understand the beauty of nature. They can use the grammar provided by Scripture to read the types with which God has filled nature and all the world.

If believers can have epistemological confidence about nature, they can also reject the prevalent myth that *science* disproves God. Or that the "brights" are the ones who understand modern science and so have rejected the "God illusion."[4] Chapter 4 shows that some of the greatest scientists in the world see design in this cosmos and that scientific discoveries of the last century have made it more difficult to be an atheist. Not that science proves God, of course. But recent science makes it impossible to disprove God and in fact lends *support* to faith. This means that modern science has been uncovering more and more of the divine *glory* on the cosmic and microscopic levels. As astronomer Robert Jastrow famously quipped (as noted above in chap. 4), skeptical scientists who thought they were scaling the mountains of ignorance pulled themselves over the final rock only to be "greeted by a band of theologians who have been sitting there for centuries."[5] They have found fine-tuning from the top to the bottom of the cosmos that reveals a creator of stunning artistry. And the deeper and closer they look, the more perfect the patterns of the universe appear to be. There is remarkable beauty in the patterns, and that beauty is traced by the beauty of mathematics with absolute precision. If this universe had been randomly assembled, such correspondence would be highly unlikely. Furthermore, scientists have found deep symmetries among matter, light, and music—yet more signs of glory that one would not anticipate in an unplanned cosmos.

Believers can also be encouraged that there are signs of glory in the human *conscience* and the world's *cultures*. Moderns have been told that morality is relative to endlessly varying cultural situations, which is said to prove that there cannot be any divine *law* to which all humans are responsible. But we have seen in chapter 5 that there is remarkable evidence that God's law is written on human hearts (Rom. 2:14–15) after all. There is astonishing evidence that across the world and through nearly all cultures there is common recognition of what we call the Ten Commandments. This does not mean that human beings or cultures follow these principles, but that they recognize that the principles *should* be followed. They are signs of the divine glory embedded in every human soul.

Shakespeare's Macbeth famously said that *history* is a "tale told by an idiot, full of sound and fury, signifying nothing."[6] Many moderns believe

---

4. This is the claim of the New Atheists; see https://en.wikipedia.org/wiki/Brights_movement.
5. Robert Jastrow, *God and the Astronomers* (London: Norton, 1992), 107.
6. William Shakespeare, *Macbeth*, act 5, scene 5, lines 2383–85.

those lines to the letter, and Christians often think that the only history with meaning is sacred history in Israel and the early church. But chapter 6 suggests that there are patterns of divine dealing with societies, shown typologically by Scripture. Even if most of history is still opaque and we are clueless about what God is doing in it, we can nonetheless observe past history to discern certain patterns that suggest God's directing. This observation can be reassuring when all seems dark.

Even the world of *animals* reveals something of the divine glory (chap. 7). In animals it is easier to see or hear God speaking to us because animals are the members of creation that most resemble people. The Bible thus refers so often to animals and uses them so frequently as types of human behavior, both good and bad. In their world it is easier to see how the world outside the Bible and church is sparkling with God's glory.

Chapter 8 should help believers make better sense of *love and sexuality*. This is particularly important in a new century when sexual difference is denied or misunderstood like never before. Seeing God's types will enable believers to see that sexual difference itself is a type of all the differences we find among people and that sexual fulfillment, which is never complete, suggests a greater fulfillment we cannot find by ourselves. They will see that intimacy in marriage is an analogy to—or *type* of—intimacy with the divine person who is Truth incarnate and that the union of man and woman in love that produces a child points to the union of three divine persons who are different.

Because of chapter 9, Christians might be able to find meaning even in activities that appear spiritually insignificant, such as *sports*. In and of themselves they do not have ultimate meaning, but they suggest the ultimate by the ways in which they resemble ultimate things in the real world of God's kingdom: God's freedom and creativity, our lightness of being, the play that is at the heart of joy, the worldly worthlessness of worship, the coinherence of time and eternity, and the fact that there will be ultimate winners and losers.

Chapter 10 helps believers understand why the *world religions* are so similar and yet so different. They are similar because they are, at one level, reflections of God's general revelation. They may also share original revelation passed down through the millennia but distorted over time. They could have received influence here and there from the Logos, the eternal Word, but without possessing the Logos. They are radically different in what they say about salvation because they all reject the God of Israel and his Messiah Jesus, who is the only savior of the world. But this chapter might help enable believers to reject the two extremes that are popular in different churches—the idea that all religions outside the Judeo-Christian tradition are realms of unmixed darkness and the notion that salvation can come through them all. Seeing that there are types of truth in religions that do not have the final truth can help dispel both of these myths.

This chapter traces the types of the Messiah in the Old Testament that are used by Jesus and the apostles. My hope is that believers will understand from this chapter how to better use christological typology in the Bible to discern types outside the Bible.

How Types Can Help the Church in the World

Today in the West arguments from religion alone make little headway in the public square. Appeals from Scripture alone are often ignored or ridiculed. Reasoning that appeals to nature, science, and history is taken far more seriously. If listeners on the other side of our issue hear us appealing to what they too can affirm in sexuality or sports or world religions or (especially) moral law, we will have a better chance of finding agreement. This is where types can be extremely helpful. They enable us to talk about truth and beauty outside the Bible that unbelievers and other religionists can also affirm.

They can also help the church resist the postmodern myth of utter subjectivity—namely, the idea that there is no final truth, only local truths that have limited application. Another way of putting it is to say that there is nothing objectively true for all times and places and peoples, but that things can be true for only some people in some cultures and situations. This position would compel the church to proclaim that Jesus saves only some people, but that others are saved by other saviors or systems. This is in fact the view of what theologians call "theological pluralism," which believes that there are gods and salvations that work for only some parts and peoples in the cosmos. According to this view, there is no one way for all. Christian orthodoxy works only inside the Bible, as it were, and not in every part of life and every part of the cosmos.

But a Christian typological view of reality shows that the trinitarian God is Creator of all the cosmos and that he has shared his glory with every last bit of that cosmos. There are types visible to all peoples, and there always have been. Only the biblical story makes sense of all the world and its types. But once that biblical world of types is known, one can begin to see that types are everywhere else. And that they all point to the God of Israel, the Father of the Son by the Spirit, whose glory fills the heavens and the earth.

Types for Seekers

Reading this book will never prove God to seekers. But it might help them to question more deeply the atheism or agnosticism that plagues them. If this cosmos really is cold and empty of ultimate love—which must be true if there is no infinite-personal God—then why is nature so full of beautiful types? Why are there such profound symmetries in science that bedazzle some of the greatest scientists? Why have many of them concluded that this universe must have been designed? Why are there so many parallels among the world's moralities? If we are really driven ultimately and only by our "selfish genes," why is there such a history-long and pan-cultural commitment to altruistic morality? For that matter, why is there a near-universal conviction that matter is not all there is and that it in fact comes from the world of spirit? If we are only animals, why is our love so different from that of animals? Why has sex always been a mystery to so many cultures, and why has it appeared to have religious meaning? Why are so many of these realms—nature, science, law, history, love, even sports—full of types of the God of Israel? Of the Triune God? Could all of these remarkable types have arisen in so many different dimensions of reality by *chance*? Are they all cosmic accidents?

These are the questions that the world of types raises. If their answers are not obvious, at least they will help seekers dig below the surface of what appears to be obvious from afar but is far from obvious up close.

Limits

The Christian typology that this book explores is not like the natural theology that the deists promoted several centuries ago. Their natural theology was believed to be accessible to all, believers and skeptics alike. They thought that ordinary reason could ascend to God using the ladder of evidences in nature (types, if you will). Their God was not the Triune God of Scripture but a remote deity that was remarkably like them. He created the world to function on its own, and he rarely intervened.[7]

In historic, orthodox natural theology God is the Triune God of the Christian Scriptures. The Bible provides the typological map that charts the types in the Book of Nature. God does not intervene in the world because that very notion presumes a separation of the world from the being of God. Instead,

---

7. For a description of seventeenth- and eighteenth-century deism, see Gerald McDermott, *Jonathan Edwards Confronts the Gods: Christian Theology, Enlightenment Religion, and Non-Christian Faiths* (New York: Oxford University Press, 2000), 17–33.

Scripture says God continually sustains the world's being (Heb. 1:3), Christ holds the world together (Col. 1:17), and in God we live and move and have our being (Acts 17:28). God fills the heaven and the earth with his glory, and we can see degrees of that glory in the innumerable types that point to his beauty and Triune life.

But the Bible is also clear that only the eyes of faith can see all this. The skeptic cannot see most of the types and will rightly understand none of them. He or she needs the spectacles of Scripture, which alone contains the grammar for the language of types. Apart from that grammar, the language of types is gobbledygook. So the seeker or skeptic needs an eye operation to be able to use the spectacles. That operation must be accompanied by a heart operation that transplants what is there with something made in another world. Only with that new heart can the eyes properly see so as to learn the language of types. That's why believing is seeing.

Appendix
Theological Objections—Luther and Barth

If the church for most of its history believed that the creation is full of signs pointing to redemption, why is a book like this needed? The answer is that Protestants have tended to so emphasize their theologies of redemption that their theologies of creation have been lost or attenuated. Even Catholic theologians in the last century, influenced by a Reformed Protestant emphasis on the noetic, or intellectual, effects of sin, have given less attention to their own doctrines of creation and typology.

To understand why Protestants have often lost sight of the fullness of creation in their laser-like focus on redemption, we have to go to the man who might be called the first Protestant, Martin Luther (1483–1546). Strictly speaking, Luther was probably not the first, but his protests (as in "Protestant") against late medieval doctrines were the most famous and influential throughout the course of the Reformation. And it was his contention about reason and the creation that set up his doctrine of justification, which he said was the word on which the church stands or falls.

Martin Luther

Let me first say that all Christians are indebted to Martin Luther. His enormous accomplishments cannot be doubted. First and foremost, he more than anyone else sent a battering ram against the castle called semi-Pelagianism that developed in the fourteenth and fifteenth centuries. To render simple a very complex matter, this was the unbiblical doctrine that we are saved not by Christ's works alone but by his works *and* ours. According to theologian Gabriel Biel, Luther's teacher in seminary, the human will and intellect were largely undamaged by sin and therefore are capable of loving God perfectly, even without the help of grace.[1] Luther went to indefatigable lengths to show that Scripture teaches that, apart from grace, we "can do no good thing."[2] Catholics too have profited from this critical teaching of Luther ever since, from the theologians at Trent to the recent Pope Benedict XVI.

But while Luther performed heroic feats for the church's understanding of salvation, he had a hard time separating properly Christian natural theology from the theologies of glory that he thought responsible for the Catholic Church's late medieval teaching of semi-Pelagianism. In his Heidelberg Disputation (1518), Luther famously asserted, "That person does not deserve to be called a theologian who looks upon the invisible things of God as though they were clearly perceptible in those things which have actually happened [*sic*] [Rom. 1:20]."[3] His targets were late medieval philosophical theologians who thought they could use reason alone, apart from Scripture, to speculate about God's attributes. Luther insisted that apart from the revelation of the cross, nothing about God can be truly known by reason. In the absence of revelation from the Bible, reason—which is never static or neutral—will immediately concoct a god whom the human self can manage. So Luther talked about a monk in his day who imagines a god who forgives sins and grants eternal life in exchange for good works. He clings to and trusts in this god. The problem is that this god does not exist. It is an idol. And this is the natural result, according to Luther, when reason looks at the created world and analogizes from its beauty and goodness to a god who has as much beauty and goodness as the monk's little mind can imagine. Not only is it a foolish exercise—for since when can the infinite God be anything like what our little minds can imagine?—but the categories of beauty and goodness are devised by the monk. How is he to know that the true God's goodness and beauty are anything like what he conceives beauty and goodness to be? Remember, this is a monk-philosopher who is deliberately setting the Bible aside and presuming to use reason alone to tell him about God. This, said Luther, is a theologian

1. David Steinmetz, "What Luther Got Wrong," *Christian Century*, August 23, 2005, 23, 25; https://www.religion-online.org/article/what-luther-got-wrong.

2. My paraphrase of John 15:5.

3. Heidelberg Disputation, in *Luther's Works* (Philadelphia: Muhlenberg Press, 1957), 31:52. The last part of this translation is curious: *quae facta sunt* is translated as historical events ("things that have actually happened") rather than things of nature ("things that have been made"). The latter translation is probably more accurate, and it is certainly closer to the Greek that lies behind the Latin. Perhaps this translation in *Luther's Works* played a role in the way twentieth-century Lutherans have regarded this critical Pauline passage and natural revelation.

of glory, who cannot imagine that beauty is found in the ugliness of the cross or that goodness is precisely where a Father permits his Son to be murdered.[4]

Yet for all of Luther's insight into the folly of unaided reason's presumptions about God, Luther joined what good Christian theology had separated: Scriptureless philosophical theology, on the one hand, and, on the other, biblical natural theology. He failed to distinguish them properly—at least not consistently enough to prevent prejudicing legions of followers against all natural revelation and Christian natural theology ever since.

How did Luther do this? By ignoring the plain sense of the Bible when it most clearly speaks of the glory of God in the creation. In his sermon on Psalm 19, one of the classic biblical texts on God's natural revelation in his creation, Luther commented as follows on verse 1, "The heavens are telling the glory of God; and the firmament proclaims His handiwork": "That is to say: 'The glory of God is preached everywhere in all the lands under all of heaven.' The emphasis is on the word 'telling,' to remind us that we should esteem the oral and external Word. The 'glory of God' is the Gospel, for through the Gospel God is known. The 'handiwork' of God is all the works wrought by the Gospel, like justification, salvation, and redemption from sin, from death, and from the kingdom of the devil."[5]

When verse 2 proclaims that "day to day pours forth speech, and night to night declares knowledge," Luther told us that "this is to say that the Gospel will always be preached and that the Christian Church will stand and remain eternally."[6]

Notice what has happened. Here, where the Bible contains a clear instance of its theology of creation—that God's glory can be seen in the heavens and earth—Luther has replaced it with a theology of redemption. Luther asserted that the heavens are not the stars and the firmament is not the sky; instead, they are the oral preaching of the Word at church and the good works that are produced by that preaching. The verse for Luther speaks not of the beauty in the night sky, but of something going on inside the church. Just as the moon is obscured by the rising sun at dawn, so too has the glory of nature been swept from view by (the image of) a preacher declaiming in a pulpit.

If Psalm 19 is one of the best-known Old Testament passages about types in the creation, Romans 1:18–23 is the best-known New Testament passage. We have just seen how Luther used it in his Heidelberg Disputation, insisting

4. I was helped to understand Luther's hypothetical monk by Carl Beckwith's superb recounting of the medieval and Reformation debates about faith and reason in *The Holy Trinity* (Fort Wayne, IN: Luther Academy, 2016), 1–112. For the monk, see 75.

5. *AE* 12:140.

6. *AE* 12:140.

that the invisible things of God mentioned in this passage are *not* perceptible through what is visible. When he commented more directly on Romans 1, he declared again that the invisible things of God, which Paul said "have been clearly perceived . . . in the things that have been made" (v. 20 ESV), are *not* clearly seen. Luther went on to explain why. He wrote that while God does indeed reveal his existence and power and even goodness through nature, and while unaided reason does indeed discern those realities, nevertheless those realities are immediately obscured by sin. Sin inevitably corrupts that true knowledge. For this reason Paul went on to say in verse 21 that human beings "became futile in their thinking, and their senseless minds were darkened."[7]

Now Luther did not discount all natural revelation, and he even adopted some typological readings of the creation. Inside a book by Pliny, Luther once inscribed the following: "All creation is the most beautiful book of the Bible; in it God has described and portrayed Himself."[8] As Heinrich Bornkamm has reported, Luther saw the morning dew as an image of the Holy Spirit; the break of day, which is neither night nor day, as a picture of the Christian, who is both sinner and saint; the red morning sky as a sign of the joyful proclamation of the gospel; summer and winter as comparable to periods of peace and trials; a mild breeze as an image of the gospel melting the winter of the heart; birds as living saints who work hither and yon and trust God to provide for them. All told, nature for Luther was a sign of God's manifold wisdom.[9] But he warned that allegory and typology should never establish a doctrine of faith but only illustrate it: "Allegory does not establish doctrine, but like color, can only add to it."[10]

Yet while Luther admitted that there is revelation in nature that illustrates the revelation in Scripture, his warnings about reason misusing natural revelation tended to dominate the thinking of later Lutheran theologians about nature. They used his admonitions about the abuse of natural *revelation* to characterize all natural *theology*. Roland Ziegler wrote: "In the hands of man, the natural revelation of the true God is turned into an idolatrous concept of god and gods. The problem of man is therefore not simply an intellectual one, but it is sin. The remedy for this is not a return to a purer, better *natural theology* but the proclamation of Christ."[11] Ziegler's inter-

---

7. Beckwith, *Holy Trinity*, 74–80.

8. Heinrich Bornkamm, *Luther's World of Thought* (St. Louis: Concordia, 1958), 179.

9. Bornkamm, *Luther's World of Thought*, 179–81.

10. Martin Luther, *Lectures on Isaiah, 1527–30*, in WA 31/11; cited in Heinrich Bornkamm, *Luther and the Old Testament*, trans. Eric Gritsch and Ruth Gritsch (Philadelphia: Fortress, 1969), 90.

11. Roland Ziegler, "Natural Knowledge of God and the Trinity"; quoted in Beckwith, *Holy Trinity*, 27 (emphasis added).

pretation is similar to that of the nineteenth-century Lutheran theologian August Graebner: "God's handwriting still covers every inch of the universe; but man's defective mental vision prevents him from making out, even with his telescopes and microscopes, what the heavens as well as the mustard seeds declare."[12]

For these Lutheran theologians, God's types in nature are useless because they are inevitably distorted by sinful human minds. They serve only to condemn, for they show that human beings have no excuse for their idolatry, since they were originally given revelation of the true God but replaced it with images of false gods. This is what happens whenever hapless Christian theologians think anything useful is made of God's revelation in nature. As a contemporary Lutheran theologian wrote, "If any constructive space is given natural revelation, it becomes natural *theology* and the consequences are *dire* for the scriptural doctrine of the Trinity and our confession of the pure gospel."[13]

Luther and these Lutherans were right about the consequences of a natural theology that presumes that unregenerate reason can be disinterested and neutral and that imagines it can "ascend" (as Luther put it) to the divine realm without the guidance of revelation. Luther wrote that when unbelievers see God in nature, they see only his wrath, for Paul wrote in Romans 1:18 that the "wrath of God," not the righteousness of God, is being revealed from heaven. The philosopher using reason alone can have a "left-handed and partial knowledge of God," but he cannot know God's will for him, particularly whether God will forgive him. Sin confuses all knowledge gained from natural revelation, so all so-called natural knowledge must die before it is to be taken up in faith. And at that point, it must submit to the revelation of God in Scripture.[14]

But what if reason is used in the way that most of the Great Tradition used it? What if it is faith seeking understanding, as Augustine first put it? What if it is a prayerful exploration, carefully mining the riches of revelation in the Bible, as it was used by Cyril of Jerusalem, Basil of Caesarea, Gregory of Nazianzus, and Augustine?[15] They spoke of faith's reason and reason's faith, faith informing reason and giving fullness to reason. Gregory of Nazianzus,

12. August Graebner, "Doctrinal Theology"; quoted in Beckwith, *Holy Trinity*, 27.

13. Beckwith, *Holy Trinity*, 87 (emphasis added).

14. Luther, *Lectures on Hebrews, 1517–18*, AE 29:111. For the "left handed and partial knowledge," see AE 22:152–53. On natural revelation having to die, see AE 22:158.

15. Cyril of Jerusalem, lecture 9, *The Catechetical Lectures*, in *Nicene and Post-Nicene Fathers*, Series 2, vol. 7, ed. Philip Schaff (Peabody, MA: Hendrickson, 2012), 51–56; Basil of Caesarea, *Homilies on the Hexaemeron 7–9*, http://www.newadvent.org/fathers/32017.htm; Augustine, *The Trinity*, trans. Edmund Hill (Hyde Park, NY: New City Press, 1991), book 15.

for example, used biblically informed reason to write a hymn to nature that inspires humility before God.[16] He used it to argue the irrationality of reason trying to know God without the use of biblical revelation from God.

Despite Luther's blasts against reason as "the devil's greatest whore," even he seemed to allow for this kind of humble and pious typological theology.[17] In the Heidelberg Disputation he wrote that it is no use trying to see God's glory and majesty "unless [one] also recognizes him in the humility and shame of the cross."[18] Notice the "unless," which implies that God's glory and majesty *can* be seen by those who embrace the shame of the cross— who know that God's beauty is in that very ugliness. Those believers can then go on to see God's glory in the creation. In fact, Luther said just that in this disputation: "He deserves to be called a theologian, however, who comprehends the visible and manifest things of God seen through suffering and the cross."[19]

Luther was brilliant in his denunciation of presumptuous natural theology that tries to soar up to heaven without the wings of revelation. He rightly protested that that flight was headed toward a dark realm of alien beings. But Luther was so obsessed with human presumption about glory that he gave little attention to believers who humbly considered the beauties of God scattered throughout the creation. *They* knew the greatest glory was in the cross, and therefore they could *also* know the glory of God that was in and beyond the physical heavens. *They* could see God's handiwork in the firmament.

Later Lutheran (and other sorts of) theologians warned that all the analogies we use to talk about God are rooted in human terms and human concepts, things in nature as perceived by our limited minds. They suggested that it borders on illegitimate to imagine that God could be anything like the things we see in nature and history—and that we should hesitate to so imagine. Yet the authors of Scripture showed no such hesitation. They regularly compared God to a rock and a storm and the sun. His wrath, they wrote, is like the ocean, and his righteousness, like the mountains. He himself is like a human father, a shepherd, a vineyard owner. Jesus said he is bread, a vine, a king.[20]

Perhaps there is a place after all for *believing* use of natural revelation.

16. Gregory of Nazianzus, *Oration* 28.23–30, in *On God and Christ: The Five Theological Orations*, ed. Lionel Wickham (Crestwood, NY: St. Vladimir's Seminary Press, 2002), 55–62.

17. "Martin Luther's Last Sermon in Wittenberg" (Second Sunday in Epiphany, January 17, 1546), in *Dr. Martin Luthers Werke: Kritische Gesamtausgabe* (Weimar: Hermann Böhlaus Nachfolger, 1914), 51:126.7.

18. *AE* 31:52–53.

19. *AE* 31:52.

20. See chap. 3 for my discussion of Scripture using these things in nature to talk about God.

Karl Barth

But wait a minute. Are we going too quickly? Haven't we learned in the last century that we have been duped on this issue? That what we think is natural revelation is not *really* that? This was the argument made by Karl Barth, the most influential theologian of the twentieth century.

Barth argued that there is no "point of contact" between things of earth and things of heaven and that when we think there is, we inevitably confuse the two, assigning something of earth to the heavenly sphere, turning an earthly thing into a god by trusting in it and loving it. If you think this sounds like Luther, you're on the right track. Barth was steeped in the Reformers, Luther as much as Calvin. Luther helped Barth to make sense of the insanity of early twentieth-century Europe, when millions of young men were mowed down in line after line as they climbed out of filthy trenches to fight a faceless enemy whom their leaders had told them was a threat to civilization. Barth was horrified to learn that his liberal theology professors had endorsed this seemingly senseless First World War, confusing German ideals with God's purposes. This realization made him rethink theology and God himself, driving him back to the Reformed scholastics whom he found in Heinrich Heppe's *Reformed Dogmatics*.[21] These theologians took seriously what Barth called "the strange new world of the Bible." Unlike his liberal theology professors, who questioned the historicity of both Testaments, these Reformed theologians in the sixteenth and seventeenth centuries believed God had inspired every word of Scripture and that the relation between each word and its historical referent was less important than the fact that the living God was speaking through that Word.

Then in the 1930s, when the most Christianized country in Europe turned against the Jews, and when it (the most educated country in history) allowed itself to believe lies, Barth turned again to Reformed theology—and Luther—to make sense of the madness. Barth was struck by Luther's rejection of Thomas Aquinas and the medieval doctor's turn to this world of being to find analogies to the Author of being. Even though Thomas said that these analogies tell us more what God is *not* than what he *is*, Luther considered all such analogies to this world to be dead ends. In the end, he believed, they turned us to our own ideas of the world and suggested that we can contribute something to the search for God, and then to our being accepted by God.[22] In Thomistic theology

21. Heinrich Heppe, *Reformed Dogmatics: Set Out and Illustrated from the Sources*, trans. G. T. Thomson (German ed. 1861; Grand Rapids: Baker, 1978).
22. Both Lutheran and Reformed Christians made these arguments against Thomas. They thought that Thomas held that saving faith comes from adding data from special revelation to what reason can find on its own and that Thomas's analogies used merely human concepts to

this was known as the analogy of being, which asserted that in the creation we can see signposts of the Creator, earmarks left by the Designer. We can use our unaided reason to study these signposts and earmarks and can conclude from them that they point to an intelligent designer—indeed, a creator.[23]

For Barth, this approach to the creation was exactly the one used by the new generation of German theologians who supported the religion of "blood and soil" suggested by an Austrian postcard-painter with a preternatural gift of oratory. This failed artist was giving hope to a generation of Germans who felt inferior after the Versailles Treaty had blamed World War I on them and left them penniless because of the draconian reparations demanded by the treaty. Hitler told them they were not only not inferior but superior, and his rearmament of Germany gave them jobs. Now they could put food on the table with self-respect. He told them he was protecting them from godless Communism, and that God raises up leaders who enable a people to find their God-given strength and destiny.[24]

For Barth, this script was the handwriting on the wall. It showed why the analogy of being was damnable, from the infernal pit—in fact, "*the* invention of Anti-Christ."[25] It claimed to find God in the creation and in a particular people. It made the human being its own creator and redeemer.

We can understand, in hindsight, why Barth connected the dots from Thomas's analogy of being to the Nazi *Blut und Boden*. But that same hindsight reveals that Barth overreached. As Hans Urs von Balthasar argued in his seminal study of Barth's theology, Barth had attacked a straw man. The analogy of being

---

interpret and replace biblical concepts. But Thomas, who was writing when the Bible was widely accepted as the Word of God and when the capabilities of reason were debated by thinkers who assumed near-universal acceptance of the gospel, was discussing in his Five Ways *not* what naked reason could do to prove God to unbelievers but how reason could show to *believers* that faith is reasonable. So it is not true that Thomas thought saving faith relied on reason, even if, as he did teach, reason could give believers "preambles" to saving faith. Saving faith, he wrote in his *Summa theologiae*, is not one of the intellectual virtues but one of the theological virtues that are "above man's nature" and from outside us. See Thomas Aquinas, *Summa theologica*, trans. Dominican Fathers, 5 vols., rev. ed. 1920 (Notre Dame, IN: Christian Classics, 1981), I-II, q. 62, art. 2; q. 63, art. 1; II-II, q. 6, art. 1.

By "preambles" Thomas meant basic truths that are *theological, not epistemological*, preambles. They are preambles only in the sense that in any ordering of Christian thinking the believer must start with these and go on from there. "For instance, it is quite obvious that one must believe that God exists if one believes that he is the rewarder of those who seek him." Arvin Vos, *Aquinas, Calvin, and Contemporary Protestant Thought* (Grand Rapids: Eerdmans, 1985), 83.

23. I do not capitalize "creator," because Thomas and his followers have conceded that the analogy of being does not point to the trinitarian God per se but only to an unnamed source.

24. For example, Adolf Hitler, *Mein Kampf*, ed. Ralph Manheim (New York: Houghton Mifflin, 1998), 65.

25. Eberhard Busch, *Karl Barth: His Life from Letters and Autobiographical Texts* (Grand Rapids: Eerdmans, 1994), 214–15.

that Barth condemned was not the one taught by Thomas Aquinas. Barth had claimed that for Thomas nature was able in its purity, apart from grace, to see the meaning of reality. And nature was able not only to see but then to contribute to its own salvation. But Thomas never taught such a "pure nature" that could of its own being, apart from regeneration, see the meaning of nature and the identity of the true God. Thomas always insisted that nature requires grace to find itself and that only the historical event of Christ's life and death and resurrection save a fallen nature. As Balthasar put it, Thomas wrote that the Word did not come to all of nature but to his own (John 1:11) and that the part of his own who received him had been prepared by grace. They were born not of blood nor of the will of the flesh nor of the will of man, but of God (John 1:12).[26]

Therefore the analogy of being, which depends on grace to see and grace to be redeemed, teaches that being is indeed "epiphanic." All of nature is created with the capacity to "show" the grace that birthed it and lies beyond it. For example, all genuine love surrenders to the other and points to the surrender of each divine person to the Trinity's plans for creation and redemption. All of the fallen creation goes through death in order to make way for new life, just as death to sin is necessary for the resurrection of new life in redemption and sanctification. In these two ways, and millions of others, the creation shows that God is the fulfillment of the world's being.[27] But only eyes that have been opened by the Holy Spirit can see this reality. In this respect the true analogy of being is different from its counterfeits in deism and liberal theology.

But Barth was never able to see this distinction or to separate *analogia entis* from general revelation in any clear way. For him, the two were of a piece. Claims for both assumed "an inborn or acquired property of man" rather than the result of an act of God, or assumed that man "has created his own faith," which we "acquire on our own," or that they both involve "an abstract metaphysics of God, the world, or religion which is supposed to obtain at all times and in all places."[28]

In his *Church Dogmatics* 2/1, Barth insisted that Romans 1:18–23 "is not speaking of man in the cosmos in himself and in general." Paul referred not to

---

26. John Webster, "Balthasar and Karl Barth," in *The Cambridge Companion to Hans Urs von Balthasar*, ed. Edwards T. Oakes and David Moss (Cambridge: Cambridge University Press, 2004), 249–50; Hans Urs von Balthasar, *The Theology of Karl Barth* (German edition, 1951; repr., San Francisco: Ignatius, 1991).

27. Hans Urs von Balthasar, *Epilogue*, trans. Edward T. Oakes, SJ (San Francisco: Ignatius, 2004), 59, 109; Balthasar, *The Grain of Wheat: Aphorisms*, trans. Erasmo Leiva-Merikakis (San Francisco: Ignatius, 1995), 31; Balthasar, "The Fathers, the Scholastics, and Ourselves," *Communio* 24 (1939; repr., Summer 1997): 391.

28. Karl Barth, *Church Dogmatics* [CD] 1/1 (Peabody, MA: Hendrickson, 2010), 245, 329, 389, 325.

some knowledge of God possible apart from knowledge of Jesus Christ, but only "the truth of revelation proclaimed by the apostle of Jesus Christ." "It is impossible to draw from the text a statement . . . concerning a natural union with God or knowledge of God on the part of man in himself and as such."[29]

In Barth's discussion of Romans 1 and of Paul's Mars Hill sermon in Acts 17, he denied any natural analogy between the creation and its creator (*analogia entis*) and any general revelation available to all apart from the revelation of Jesus Christ.[30] The rejection of the analogy and of general revelation went together.

What about Barth's appeals later in his career to "little lights" and "parables of the kingdom"? Did those discussions represent a change of mind on general revelation? Apparently not. Barth argued that the occurrence of such parables was not to be ascribed to "the sorry hypothesis" of natural theology. As George Hunsinger explained, Barth could not accept any true apprehension of God without personal conversion.[31] The notion that there could be objective revelation that was there even if a person could not apprehend it was impossible for Barth to accept.

James Barr agreed that the later Barth did not change. "There was no talk of a revision, still less of an abandonment, of the violent earlier attacks on natural theology. . . . Since this is so, we are justified in taking the position of complete denial of natural theology[—which is] Barth's position in his Gifford Lectures, in his controversy with Brunner, and in the earlier volumes of the *Church Dogmatics*[—]as the classic Barthian position."[32]

The great Lutheran theologian Wolfhart Pannenberg studied under Barth and saw this problem in Barth's theology. Pannenberg observed that Barth could not distinguish between natural knowledge of God and a natural theology constructed by autonomous man. As a result, according to Pannenberg, Barth created a false dichotomy—either Enlightenment-style natural theology that thinks natural revelation is enough for saving knowledge of God or no general revelation at all. Either knowledge of God apart from knowledge of Christ was something *possessed* by a human being *for his or her disposal*, or there was no knowledge of God at all apart from revelation of the gospel.[33]

The Dutch Reformed theologian G. C. Berkouwer joined Pannenberg in criticizing Barth for failing to distinguish between natural theology of the Enlightenment sort and explicitly *Christian* natural theology based on general

29. *CD* 2/1:119, 121.
30. *CD* 2/1:117–23.
31. *CD* 4/3.1:117; George Hunsinger, *How to Read Karl Barth* (New York: Oxford University Press, 1993), 275.
32. James Barr, *Biblical Faith and Natural Theology* (Oxford: Clarendon, 1993), 13–14.
33. Wolfhart Pannenberg, *Systematic Theology*, 3 vols. (Grand Rapids: Eerdmans, 1992), 1:73–118.

revelation. More recently, Alister McGrath added a similar critique, along with a new call for revival of a properly Christian natural theology.[34]

Now we must get into the weeds, to see how Barth misinterpreted Scripture. Barth went to the classic texts, not only Acts 17, as we just saw, but also Psalm 19 and Romans 1. On Psalm 19, he pointed to verse 3, "their voice is not heard," arguing that the voices of creation are dumb, mute. After all, he wrote, the Old Testament shows that no one outside of Israel knew the true God. On Romans 1 Barth argued, following Luther, that all the so-called revelation of God to man through nature results only in condemnation. Therefore, Barth reasoned, since the testimonies of God in nature are invariably misunderstood, they are not revelation at all. They falsify rather than illumine. The only true knowledge we have of God is in the face of Jesus Christ. By implication, all the supposed types that observers say they find in nature and history and that point to the true God are counterfeit, pointing instead to things other than the true God, merely imagined in likeness to the observers. In a word, they are idols. The search for types is a wild goose chase, with a pagan god at its end.

But Barth was practicing *eisegesis* rather than *exegesis*. He was reading into rather than out of the text. When the psalmist said of the voices of the creation that they are "not heard," he probably meant that their voice is not understood rather than that it is not sounded. For he went on to say that these voices "go out through all the earth" and reach to "the end of the world." The point seems to be that their voices are sounded to all the world, not just Israel. *Something* is being proclaimed to the world outside of Israel, even if it is not always understood or received.

And in Romans Paul said the same thing. In seven different ways he claims that God is making himself known to what seems to be every human heart, on which he has "written [*grapton*]" his "law" (2:15). That is the first way. Back in Romans 1, he claimed that

what can be *known* [*gnōston*] about God [the 2nd way]
is *plain* [*phaneron*] to them [3rd way],
because God *has shown* [*ephanerōsen*] it to them [4th way].
Ever since the creation of the world, his eternal power and divine nature, invisible though they are, have been *understood* and *seen* [*nooumena kathoratai*] [5th and 6th ways]
through the things he has made. So they are without excuse;
for though they *knew* [*gnontes*] God [7th way],
they did not honor him as God or give thanks to him. (vv. 19–21a)

34. G. C. Berkouwer, *General Revelation* (Grand Rapids: Eerdmans, 1983), 154; Alister McGrath, *The Open Secret: A New Vision for Natural Theology* (Malden, MA: Blackwell, 2008).

Barth was right that Paul suggested that this general revelation simply led to condemnation. The apostle said that these same human beings "exchanged the truth about God for a lie and worshiped and served the creature rather than the Creator" (1:25).

But we must remember three things. First, Paul was speaking of the universal tendency of every human being to turn away from God to self and world. This was true of every believer before the grace of God turned him or her back to God. It speaks of the fall, not redemption from the fall—of the tendency to misread the signs in creation, not the legitimacy of the signs themselves. Just because our sinful tendency before redemption is to misread does not mean that, once redeemed, we cannot learn to read properly.

Second, Paul repeatedly declared that the message comes through loud and clear, that there is a Creator who is divine and eternally powerful.

Third, Scripture suggests that some fallen creatures see *something* in the signs to encourage a search for the true sign-maker: Paul told the Athenians on Mars Hill that God "allotted the times of [human beings'] existence and the boundaries of their places where they should live, so that they would search for God and *perhaps grope for him and find him*" (Acts 17:26–27).

So Psalm 19 and Romans 1 teach that there is natural revelation from God. God speaks through nature of his existence and power and deity. Most use this revelation most of the time for idolatrous purposes, but it is revelation nonetheless. Scripture suggests that some unbelievers use this natural revelation as an incentive to search for the true God. This search, if it is successful, always leads to the trinitarian God of Scripture and is both inspired and led by the Holy Spirit. Human nature by itself is powerless to see the meaning of the signs or to follow them to the true God. But *God* uses his signs to open eyes to his glory in the creation.

What can we say about Barth, then? He rightly warned of our temptation to confuse culture with Christ and disastrously so. But his rejection of Scripture's testimony to natural revelation was "more the result of an *a priori* view of revelation than an unprejudiced reading of the text itself."[35] So Barth departed from the majority view of the Great Tradition that while nature affords no *saving* knowledge of God, nevertheless true knowledge is available to the unregenerate, and that the regenerate have available to them a near-infinite panoply of revelations in human beings and the world testifying to the truths of redemption by the Triune God. Barth thus departed from Basil, Gregory of Nazianzus, Augustine, Thomas, Calvin, and Edwards on this understanding, and even from many of the Lutheran and Reformed scholastics.

35. Berkouwer, *General Revelation*, 154.

Scripture Index

Subject Index